Medal Man

Medal Man

Dad, Me and the Second World War

MARK SMITH

PENGUIN MICHAEL JOSEPH

UK | USA | Canada | Ireland | Australia
India | New Zealand | South Africa

Penguin Michael Joseph is part of the Penguin Random House group of companies whose addresses can be found at global.penguinrandomhouse.com

Penguin Random House UK
One Embassy Gardens, 8 Viaduct Gardens, London SW11 7BW

penguin.co.uk

First published 2026

001

Copyright © Mark Smith, 2026

The moral right of the author has been asserted

Picture credits can be found on page 303

Penguin Random House values and supports copyright. Copyright fuels creativity, encourages diverse voices, promotes freedom of expression and supports a vibrant culture. Thank you for purchasing an authorized edition of this book and for respecting intellectual property laws by not reproducing, scanning or distributing any part of it by any means without permission. You are supporting authors and enabling Penguin Random House to continue to publish books for everyone. No part of this book may be used or reproduced in any manner for the purpose of training artificial intelligence technologies or systems. In accordance with Article 4(3) of the DSM Directive 2019/790, Penguin Random House expressly reserves this work from the text and data mining exception

Set in 14/17 pt Garamond Premier Pro
Typeset by Six Red Marbles UK, Thetford, Norfolk
Printed and bound in Great Britain by Clays Ltd, Elcograf S.p.A.

The authorized representative in the EEA is Penguin Random House Ireland, Morrison Chambers, 32 Nassau Street, Dublin D02 YH68

A CIP catalogue record for this book is available from the British Library

ISBN: 978–0–241–73810–8

Penguin Random House is committed to a sustainable future for our business, our readers and our planet. This book is made from Forest Stewardship Council® certified paper

For Tilly and Molly

Introduction

It was standing there, big and white. I'd seen it before at an air show and witnessed it flying, but I'd never been this close.

When I got near it, walking up to it on the grass, I thought, 'Blimey, it's huge – it really is a big thing. Big engines, big aeroplane.' And it was gorgeous – an impressive machine sitting on its wheels, ready to take me flying over London.

I'd always imagined what it would be like to fly in a PBY Catalina, the flying boat that my father, Les Smith, flew for more than 1,000 hours during his wartime career in the RAF. It was Dad's Catalinas that formed the backdrop to all his stories of training, of flying top cover over the Atlantic convoys, and of secret missions against Japanese forces in the Far East.

And it was in one of these planes that Dad's greatest friend in his crew, young Harry Shirt, had been killed by Japanese ground fire one night in April 1945 over Sumatra, in an event that haunted my father throughout his life and until his dying day.

I had been invited to fly in the only Catalina still operational in Britain, based at Duxford in Cambridgeshire, on a beautiful early summer's day in May 2025. The idea was that we would do a little loop down over the City of London and back, a flight that would take no more than an hour. Alongside me was Steve Foster, the son of Dad's second pilot, Don. I'd seen Steve off and on over the years, and we hugged a greeting as we met with the rest of our flying complement.

'You know something, Steve,' I said to him, 'this is going to be the first time a Smith and a Foster have walked out together to a PBY Catalina for eighty years!' We laughed like two excited little schoolboys.

It may have looked big from the outside, but inside it was tiny – cramped, uncomfortable, all painted green. And when the Pratt & Whitney Twin Wasp engines started up, it was extremely noisy and rattly – and that was while we were still on the ground.

We climbed aboard via a ramp at the back, entering between the two blisters in the fuselage that would have held two .50 machine guns. There were no guns on this plane, but I could well imagine how tight the space must have been with the weapons on their stands and their ammunition as well.

Then I made my way forward through a bulkhead, past where the Flight Engineer sat and into a compartment behind the two pilots. 'This is where your father would have sat as the Radio Operator,' one of the crew told me.

In the main compartment there were eight seats, and I was sitting next to Steve on the inside so it was hard to see too much, but I was able to watch the two pilots, especially the first pilot. I could see his feet and his hands, and I could see a red lever that said 'Wheels Up' and 'Wheels Down', and when we took off he grabbed hold of that red handle and turned it, and I knew we were airborne.

The take-off run was so slow. More of a trundle than a

sprint – and in this respect, as with so many others, it was absolutely nothing like a modern holiday jetliner. The state of the wheels apart, the first thing I noticed when we were flying was how bumpy it was. Oh my God, this was something else – continuous rocking and rolling, properly uncomfortable.

The funny thing was that I didn't feel nervous about the flying, but I was terrified I might throw up and disgrace my dad. It struck me then that we were doing sixty minutes in a Catalina, whereas my father and the crew led by Flight Lieutenant Johnny Ayshford would sometimes fly for up to thirty-six hours in one of these.

It was amazing to see the Thames and the familiar landmarks of the City, as we toured the centre of London at about 1,500ft. As we approached the Shard, I texted my nephew William Dunstan, who works there and told him we were about to overfly him. He rushed to the window and took a photo.

All the while, above me, I could see the pilot's hands wrestling with the controls keeping this wild beast in order. I thought of my father, and I thought of Harry in that tiny little space, and, honestly, I was in total awe of what they did and what people like them went through in the Second World War.

This was nothing like flying as we know it today, and, when you think about it, even in 1945 aviation was still a relatively new thing. Wartime RAF crews flew for miles and miles. In Dad's case, this was over the Indian Ocean, relying on two engines that could break down at any moment, leaving the plane to simply fall out of the sky. The chances are they would never be found.

It reminded me of the courage those young pilots who flew Spitfires or Lancaster bombers needed just to climb into their cockpits every day. Being inside a Catalina completely turned on its head what I thought it might be like. The reality was about 25,000 times worse than I had ever imagined.

At one point, I looked up and noticed the pulleys and wires that controlled the rudder. I remembered my father saying that between the two blisters there were two wires and two pulleys just above the guns. At the end of the fateful flight when Harry died, they landed and discovered a bullet had bent the pulleys but not broken the wires. If it had broken them, that would have been it; they would have all been dead. I stared at the arrangement of wires above me and thought, 'There but for the grace of God . . .'

Another thought burst into my subconscious: Dad describing how the bottom of the airframe – the keel – was full of blood as they flew back to the airfield at Red Hills Lake outside Chennai, or Madras in Dad's day. Can you imagine that? I looked at the bottom of the plane, as if to check, as the recollection made my own blood run cold.

I could sense my father so close to me that day. Everywhere. Smoking his fag. Earnestly carrying out his duties as Radio Operator using secret signalling techniques or Morse code, helping to drop propaganda leaflets over Japanese-occupied territory or doing more routine duties like preparing the plane for landing or mooring up on the lake. For one hour I not only remembered Dad's stories all over again, I felt I was *in* them because I was in a Catalina with him alongside me. And it was a rare privilege – to fly in a Second World

War aircraft, even if on this occasion we were not able to land on water like he did.

As we made our way back to Duxford, over the patchwork quilt of Home Counties farmland, I pulled my phone out and made a little video to myself. 'Well, here we are in a Catalina, the noise is incredible,' I said as the engines rumbled on above me. 'How you did this Dad, I'll never know.'

Chapter One

I grew up in the past. On my dad's side, I was the first person born into the family for over four decades when I came along on Christmas Day in 1963. I have no brothers or sisters; there is nobody else, only me.

And what I ended up with was a family of old people. My dad was forty-one when I arrived, and my mum thirty-nine. I have four cousins on my mum's side. Barry and Tim are slightly older than me, Peter and John slightly younger. But them aside, there were just a lot of old people.

My nan – my dad's mum – was born in 1894. Dad's dad was born in 1896. My other nan was born in 1900, and her husband in 1899. All of my dad's aunts were born in the 1890s or early 1900s. Dad's big brother, Uncle Vic, was born in 1915. His sister, Kathleen – we called her Auntie Bob – was born in 1918. Uncle Tom in 1915.

So I grew up with all of these people – relatives who in Dad's words 'had history'. And I was always conscious of the fact that, being a boy of six or seven, I couldn't say, as they habitually did, 'D'you remember, forty years ago, when Walthamstow first came under attack by the Luftwaffe?', or whatever it was. I was desperately sad not to be able to join in on those fantastic family conversations about the past and often about the war.

The frame of reference was set so far back. I remember saying to my nan once, 'Have you ever seen the queen?'

'Yes,' she said. 'Well, I did see Queen Victoria once.'

And I said to Auntie Doll, my nan's sister, 'So, the *Titanic* sank in 1912.'

'Yes, I know,' she replied.

'Well, how old were you when that happened?'

'What? In 1912? I was twenty-one.'

And I asked my nan whether she saw the soldiers going off to the war, which was probably a silly question because Grandad was in the trenches, and I meant the First World War. 'Oh yes,' she said. 'I saw them marching off . . . to the Boer War.'

They used to joke that I looked like 'Uncle Henry'. He wasn't a living relative but Henry Dickerson, my great-great-great-grandad, who was born in about 1832 or 1833. One day, I asked Auntie Doll and Auntie Hilda, another of my dad's aunts, whether they had any photos of him. They laughed at that. 'I wonder what he looked like,' I mused.

'He looked like you, Mark,' said Doll. 'You're a bit taller, but there's a clear likeness.'

I was pretty astonished to hear this. 'What d'you mean he looked like me? How do you know?'

'Oh,' said Hilda, 'we knew him, of course. He was "Uncle Henry" to us.'

I know this might sound a bit weird, but I have spent my entire life wanting to be sixty years old so I could kind of catch up. And when I finally made it a couple of Christmases ago, Lizzy Dunstan, my sister-in-law, said, 'You are the happiest sixty-year-old the world has ever seen.'

She was so right. Everybody else gets to that milestone and thinks, 'Oh no . . . I've gone bang.' All I could think of is that I had finally reached the age when I could say, like they did, 'Fifty years ago, I remember when . . .'

It's been a long journey to get here. In 1973 on Christmas Eve, I was sitting on the floor in our front room. We had just come back from my nan and grandad's, where we had been at a family thing, and it was about ten to midnight. As we waited for the minutes to tick by, my dad looked at me and said, 'Just think, at midnight you'll be in double figures. You're getting some history, Son.'

And suddenly I felt a little bit prouder. I *was* getting there . . .

My link with our family's past wasn't something I could read about in a book. It was a past that people talked about, told me about, and had lived through. Christmas Day was always the best one for stories, when Mum and Dad used to put on a big family party because it was my birthday as well. Incidentally, I was spoiled rotten as a child, and from an early age was gifted a 'half-birthday' on 25 June, so I never missed out on presents or extra pocket money.

On Christmas Day, our front room at 1 Fernhill Court on Forest Road in Walthamstow would be full of wonderful aunts and uncles, and nans and grandads, and cousins and all sorts of people. And it was usually Uncle Vic, sitting on the hardest, most uncomfortable chair in the house – because Uncle Vic was a hard man – who would hold forth. It would be that stage in the afternoon, after *Morecambe and Wise* and after the queen, when things had gone a bit quiet on the telly and Mum would be handing round the crabsticks and smoked salmon sandwiches. Uncle Vic would sit there and say, 'D'you remember the night when that oil bomb' – an incendiary device – 'came down on the corner of Ruby Road?'

And everyone would go, 'Oh yeah, we remember that...' And then they would be off talking about it as if it had happened yesterday.

That story would lead to other family favourites, like the one about how the kettle got knocked over by the first bomb that hit our neighbourhood in 1940. Or the one about Auntie Hilda pouring tea from a flask as a bomb went off, and her head ending up getting stuck in the same position for three weeks... they'd laugh at that one, including Hilda herself. And I'd be there, sitting on the floor on my most favourite day of the year, listening to this wonderful oral history.

Being with people who were older than me never left me feeling isolated or lonely – it was my normal – and, in any case, I had friends of my own age. My best friend at the time – he still is – is my mate Phil Nobo. We met on our first day at Hyland House Primary School at the top of Forest Road, near the waterworks, when my mother sat me down in my new classroom and said to the boy sitting next door, 'What's your name?'

'Phi-lip,' he said slowly, making the most of each syllable.

'Well, Philip,' she said, 'this is Mark, and you two are friends' – and we still are.

Now, Phil had a horrible childhood. His dad was a juggler

in the circus, and his mum was a 1960s babe in white plastic knee-length boots and miniskirts with long black hair. She was probably about fifteen or twenty years younger than my mum. Her front room, across the road from ours, looked like a set from *The Sweeney* – lava lamps, orange wallpaper and big flower paintings. She married a guy called Bill, but the moment she did that she upped sticks and left, leaving Bill, as Phil's new stepdad, to look after him.

But Bill, bless him, was a printer and worked nights. From about the age of nine, Phil was left on his own all night, every night. He used to live at my house, pretty much. He would call my mum and dad 'Mum' and 'Dad', because we took him in and looked after him. It was great for me. He was my best friend and new brother all wrapped into one, and he practically lived with us.

We used to watch horror films together – *Appointment with Fear* on Monday nights on ITV. When it was over, I would say, 'OK, night, night,' and Dad used to walk Phil home to a completely empty house. Dad would stand outside waiting for him to turn the light on, so he knew he was safely indoors, and then come back home. Funnily enough, it wasn't until Dad's funeral in 2004 that I found this out, when Phil and I were discussing it at the wake. I knew Phil went home at bedtime, but I never realized Dad would walk him back and wait for him the way he did.

If you're wondering whether I had a normal boys' rough-and-tumble childhood alongside all the stories and the living past, I certainly did. And it was Phil who made sure of that. He was my foil. We would go off skateboarding together, and fishing, and playing football in the garden, and all that sort of stuff. (He was actually a terrible footballer, but I've known him long enough to let that go.)

But because Phil lived at our house most of the time, he also knew my relatives and heard the same stories from my aunts and uncles. And they have done the same job for him as for me – engendered in him a love of history and storytelling. These days he designs computer wargames while also running an import–export business.

My grandad on my dad's side was called Dick. His real name was Walter. He was a Schmidt – Walter Clarence Schmidt. Before Dick there was George Schmidt, and then another George Schmidt, and the one before him was Jacob Schmidt. In 1841, Jacob came to England from Kassel, in the Rhine valley in central Germany, not far from the Möhne Reservoir of *The Dam Busters* fame. Jacob was a Professor of Music, and he settled in London.

I think he was Jewish, and I think he worked out that nobody liked Jewish people in Kassel, so he came to England. He used to say, 'I can't not be German because I can't speak English, but I don't have to be Jewish.' Jacob married and had George, who had George, who had Walter. Jacob may have been a musician, but his descendants were mostly butchers, among them both Georges and my grandad, who was a master butcher of Smithfield meat market during the Second World War. His job was carving the condemned meat – meat that had come in from America and elsewhere that had gone off, but parts of which could be saved for general consumption in wartime.

It was Dick who changed our family name from Schmidt to Smith. In his school register he is listed as Dick Schmidt, but in 1914, on 8 September, he queued up near St Paul's Cathedral in the City to enlist. They asked him his name, and he said, 'Walter Clarence Smith.' And that was the day we changed our name.

Dick was in the King's Royal Rifle Corps. He went to France in 1915 and was gassed and wounded at the Battle of Loos in the autumn of that year. He came home and got better, and then they sent him back. During his second tour his battalion attacked an infamous trench called the Switch Line, an earthwork that claimed many lives, which ran between High Wood and Delville Wood on the Somme.

I know pretty much exactly where they went over the top because there is a telegraph pole in more or less the right place there today. It was 1916 and Dick was a machine-gunner, and, as the No. 1 on the gun, he carried the tripod. The No. 2 carried the gun. Where Dick stopped and put the tripod down, that was where they were going to fire from, and the No. 2 would slap the gun down on top of the tripod and they would open fire.

So Grandad had the tripod over his back but, as they scrambled forward, a German shell burst over the top of them. There was a purple flash, and he got blown off his feet. He woke up several hours later and discovered that a shrapnel ball – one of 300 metal balls in a shell – had gone through his wrist, between the bones. He had been gassed, he had been wounded before, and now he had been wounded again, and he had trench fever – rheumatism – to boot. All this and he wasn't yet twenty, bless him. He got picked up and taken back, and in October 1916 he was discharged from the army and went back to being a butcher. The No. 2 he was with just disappeared, vaporized in the explosion that ended my grandad's service in the army.

Dick was a hard man. I once asked Dad, 'Did you kill anybody in the war?'

'I don't know,' he said, after pausing to consider his answer. Then he added, 'I asked *my* dad that question, and he said "More than 500" as a machine-gunner.' That was one of my first lessons in the scale of the slaughter on the Western Front, and I sat in silence thinking about it.

So Dick is the beginning of my story in a way. I think my father was as proud of his father as I am of mine. My greatest regret is that I never knew Dick. He died in 1959. He was, by all accounts, a very determined individual. Despite his injuries, he was in 1920–21 the goalkeeper for what is now Leyton Orient football club – 'Come on you O's!' – and he went on to have three children. The funny thing was, his wife – my nan – would not allow him to talk about the war apart from on Christmas Day, something that helped to start our family tradition of storytelling under the Christmas tree.

Dick never stopped wanting to serve his country. When the Home Guard was set up in May 1940, he and my other grandad were among the first to volunteer at Walthamstow dog track. Neither of them made it. My mother's father, Ted Riley, was rejected on the grounds that he was a printer, and he was required to continue with that work. Dick was rejected because, they said, he was already too badly hurt from his days on the Western Front.

He was doing all right, though, on his army pension. In fact, in about 1936 the army wrote to him and said if he gave up his lifetime pension he would get a one-off lump-sum payment instead. Dick decided to accept the offer and received a payment of about £65. Instead of stashing it away under the mattress or in a bank, he put the whole lot on a horse called Socrates. It was forever after known in the family as 'Soc Crates', and it was never forgotten because it came in and won, earning Dick enough money to retire.

Ted Riley also fought in the Great War. He was in the Rifle Brigade and was on the Somme during the Spring Offensive in 1918, one of the last big series of attacks by the German army before the Americans joined the war. I knew him until my early thirties, when he was in his nineties. He would often say, 'Oh, I was in the trenches – it was horrible, and I remember it.' But you would be lucky to get much more out of him . . . bar one occasion.

We were watching the snooker on telly one afternoon. It was a Friday and Ted must have been about eighty-five. He was sitting in his chair, and something must have triggered a vivid memory for a fleeting moment. Suddenly he said, 'There was this German aeroplane that was coming down the line, and he was machine-gunning everyone in the trenches. I jumped up on the firestep and got this machine gun and gave him a burst as he went by.'

There was a pause, then Ted said, 'Oh look, he's potted the pink.'

Incredulous and transfixed all at once, I tried to get him to carry on with his story. 'Grandad? Grandad? German plane . . . coming down the line . . . ?'

But he was having none of it. 'Oh, I dunno what you're talking about,' he said. And that was it.

Both of my grandfathers were soldiers who became

soldiers because it was their time. They didn't go to be soldiers because they were from a military family, although Ted became a regular after the war. They did what England expected. They stood up and went, and they didn't always come back in one piece. But they never shirked the idea or the responsibility that they were going to go.

You could describe my family as Victorian in its values. Certainly, my dad's family. His parents and aunts and uncles, and the rest of them, were formal in that Victorian way. They shook your hand. They did not hug you. They did not say, 'Oh, you fell over. Ah, bless . . .' It was more likely to be, 'Stand up. Dust yourself off and get going.' It wasn't horrible. If you did fall over and hurt yourself, obviously everyone was going to be sympathetic, but the overall theme was always, 'Get up and get going, Son.' That's what they did in the trenches and that's pretty much how I grew up.

Looking back, my early childhood was special. I had the best time ever and loved every second of it.

Chapter Two

In my nan's house, there was an alcove next to the fireplace in the front room on the right-hand side. And in that alcove were shelves, and on the shelves were pictures. And my favourite picture was of Dad in his flying kit in the back garden of that house. So I knew from an early age that he was an airman.

I've still got the picture. It came from Nan's to Auntie Bob's, and from Auntie Bob's to me. In fact, there are two pictures. There's the full-length one of Dad in the garden with his big knee-length flying boots on, his bulky Sidcot flying suit, his flying helmet and his Luxor goggles. His gloved hands are held together in front of him at his waist, and he has an easy half-smile on his face, a proud young trainee gunner in the RAF. Then there's another one – this time head and shoulders – with Dad wearing his leather B-Type flying helmet, his goggles and his suit. They were both taken in 1942 during his training phase, when he had been sent to air-gunnery school at Evanton in Scotland.

At some point me and Dad went out and bought a model aeroplane, an ordinary Airfix kit. It wasn't a Catalina flying boat, which Dad flew in, but probably a Blenheim bomber because he flew in one of those for a while as well. And we sat on the floor, me and him, and we made this thing, and, as we put in the gun turrets, that's when he started to talk about what he did in the war.

'This is where I used to sit,' he said, as we finished glueing the guns in place. 'And that's the kind of thing I would be looking out of, scanning for enemy planes,' he added, pointing at the Blenheim's dorsal gun turret.

And I've always remembered it because he put the cockpit in backwards. I can still see him sitting there laughing about it – he'd completely cocked it up with the pilots' seats facing the wrong way. But we carried on, and when we'd finished we painted it with camouflage colouring, splodgy green and brown.

At about the same time we went to an airshow at North Weald Airfield, not far from Walthamstow, north of London, and as we watched the display Dad started talking about being in an aeroplane. Nothing too specific. It was the odd remark about what it would be like to fly some of the manoeuvres we were witnessing above us.

Naturally, I was curious to hear more, and one day I stopped him and asked him, 'What *did* you do in the war?'

He said, 'Ah . . . well, Son . . . that's a long story.' And that's when he told me in detail for the first time about being an Air Gunner and what it was like to sit in the blister turret of a Catalina flying at night over the Bay of Bengal.

And he also told me something else – his service number. And I tried desperately hard to remember it because, at the age of six, it seemed like something important and something that I needed to remember: 1389595. 'One-three . . . eight-nine . . . five-nine-five,' I would slowly enunciate.

I used to sit in bed trying to remember it and I would be annoyed with myself when I got it wrong. I never wrote it down because Dad told me you weren't allowed to do that; you had to memorize it. So I had to ask him each time. I would say to him every now and again: 'What's your number?'

And he'd rattle it off, 'One, three, eight, nine, five, nine, five.'

And I'd repeat it, a little more hesitatingly, 'One, three... eight, nine, five... nine... five.'

Why I was so fixated on it, I'm not sure. I think I wanted to be part of his story. Not merely listen to it but be *part* of it. And one way to do that was to remember the same number as Dad did. He would tell me his father's number in the First World War – R695 – and because he could remember that, I knew I had to remember my dad's number. It made more sense to me to think of it like that.

It was something that was a burning necessity for me. If you talk to Phil Nobo, he will also have remembered at least part of Dad's number because I drilled it into everybody. And I think Dad did that too to a certain extent. And when PIN numbers for everything came along, that was how he did it, using his service number for bank cards and so on.

When he was eighty, I had a picture of him painted based on the photos in the back garden. It was done in watercolour, and I called it 'Smith 595' because that number meant a lot to my dad, and I think I wanted it to mean a lot to me too.

The number was something in my head. Other things were more tangible, like Dad's Air Gunner's badge. This was the brevet worn on uniforms by Air Gunners in the RAF during the Second World War. It featured the initials 'AG' flanked by a brown wreath, alongside a white wing on a dark blue background. I quite liked that and imagined wearing it on my own uniform one day.

Then there was his watch that he wore on all his flights. It was an Eterna with a simple brown face on a metal strap. He had bought it off someone in Africa, and the inference was that it had come from a German soldier. With the watch was Dad's original wedding ring that had cracked on his finger when they were trying to move a radio set around the aircraft while it was being shot at. It had stuck into his finger, and when I was a kid I used to hold his hand and could feel the ruptured bone. He'd say, 'Oh, that's where I broke it on the aircraft.'

In the cupboard in the hall, right at the top, there was a brown bag – a military-style canvas one. It had the initials JX311 on it, which corresponded with one of the Catalinas he flew in.

Now, this was the one thing that I never got to see inside, ever. Not once. But Dad would sometimes bring it down and things would come out of it. There was a Japanese toothbrush that had come back from a soldier who had been killed. There were boxes of matches that they used to drop over Japanese-occupied islands in the Far East with messages intended for the locals on them, like: 'We are your friends, we are better than the Japanese.'

And there was always a brown flying sock in the bag.

'What's the sock for?' I would ask.

There was only one and he would say, 'That's where I used to keep my money.'

On the day of his funeral, I came home after the wake and sat down in the front room and thought, 'You know what? I'm going to have a look.' And I went up and got the bag. I sat there for quite a long time before I opened it. It still felt like forbidden territory, all those years later.

On top was the sock, still there as it always had been, and there were the matchboxes. And then I realized the bag was not full of other bits of military memorabilia as I had imagined, but the letters my mum had written to him while he was out in India and flying over Burma (now Myanmar). There were hundreds of them, testifying to her love for him and the support she gave him while he was on operations abroad.

In January 1945, in her 193rd Air Mail letter to Dad, she wrote about not knowing where to begin when it came to trying to find a home for them to live in when he got back. She signed off a very chatty letter as follows: 'Although we've had our quarrels, we've really loved each other deep down haven't we Les, and now we're husband and wife and, oh my darling, I love you with all my heart. Kiss me precious, and God bless you and keep you safe for me, your ever and adoring wife, Joan.' Then she added thirteen kisses.

Dad's uniform was another treasured keepsake, and I was allowed to put it on, along with his RAF hat. I even found myself a blue shirt and black tie so I could wear it properly and look the part. My nan would pull the sleeves up and pin a pleat in them so they would fit, concealing Dad's warrant officer's badge.

'What's happened to my badge?' he would ask for fun.

Dressed in that uniform I *was* Dad. Not a pilot like most schoolboys would want to be, but a Wireless Operator/Air

Gunner as he had been. I still wanted to be one of those long past the time the RAF had dispensed with roles like that in modern jet fighters and bombers. In fact, I wanted to be one until the day I accepted that I could no longer see the blackboard at school without glasses. It had gone fuzzy. It was then that I knew that being an Air Gunner was never going to be on the cards for me.

Sometimes I would go round the houses in uniform. One afternoon after school in full kit, I went to see my nan Nelly and her husband, Ted, who were living in sheltered accommodation down the road. I walked into the community room, and they were sitting together with lots of old ladies. One of them said, 'Oh, you look just like my son.'

'Really? Do I?'

And she said, 'Yes, that's an Air Gunner badge on your uniform, isn't it?'

'Yes,' I replied, proudly pointing at the brevet on my chest.

And then she said almost matter-of-factly, 'My son was an Air Gunner, but he was killed in his aeroplane.'

Those words hung there in the momentary silence in that room as I considered the implications of what she'd said. I never wore the uniform again after that.

I can't remember the first time I was allowed to look inside Dad's logbook. It occupied a position of importance among his wartime stuff that was a cut above everything else. It was on the shelves next to the photos of him, and he would take it down and we used to sit on the floor together and look at it.

It was a light-greenish coloured canvas notebook with 'Royal Air Force' picked out in capitals on the cover.

Underneath was printed 'Navigator's, Air Bomber's and Air Gunner's Flying Log Book'. Below that, where it said 'Name', my father had written simply 'Smith, L. A.'

Dad was issued with it from the moment he started flying, and it told me everything I needed to know – the date, the time, the squadron, the aircraft, the crew, where he went, how long they flew for, and what job he did. It told me whether they were operating in daylight or darkness – red ink for darkness, black for daylight – and it included an all-important 'Remarks' column, which often contained vital reflections on a mission, or details of what had happened, sometimes with a photograph attached.

Dad was good at telling a story. And the bit that always fascinated me was that he could open any single page of that logbook, and it took him and me from our front room in Walthamstow to that aircraft and its gun turret, wherever it may have been – flying out of Scotland or Northern Ireland over the Atlantic, or from India on a clandestine mission over Burma evading Japanese radar.

And not only that, it was so precise. He wrote it, so it was always going to be precise, because he liked everything to be just-so. But the very nature of it was about specifics. It was a minute-by-minute account, to the extent that on any particular day he could tell me exactly what he had been doing.

Uncle Vic's stories about being blown up in the Blitz were interesting, but they were often a bit vague. People would chip in to correct him or suggest a completely different setting. And then someone else would chirp up. Those exchanges were good value because people would discuss their conflicting recollections and make the story last longer.

But when Dad was doing the telling it was quite different. It would be 12 August 1944. He would be flying out of Lough Erne in Northern Ireland. He would have taken off in Catalina JX647 at 0600 hours, and he knew exactly where he had gone and what he and the rest of the crew were looking for (most likely German U-boats harassing Atlantic convoys).

And I was there in that grey sky over the Atlantic looking for submarines. I was there in that gun turret all the time. Every time.

The logbook used to come with him for bedtime stories. He would find a date close to whatever day of the year it was, and tell me what they had done. Even if it was a training flight, he would still remember the details of each particular trip. But they were the worst bedtime stories ever because I never used to be able to go to sleep afterwards. I would hang on every word and would be wide awake imagining being in the Catalina alongside him, and I'd ask questions along the way. 'What's a No. 1 stoppage on the guns, Dad?' And he'd explain how the guns would jam, and then I'd ask about how they cleared them. He would sit on the bed patiently explaining it all to me.

In the logbook there were photographs of the crew, so I quickly got to know who was who, and I came to think of them as real people. There were occasional travel snaps too, like pictures of the Pyramids and the Sphinx, and there was a picture of Dad's big pet dog, a stray that he befriended in India which he loved. The sad thing was it got bitten by venomous ants, and he had to shoot it to put it out of its misery.

As logbooks go, Dad's is pretty knackered – the cover has a ragged fold down the centre and the pages are frayed at the edges, testament to its long use during and after the war. Dad continued filling it in throughout his teaching career after he left the RAF, so it has details of the flights he took to various places to deliver lectures on education. That habit has worn off on me. I started keeping my own logbook after Dad, Mum and I flew to the States in 1973 when he was invited to lecture at two universities over there.

Amid huge excitement, we climbed aboard a BOAC 747 at Heathrow – a first-ever flight for both me and Mum – and, once airborne, a hostess informed me that I could join the Junior Jet Club. What's more, I would get a badge and my very own logbook. I was over the moon. But then she told me that they had run out of logbooks and mine would have to be sent later by post. Of course, I was heartbroken to hear that. But it duly turned up, and ever since then the details of every flight I took either went into that one, or subsequent ones when that one was full.

When we cleared Mum's flat after her death in 2007, Dad's RAF logbook was still on the shelf, and I carefully picked it up and put it on top of a pile that was coming back to mine. When we had finished clearing the place and tidied up, I went back home and my first thought was to find it and put it away safely. But it was nowhere to be seen. I searched the house looking in places it couldn't possibly be and asking everyone who had been at Mum's that day whether they had seen it or could have accidentally thrown it out.

Beside myself, and with a rising sense of panic gripping my chest, I went back to the flat and, after scanning the empty rooms, started going through the dustbins outside at the back. It was dark and there were a lot of them because the bins serviced all the flats adjacent to Mum's. For about two hours I went through every bin, but there was no sign of one of our family's most treasured possessions.

Fearing the worst and sick to my stomach about it, I went back home and had another look in the dining room. And there it was, sitting on a chair obscured by the tabletop overhanging it. 'You effing idiot, Mark,' I muttered to myself. The relief coursed through my veins. I had it back and I swore (loudly) I would never allow that book to go awol again.

My grandad, Dad's father, would sometimes say his son had taken the soft option by joining the RAF and spending the war flying about in a comfortable and warm aeroplane (Catalinas were neither comfortable nor warm).

I suppose one reason why I love that logbook – a document classified in the RAF as 'Form 414' – is the way it records the evidence to show that Grandad was wrong. That thing is the proof that Dad did his bit, and I think that's why it meant so much to him. For me, it was always the reference point. If Dad started a story about his wartime service, at some point he would go and get the logbook because that was the bible. There was no memory loss involved. Here was the written document where the details were set out. This was it . . .

Chapter Three

I guess you could call me a born collector.

I like to collect stuff, to find it and own it and then hold onto it. If you're not a collector, people don't really understand the appeal of it and how it can become a way of life. For me, the key part of collecting is completing the set. I like that. You set yourself a goal and you have somewhere to go, and you have to fulfil that goal.

Being given my dad's medals was the first step on this road for me. It happened when I was five and a half years old in 1969, during a visit to my nan's.

My primary school was at the end of the road where we lived, and on Fridays I would come home at half past twelve. Then I would be taken on the bus to Nan's – Dad's mum – who still lived at 74 Blenheim Road where Dad was born. I would be left with her and muck about there, going out in the garden to see Grandad's old greenhouse from his flower-growing days and all the other bits and pieces.

In the parlour among Dad's stuff, there was a box with his air force badges in, and Nan would let me take them out. I had no idea what they stood for or why they had been awarded, but I used to enjoy playing with them. I would make a little display before carefully putting them back and giving the box back to Nan.

On this day it was my half-birthday – 25 June – and, as she took the box from me, she said, 'Well look, Markie, you really like these don't you?'

'Yes, Nan, I really do,' I replied.

'Well,' she continued, 'as long as you promise to look after them, you can take them home.'

'Can I?' I said, wide-eyed with excitement.

'So long as you promise me you won't lose them or damage them?'

'I promise Nan,' I said.

To say I was one very happy little boy that day would be an understatement, as I cradled the box on the bus containing a 1939–45 Star, Burma Star, with Pacific clasp, 1939–45 Defence Medal and the 1939–45 War Medal.

It was the beginning of a lifetime passion. No, the beginning of a lifelong obsession. I committed myself to look after those medals for as long as I could, before handing them on to someone else who would look after them when I am gone.

Of course, Dad's medals were special, but as a young lad I was already collecting all sorts of other stuff from the two world wars. From Nan, for example, I got Grandad's fire watcher's steel helmet that he wore during the Blitz, and someone else gave me a pair of wire cutters. They were stamped '1917' and may have been used in the First World War, and had been lying in a shed somewhere. What a thrill it was for me to have them as I imagined them being used to cut the wire on the Somme.

When I went to senior school – a private day school in

Snaresbrook called Forest School – I quickly earned a reputation as the bloke who did the military stuff. I joined the combined cadet force at the first opportunity and made fast friends with a kid called Gordon Ramsey. His dad wrote a quarterly history magazine called *After the Battle*, which me and Phil loved. So now I had another solid mate in Gordon, who collected German helmets and flying kit and old bullets and even dug up aeroplanes with his dad at the weekend. I was off then, really, and never looked back.

Dad and I had started collecting medals, and every time we got one we would record it in our logbook and then write a story about the man whose medal it was. It was through this process that it began to dawn on me that collecting was a way of owning a piece of history. You could hold something in your hand that had been there on the battlefield, and the young Mark Smith wanted all of it. At some point – I'm not sure when – it also dawned on me that you could actually go out and buy this stuff, which opened up endless possibilities.

One of the first medals Dad and I got – it was No. 20 in our collection – was an India General Service Medal 1936–9. We bought it in a junk shop in Buckhurst Hill, up the road from Walthamstow. I was about nine years old, and finding and buying this medal with its green ribbon was incredibly exciting. With it safely back home, we got the medal book out and wrote its description down, and then Dad helped me understand where it was from and what it stood for.

The bar on the medal was stamped with 'North West Frontier' which, today, is in Pakistan we discovered, but was formerly a province of India.

'So, Son, where is the North West Frontier?'

'I don't know,' I replied.

Out came the atlas, and we found the right page and identified the border area between old India and Afghanistan.

'What would it be like up there?' he asked. 'Probably damn cold in the winter with snow,' he continued. 'And what about animals?'

'Tigers?' I offered.

'Yes, tigers. So tigers and snow. You can imagine this guy must have been tough. And he would have been a Muslim.'

'What's that?'

And so Dad explained what the Islamic faith was. And then we moved on to discussing how they got guns up into the mountains, and we sat there for hours chatting away, all on account of this one medal from a shop up the road.

And then something happened that had a profound effect on me. Dad asked me a simple question.

'The bloke who owned this medal – why d'you think he wanted to be a soldier?'

'I dunno,' I replied. 'Maybe to be a hero and have a gun or something?'

'Hmm . . .' He paused. 'Maybe he was just hungry and being a soldier was the only job he could get. Maybe he didn't have a choice.'

And that's when collecting medals stopped being a thing about inanimate stuff, when it all changed and when I started to think of the people behind the medals. Who were they? What did they do? Where did they come from? What made them go to war? What was their life like? From then on,

I started to think of the medals as the people they represent. The medals are 'people' that I am looking after until it's time to hand them on to someone else.

With Dad's medals I know all the details because I was brought up with the stories – endless tales about his war. They have made me want to be close to all of the people whose medals I have.

In the medal collecting world, what you want to be able to do is take each medal and find the person who was awarded it and what they did – you want to be able to put them on the battlefield, in that trench, or in the corner of that building, at that moment in time. For the most important set of medals that I have, and the ones that started all of this – Dad's medals – I have the best set of facts available: the memories of listening to Dad.

On the *Antiques Roadshow*, people say to me, 'Oh, my dad never liked to speak about the war, so we really didn't know what he did.' Well, I have the complete opposite experience. My dad never stopped talking about it. And what I want people to understand on the *Roadshow* is that you can bring out these people's stories, from their artefacts, their medals, their citations and their letters and photographs. I want people to recognize that these fathers, mothers, grandads, uncles and aunts, who didn't talk about this stuff, actually have fantastic stories to tell, and if only we can unlock them, they are amazing to hear.

So what I've got in my medal collection is about 7,000-odd people whose stories I have unlocked to a certain extent. You can only go so far, but every now and again you find something else about someone, another piece of the jigsaw of their lives, and the medal in question comes back to life just that little bit more.

Of course, there's a bit of envy in me of those who lived through the wars, and of romanticizing war in general in my outlook. I've always been fascinated and enthralled by people's memories of those times. But when I started to collect things that had been there – the wire cutters for example, or a simple wooden cross that marked the grave of a British soldier on the battlefield at Ypres and now sits on the windowsill in front of my desk – these things became time machines that took me back to those days. And they enabled those times to become mine. I can pick up a German helmet that I got in a barn in Normandy that was there on D-Day. I don't know who the bloke was who wore it, but I know what the people he was with were doing, who they were and where they went, and that's the fascinating bit for me. I always say to Fiona Bruce on the *Roadshow* when we're filming, 'You're not holding a medal, you're holding a time machine. You are holding a door that opens that moment in time all those years ago.'

One of the best examples of that was a sword that was held by the Royal Artillery Museum in Woolwich in South East London, where I was curator for twelve years. It's a thing called a basket-hilted broadsword that was used by highland soldiers in the eighteenth century and is characterized by a basket-shaped guard that protects the hand. It's often known as a claymore, and this was a really poor example – a blacksmith-made, cheap piece of rubbish. No one there paid any attention to it whatsoever.

But it had a ticket on it, and one day I got hold of this

thing and read what it said on the ticket: 'Picked up by Lt Hope in front of his gun after the Highland Charge at Culloden.' What? That knocked me for six.

Suddenly, holding this thing, feeling my hand gripping it, I was there on that freezing day in April 1746 when the Duke of Cumberland's forces crushed the Jacobite army led by Charles Edward Stuart near Inverness. I could smell the powder of the guns, and every hair stood up on my arms as I held onto this thing because it's just incredible to still have it. And that's what I love about this stuff.

Four years after Nan let me look after Dad's medals on that momentous half-birthday, Dad bought me a poster called 'Decorations and Medals 1793–1973', and a new line of collecting was launched. The concept now was trying to collect a set – in this case, all the medals listed and described on the poster. Dad and I set about our task with gusto.

Every time we found one, he would make a small mark in pencil next to its entry on the poster, and slowly those marks spread across it. But I learned something else from the project. You can't expect to find everything you're looking for just like that. In fact, it took me forty-seven years to complete the search for every medal on that poster, finishing it many years after Dad had died. You need to be patient and accept that some prizes may forever remain out of your reach.

The poster has inspired other similarly ambitious long-term projects. My most ambitious project is to collect a medal for a man killed on every day of the First World War. So far, I've got medals for 862 days of the 1,553 in total that cover the entire chronological span of the war. So I am over halfway there. The hard ones, by the way, are the days during the months of January and February when it was often too cold to fight. But people were still killed during those periods by shellfire.

For the Second World War, this kind of diary-based project is not possible because the conflict was so widespread and complex. Instead, I collect groups of medals for the main actions, for example the Battle of Britain, Dunkirk, D-Day, Kohima, Monte Cassino, Tobruk and the Atlantic convoys.

But medals of all kinds still enthral me, and they always will. The hard part these days is trying to find excuses *not* to buy the next one.

Chapter Four

Dad wrote a memoir of his career in the RAF. It sits in a box in my study and tells me what happened almost hour-by-hour. It's the standard by which all my other medals and my research around them is judged: his own detailed account that places him in a Catalina flying boat over the Bay of Bengal on special operations in the early days, weeks and months of 1944. Dad's memoir is like a piece of granite, and it forms a substantial part of this book. It's the one thing I have left – that solid lump that lives on in the box behind me.

I know this is going to sound strange, but the truth is that until I sat down to write this book I had never actually read Dad's memoir. It had sat unpublished and unread in a box next to a filing cabinet in a corner of my study like a reassuring old friend.

I always used to check it was there, a neat pile of nearly 330 typed sheets as Dad had left it, but that was all I needed. It remains one of my most valuable possessions, and looking at it is all I need to do to remind myself of him and how much I miss him.

Why I hadn't read it before now is a difficult question to answer. I would say the real reason is that I have always known the stories of Dad's war, because he told them to me over and over again. So I have always known them. I wanted those stories to remain alive in my mind and my memory, and not end up between the covers of a book, frozen on the page. I wanted to remember them as he told them to me: full of life, laughter and pride in what he and his crew had achieved.

I can see him sitting on the floor with a fag in his hand telling me about flying a Catalina over the North Atlantic, or sitting on the end of my bed with his logbook in hand. That's my living memory of him. It's like when young people get married, I'll say to them, 'Look. Every now and then, stop and look around the room, and remember who is there and where they are. Don't rely on a photo. Remember where Auntie Floris was sitting, remember where your brother and your father were standing. Treasure and nurture those memories of what you lived through on your most important day.'

I thought that reading Dad's memoir might break the spell. Then it would be in a book, and I could pick it up and read and reread it, and my memories would start to take second place and would gradually fade. I didn't want that.

Dad had never planned to write about his war, but then, in March 1997, when he was seventy-four, the North West Essex and South East Herts Branch of the Aircrew Association invited him to give a talk entitled 'Special Duties Operations in the Far East'. In the audience that evening were several members of his Catalina crew, including his old skipper, Flight Lieutenant – now Group Captain – J. M. Ayshford, and the second pilot, Flight Lieutenant Don

Foster, and me, standing by with a few visual aids to help things along.

The talk went well, and at the end the president of the branch, Air Vice-Marshal H. Alan Merriman, told my father his story was unusual because of its special-operations detail. He said it should be written down 'for the record'. Dad did not need a second invitation and sat down to write in June 1997. He borrowed a computer from my then girlfriend, Helen, and enjoyed the process.

The writing and the research took him the rest of that summer. On one occasion we went together to the National Archives at Kew to see the operation record books for his squadron. He wanted as much detail as he could find. He and I spent many hours discussing it, with me in the encouraging role, helping him to go back all those years to his early twenties.

I promised him I would publish his memoir, and I know he wanted that to happen and tried a few publishers himself, but with no luck. He told me that people weren't interested in the war – *his* war – any more. It was a sad moment.

So here we go. It's time for me to read it and share it with you. Let's see what we find . . .

I had no idea how Dad would start this project. But the first surprise is that, long before he turned up at the RAF recruiting office in Romford, he witnessed the aftermath of Dunkirk, when thousands of Allied soldiers who had been driven out of France and the Low Countries made their way across the English Channel.

They had come back on warships, merchant vessels and

the famed armada of Dunkirk little ships, and my father was waiting as some of them disembarked on the Thames. In the dying days of May 1940, he was a seventeen-year-old clerk working for a pepper importer in the City and still determined – despite the disruptive influence of the war – to finish the third year of a National Certificate in Commerce that he was studying for at the weekends. He happened to be on hand to watch a little bit of history as the troops came home.

> I witnessed depressing scenes as I stood on London Bridge, when partly dressed, largely unarmed soldiers who had been rescued from the beaches clambered ashore from small boats manned by courageous civilians. I too had been caught up in that incredible phenomenon known as the 'Dunkirk Spirit', a very real outpouring of mass optimism as the RAF took on the Luftwaffe daily, with cricket-like scores indicating marginal or considerable victories for the 'home team'.

Then a few months later in September at the onset of the Blitz, when German bombers began targeting London in a bid to break Britain's will to resist ahead of a possible invasion, Dad was there when some of the first Luftwaffe raids on the capital took place. On Saturday 7 September, he watched hundreds of bombers escorted by twice as many fighters launch a daytime raid on the Docklands at teatime.

> It was an awesome sight seeing so many planes in close formation flying relatively low over Walthamstow, the fighters much higher looking like silver gnats weaving

at speed above them. The smoke from fires caused by the bombing of the East End of London soon became a feature of the sunny afternoon sky, and people out shopping had a grandstand view of the terror of mass air raids on cities.

One reason Dad was so determined to complete his studies was that he was convinced that having a recognized qualification, in what today would be termed accountancy, would boost his chances of being selected for service in the RAF. This was a highly competitive business, and hundreds, if not thousands, of young men who volunteered to fly were being rejected for one reason or another. But there was precious little time in the evenings for him to complete his course assignments, not least because, along with his father and Uncle Vic, Dad was also carrying out fire-watching duties at Blackhorse Road School in Walthamstow, not far from the family home:

> Using his experience of trench warfare during the Great War, my father taught Vic and me how to differentiate between upward rushing shells from our own guns, including bits of shells from anti-aircraft fire, and downward falling missiles dropped by German planes.

It was not long before Hitler's Blitz hit close to home when a good friend of Dad's was killed, along with his family, when a bomb scored a direct hit on their air-raid shelter in Higham Hill: 'Frank Deadman was one of the finest cricketers in the town . . . His violent death at the age of eighteen shook me, scared me. Then two days later Uncle Vic and his wife Lil were blown out of their marital home by a landmine that dropped nearby, killing all who were at the centre of the blast.'

With his mum evacuated to the village of Llandybie in South Wales to help her recuperate from major hip surgery, Dad was growing ever more impatient to join up. He had decided that his role would be as a Radio Observer in an aircraft crew, but he was still too young. He would have to keep his plan secret – he told no one in the family of his intentions – until the new year. In the meantime, the raids continued.

There was a fairly heavy one on 27 December after a lull over Christmas. But this was a mere curtain-raiser to what happened two days later when over 1,000 bombers in three waves set out to destroy the City of London financial district. The mixture of high-explosive and incendiary bombs produced a devastating effect that became known as 'the Second Fire of London', when St Paul's Cathedral miraculously survived the destruction all around it.

The day after, always on time, Dad attempted to go to work as normal. His train from Walthamstow to Liverpool Street was delayed but it did get there eventually.

> As I walked along Bishopsgate and then Gracechurch Street, the damage on view was mind-blowing. In Eastcheap I found the road covered with worm-like hoses, limp in the smoke-filled winter air. A deliberately dropped delayed-action bomb found its time to detonate on my left, but nobody in the street moved and the new pall of smoke from yet another destroyed building merged into the thundercloud of smoke and fire that engulfed the streets.

Dad did make it to the office that morning, but the manager – a man named Ansell – quickly realized there was no point in anyone being there and sent him home. Once again, miracle of miracles, his train from Liverpool Street got him back home to Walthamstow. The following day, New Year's Eve, he was put on night-time fire-watching duty alongside Ansell, a veteran of the First World War, and the office boy, who was called Wigg. That first night proved uneventful, but the following Saturday was action-packed.

> Wigg and I had been joined by our mutual friend and colleague in spotting activities, Harry Cason of the Royal Navy. We were glad of his company during a hectic night, involving handling three incendiary bomb incidents and the dangling cable of an escaped barrage balloon. When morning came Cason pronounced, with some feeling, that we would be far safer in the armed services and that kicking fiercely burning incendiary bombs from City rooftops was a mug's game. I had to agree with him. The time had come for me to join the RAF as quickly as possible.

Joining or volunteering for the RAF, even in 1940 and 1941, when Britain faced its most perilous days, turned into quite a business.

Dad's first attempt in February 1941 ended in farce, when he turned up at the wrong RAF office in Central London. A couple of weeks later, he met an old friend from school, John Field, on the trolleybus on his way home from college. Field had been a football and cricket teammate and was now working locally in an engineering factory. His ambition was to join the RAF as a pilot, and he told my father about a recruiting centre in Romford he'd heard about.

They decided to go together, and the following Saturday Dad found himself standing outside a large Victorian house in the middle of Romford. As he and Field entered, they were guided by an RAF corporal to a room where six volunteers were already waiting. It would prove the beginning of a long day that tested my father's patience.

Finally, they were called through.

> I almost ran into the place, ahead of Field who seemed hesitant. The hall contained twenty trestle-type desks at which sat airmen clerks who faced civilians in their late twenties and early thirties. An airman told us to proceed to the stage at the far end of the hall where an officer sat mulling over piles of papers. 'He interviews recruits for aircrew,' the clerk explained. 'He's the Commanding Officer.'

> Field was dealt with in five minutes. His application to be a pilot was accepted on the basis of his having attended a craft school and because he had then completed an apprenticeship as an engineer. The officer – a squadron leader – remained seated. He turned to my father. To start with things did not go well.

> When he asked me which role I wished to perform, he was not impressed when I told him that I was keen to become a Radio Observer. I knew what the job entailed: the use of radio and airborne radar, preferably in a night fighter. The squadron leader said he couldn't see how my commercial experience and studies in that area would

transfer to high performance as an air navigator, with or without radio connections.

But then, weirdly, the interviewer seemed to have a change of heart. Suddenly he could see Dad's potential and decided his qualifications proved that he knew how to learn.

'With your record, Smith, you will find that the RAF will give you plenty of opportunity to use your learning skills, and I feel sure that you will make an effective member of aircrew, no matter which job you are given. You are accepted,' he told me.

Field and I were like excited schoolboys on the bus back to The Standard at Walthamstow. We parted company at about 7.00 p.m., and the surprising thing is that I never saw him again. I've no idea what happened to him. I certainly failed to pick up on the grapevine of school contacts that he became a pilot. My career, however, had just started and I was eager to get on with the job.

The fact that Dad had succeeded in volunteering for the RAF did not wholly delight everyone in the family, especially his mother – my nan. He confirmed the news after he had returned to Romford a few weeks later for a medical.

Mum had been away in Wales when I had volunteered, so on that day I had gone directly to Vic and Lil's on my return from Romford, and they became the first in the family to hear what I had done. Lil cried on hearing my news, like a surrogate mother. Later that evening, when I told my father that I had joined up, his first reaction was one of surprise, and then he approached me to shake me warmly by the hand.

My grandmother, bless her, having returned from Wales, had seen Dad off early that morning and was at home to welcome him back. She also cried when Dad told her he had passed the medical, knowing that it made certain that he would be joining up.

She had good reason to be upset, knowing that she would have to face again the heartache of seeing a loved one go to war, having strong memories of my father's forays to France and Flanders in the Great War. I felt sad and selfish. I had achieved a significant part of my ambition, but at what cost to my family? Now the die was cast. There was no turning back. We all had to face up to the fact that the baby of the family was off to war.

After passing another medical and sailing through selection as an aircrew in the role of Wireless Operator/Air Gunner, Dad was placed on the RAF reserve list and posted to Liverpool Street station as a relief clerk 'on war service'. Little did he know that his exceptional performance in this role would delay his longed-for call-up to active service.

The job at Liverpool Street involved helping to keep the vast station running during the Blitz. With its eighteen platforms, it was a key target of the Luftwaffe, and despite the blackout it took direct hits from incendiary devices or high-explosive bombs almost every night. Dad was quickly promoted to Senior Relief Clerk assisting the General Manager of the station.

Early in his tenure, he invited a girl from his previous employment out to the pictures after work. After leaving the cinema at 10 p.m. and then sitting around chatting to her for an hour or more, he realized he had missed the last bus home. It was to be an eventful journey.

> The moon was full as I set off for the six-mile walk to Walthamstow at 11.15 p.m. At that point, the air-raid sirens sounded and the thumps of gunfire quickly followed. This was not unusual; but the noise made by the attacking aircraft was unusually loud. I had heard this concentration of engine power before, and I knew that London was in for an air raid of massive proportions. I seemed to be walking towards the area under attack, but only occasionally did I have to take evasive action. I could see bomb-bursts ahead of me and to my right, and I gained the impression that there were a large number of Me 110 fighter-bombers active among the main bombing force.

There followed a lull as Dad reached Ferry Lane, a two-mile-long road that crosses the River Lea.

> Soon I heard the familiar crunch of bombs exploding and I could see that the areas of Stratford, Leytonstone and Leyton were under heavy attack from a mixture of bombers and fighter-bombers.
>
> The anti-aircraft guns made as much noise as the bombers. As I reached the halfway point of my Ferry Lane jaunt, the guns to my right opened up with rapid fire, and they came under machine-gun attack from a few of the raiders. It was then that I caught a glimpse of a

large formation of German bombers crossing my path. In the clear, moonlit sky, the silver glints made by the aircraft were easy to see, implying that they were at no great height and the bursting shells seemed to be both among them and above them.

Dad got home after 1.00 a.m. and managed a few hours' sleep before getting up in time for his early train to Liverpool Street.

When we pulled into platform 3, I could see the station had been hit several times during the night's raids. As I walked to my office above platform 18, I was amazed to find so much glass on the floor. It had come from the enormous arched roof of the station. I had not realized we had that much of the stuff left after the months of bombing we had already endured.

Platform 18 was a real mess. The train standing there looked as if it had been burgled. The platform now supported two pyramids of building rubble, debris from two large holes in the wall of the station where bombs had entered at an angle before exploding. I could see moving traffic on Bishopsgate from where I was standing, a very odd experience.

Men from the Heavy Duty Rescue Service were beavering away trying to clear this rubble as they searched for trapped people. Tragically, they found a loving couple who had been using a station bench as a bed, crushed to death. The search for casualties continued as I went to my office to pick up the manifest for the train that was trapped on that platform.

It was there that I heard on the news that thirty-three enemy aircraft had been shot down during a night of fierce bombing, and three of them had fallen to the guns of our ace night-fighter pilot, 'Cat's Eyes' Cunningham. I knew what that meant and I applauded silently the skill of the Radio Observer who had provided Cunningham with his uncanny night vision. That was the job I wanted.

As spring turned to the summer of 1941, the Blitz came to an end, though the night raids over London did not stop completely. But Hitler was turning his attention to the invasion of the Soviet Union and the prospect of an invasion of Britain receded. Dad continued in his role at the station. Among his duties were caring for the coffins of dead soldiers being transported back home for burial. He was also tasked with clearing prostitutes from the station concourse, and was given responsibility for plunging the station into darkness when he received a coded signal to do so from Air Raid Precautions headquarters.

In addition to his routine duties, he occasionally found himself dealing with deliveries for King George VI, who spent much of the war at Buckingham Palace.

In late June, I caused a royal fuss when I intercepted a consignment of three dozen punnets of summer fruit in the 'To be called-for' department in the station's front office. I telephoned Scotland Yard, gave my Railway Code, and asked the officer to get a message to the king's staff to hasten collection in view of the perishable nature of the goods involved. Thirty minutes after my call, a small fleet of taxis arrived together with a number of civil servants to collect the king's summer fruit. I received an official commendation for my handling of this consignment. Henceforth, the king's golf bag, golf shoes tied to it, would arrive with clubs poking out for onward transportation to Sandringham. Such was the trust the palace placed in the honesty of the staff at Liverpool Street. Apparently, I was making a name for myself without knowing it.

To his horror, Dad discovered that his boss was so impressed with his performance that he had applied to the Air Ministry to have his call-up cancelled. His role was henceforth to be considered a 'reserved occupation', meaning Dad would continue at Liverpool Street indefinitely. Far from being flattered, my father was furious, and the moment he got home he wrote to the ministry requesting an immediate call to the colours to honour the contract he had signed seven months earlier.

In response, his mobilization papers arrived at 74 Blenheim Road, Walthamstow in mid-September.

Chapter Five

I'm very parochial, in as much as I'm very happy when I'm at home – and I feel I've come home when I get off the train in Walthamstow. When I go to other bits of London, that's London. This is home.

Walthamstow was difficult to spell and pronounce when you were small. It's an old Saxon word, 'Wilcumestou', that is mentioned in the Domesday Book of 1086. It means 'Place of Welcome'.

Now a suburban town about seven miles north-east of Central London within the London Borough of Waltham Forest, it would have been one of the first places travellers from the north or East Anglia came to on their way to the capital.

The oldest part – the 'village-y' bit – where St Mary's Church is, has always been there. The church dates from the twelfth century, and the timber-framed house on Church Lane known as 'The Ancient House' goes back to the fifteenth century.

The Smith family and Walthamstow go back a long way too. My great-grandad, George, probably came to the area around the late 1890s when he opened a butcher's shop down by what is now the Crooked Billet roundabout, where there was a pub of the same name.

Prior to that George had been living in Whitechapel and worked as a butcher for many years at Leadenhall meat market in the City. The family story goes that when he was in Whitechapel he was taken in for questioning by the police to see if he was Jack the Ripper. It was after the second of the five murders attributed to London's storied Victorian-era serial killer in Whitechapel and Spitalfields that George had his collar felt.

Annie Chapman, a forty-seven-year-old prostitute of 29 Hanbury Street in Spitalfields had been strangled and then had her throat cut before her body was extensively mutilated. The police believed her killer must have had some anatomical knowledge because of the way she had been disembowelled, and they worked on the theory that the murderer could be a doctor or a butcher.

But doctors were rich, upper-class people, they reasoned, so they concluded it couldn't possibly be one of those. It would have to be a butcher, and witnesses who saw Chapman on the night of her death thought she had been with a foreigner. So George Schmidt, the butcher with a foreign name who worked at Leadenhall market, was brought in for questioning, but that's as far as it went.

What I do know is that my grandad Dick, George's son, was at elementary school on Blackhorse Road in Walthamstow long before the First World War, so we've been in the area for well over 100 years and, like most of my forebears, I've spent my entire life in Walthamstow.

It's a funny thing, but I've never thought about leaving, and I find it difficult to understand how I might ever do that because this is our place, it's where we're from. And I can still see them, all of them – my parents, my grandads and nans, my uncles and aunts – walking along the pavements and popping in and out of the shops.

On Wood Street, where the railway station is and where the Co-op is now, there used to be a little parade of shops. There was a butcher's and a sweetshop, and there used to be a couple of benches there. And I remember driving by one day and there was Dad sitting outside the butcher's shop on the bench. When I drive past there now I still see him, sitting on that bench, and he seems as real to me now as he did then . . .

I used to go shopping with Mum on Wood Street. And those trips frame my memories of old Walthamstow, the place that defines me. We used to walk from the top of Forest Road where we lived and then go shopping all along Wood Street to the station end, then turn the corner and walk back up the hill. I used to enjoy listening to Mum's stilettos clicking on the pavement – a crisp rhythmic sound that reminded me of breaking a bar of Bournville chocolate.

It was a different place to today, in as much as it had a street of shops which were very old and very *interesting*. As you came into Wood Street there was a supermarket on the right-hand side, which was a new concept in those days. It was called Neemans and opposite was the public library where I got my first books about medals. Then you moved along and there was a butcher's shop, an old-fashioned establishment with the joints, chickens, rabbits and game hanging in the windows. The butcher had been taught by Grandad Dick, so when we went in we were treated slightly differently. It felt like we got a bit extra.

Next door was the fishing tackle shop. While Mum was

in the butcher's, I would look through the windows at the fishing stuff. It was a dark, gloomy shop run by an old man, and he had glass cases full of stuffed fish – pike, perch, carp, bream and things like that. And I've always wanted one of those cases stuffed full of fish that I had caught. But we'll come to that. 'One day I'll get one of these,' I promised myself as I pressed my nose on the glass casing.

You could get boxes of maggots in that shop, and I used to delight in showing Mum my half-pint of writhing, wriggling little creatures, which made her flinch. Me and Phil Nobo bought our tackle and rods there, and we used to go fishing at Ferry Boat where there's a famous pub, the Ferry Boat Inn, on the side of Low Maynard reservoir. It's an area of wooded islands and marshes that divides Walthamstow from Tottenham, near where Dad had walked home that night after he missed the last bus during the Blitz. But I never caught anything, ever. No joke, I never caught a single fish.

One day me and Philip found a dead one. It was a biggie. I don't know what it was, but it was probably ten inches long and it had gone sort of greyish, as dead fish tend to. One way or another it was very dead, and we decided we would take it home and show everybody we had finally caught something. So we got it home and proudly had our photograph taken with it. Then we tried to stuff it like I'd seen in the shop. We used grass cuttings, but the scales were coming off in our hands and the poor creature was going to fall apart before we'd got the job done. Eventually, it was Uncle Tom who said, 'I don't think this is going to work,' and he magically made it disappear. By that time the old fish was stinking to high heaven.

Next to the fishing tackle shop was the newsagent's where my favourite comic, *Warlord*, came from. It was delivered on Thursday mornings along with the *Daily Express*, then a broadsheet, which arrived every day with the milk. If I was with Auntie Bob, she would buy me other comics like *The Beano* and *The Topper* and a packet of Rolos. After that it was Percy Ingles, the bakers, and then it was the most magical shop on Wood Street – J. E. Telford, a toyshop I used to call 'Mr Telford's'.

It had *everything*: model railways, Action Men, Dinky Toys, Airfix kits, Scalextric sets, cap guns and marbles. The Action Man uniforms would be hanging from a frame on the ceiling. You would say which one you wanted, and Mr Telford would use a wooden pole with a brass hook on the end to bring it down.

In the centre of the shop there was a roundabout with toy cars on it that went round and round for sixpence each. Mr Telford's was where I got my model aeroplanes and where Dad bought my railway set for Christmas in 1967. We would get our fireworks for bonfire night there, too, and it was always a special occasion because Dad's birthday was on 6 November, so we had a double celebration.

Opposite was another toyshop, called the Kay Shop. If I was with Auntie Bob, whose real name was Kathleen and who was often known as Kay, we would go in. She would buy me another Action Man for my collection, or a paratrooper uniform or something for the twenty or so I already had. Next to that was Mr Moffat's, the chemist. He wore a white coat, and it was another dark interior with big jars in the window full of drugs, powders and potions. Inside, everything was in drawers or jars, and it was a hushed atmosphere, like the library but without the books.

Then there was a sweetshop where Dad used to go on Saturdays and buy liquorice cuttings. It was all on display – bonbons, gobstoppers, toffees, boiled sweets, you name it – and it was quite low down so children could see what they wanted. The dogs could too, and stuff would get licked before your quarter of aniseed balls, or whatever it was, made it into a paper bag. Dad would get his cigarettes in there – Player's in a white box.

A couple of shops along from the sweetshop was our local record shop. One of the first albums we bought was *Big Western Themes*, a collection of cowboy film scores from westerns like *The Big Country* or *The Magnificent Seven*. The first record I bought with my own money was 'Tiger Feet', the runaway mid-1970s hit by Mud.

We had a record player at home and Dad had a 10-inch 1951 recording of the Swedish tenor Jussi Björling singing the opening aria from Bizet's opera *The Pearl Fishers* alongside the American baritone Robert Merrill. That celebrated duet used to get played every Sunday morning, and it remains my all-time favourite, so much so that it will be the last piece of music played at my funeral.

It's just an incredible aria, and the two voices of Björling and Merrill are absolutely perfect. Far better, in my opinion, than Bryn Terfel and Andrea Bocelli, who have also recorded it. They're good, but not on a par with Jussi Björling and Robert Merrill.

I always wanted to go and see that opera, and one day I got tickets for Opera in the Park at Holland Park in West

London. *The Pearl Fishers* is about two-and-a-half-hours long and it starts with the aria. They never sing it again and the remaining two hours and twenty minutes are interminable – absolutely awful, which is amazing because Bizet got it so right with the first bit. After that, what a load of old rubbish it is. I've never gone again and never will. It's a shame – I wished he'd only written the opening and then gone home and left it at that.

After another sweetshop, a bicycle shop and a wet-fish shop, you came to A. Pamphilon and Sons Ltd. This was an emporium – otherwise known as a hardware store – on three floors with a wonderful smell of polish and paraffin that sold everything from taps to pint mugs, light bulbs and floor mops. Beyond that there was a tobacco importer, and then you got to the station and turned left, and that was more or less it from start to finish.

While Wood Street was our local secret, Walthamstow was famous for its never-ending market on the High Street, which opened Thursdays to Saturdays. Bustling, noisy, smelly and vibrant, it attracted shoppers in their thousands, stretched for over a mile and is still reckoned to be the second-longest street market in Europe after Rome's Porta Portese.

We would walk past the traders shouting out their wares, selling everything from vegetables to curtains and clothes, and Mum would grip my hand. 'Don't let go, don't disappear, don't walk off,' she would say as we fought our way through the throng towards her Uncle Bert's fish stall.

There was another toyshop down there, called Percival's, and one Saturday morning – a couple of days after my half-birthday in 1969 when I got my dad's medals – he bought me a policeman's uniform and a camouflaged soldier's uniform with a plastic steel helmet from there.

But the shop on the High Street that really changed my world was H. M. Stores – an army-surplus business run by a brother and sister who were Jewish. This became my Mecca because hanging up outside were iconic Second World War military items of clothing and kit. They had Irvin flying jackets, Sidcot suits like my dad had worn, webbing, battledress and all sorts of hats, helmets and caps. And – oh my God – the smell. The smell of that shop was *un-be-lievable*. Mouldy old uniforms and a musty scent of damp military clothing. We went in and, oh lord, it was beyond Aladdin's Cave.

When I got the uniforms from Percival's home, Dad pointed out that I now needed a kit bag. So we went back to H. M. Stores, and he bought me what turned out to be a 1943-pattern lightweight gas mark carrying case. It cost sixpence. We took it home and he wrote my name on the front with his service number – 'Warrant Officer Mark Smith 138959'.

To the north of Walthamstow is Epping Forest, which stretches for thirty miles up towards what is now the M25 orbital motorway. During the summer holidays, Phil would come round on his bike and that's where we'd go. We'd come out of Mum and Dad's, go past our school, cross over the bridge on Forest Road, and then we were into the beginning of the woods.

There's a place up there we called 'the bumps' – lumpy things we used to ride our bikes over. And there was a bit we called 'the glade' where me and Phil and a few other blokes used to play cricket or football by the stone memorial to

Gypsy Smith. That would be Rodney Smith, by the way, a famed Romany Gypsy preacher known as the 'King of the Gypsies.' He was born in a tent in Epping Forest but died on the way to New York, on board the *Queen Mary*, in 1947. We'd be up there all day and then ride back home for tea.

So that's how I remember it, but I have to admit, Walthamstow has not always been the most prosperous of places. And certainly, in the 1970s, when I was growing up, and the early 1980s it was a fairly dodgy place, really. A lot of the shops started to disappear, including the lovely old fishing shops and Pamphilon's, and in their place came tacky fast-food joints and betting shops.

It got pretty run down, and there was a lot of vagrancy with drunks wandering the streets. The market changed from that wonderful, vibrant collection of traders to a place of knocked-off T-shirt sellers and people hawking rubbish. And the High Street wasn't a place you wanted to go to, and nor would you want to be on the streets much after dark. The pubs went downhill, with hard, miserable characters in them who didn't like youngsters walking in. It became a time when, if you were asked where you lived and you said 'Walthamstow', people looked twice at you as if to say 'Oh, really?'

But then in the early 2000s things started to change. We started to go back down the High Street. A few new stores had opened selling fresh produce, and suddenly you could start to feel a bit of a buzz about the place. It all changed when Orford Road – a little street where the old town hall used to be – became the place to go in Walthamstow to eat out.

I remember thinking to myself 'We've got a restaurant!' when the first one opened. There's now a big Italian there, a place called The Village Kitchen, a tapas bar, a Thai restaurant, and Orford Road has become partly pedestrianized with an antiques shop and a bakery. The pub, the Queen's Arms, used to be a horrible place, but even that has become trendy. We took Mum there for her last birthday, and now, most Sundays, you will find us on the sofas there enjoying their amazing roast dinners served by the lovely Charity.

On Saturdays and Sundays, Orford Road is humming, and the hilarious thing is that people sit outside on the pavements. I mean, who would have thought you would ever sit outside on the pavement in Walthamstow? If you said to Mum and Dad we're going to Orford Road, and we are going to sit outside and have a latte and croissant, they would stare at you like you'd fallen out of a tree.

At the same time, the kind of people who have come to live in Walthamstow has changed, with the migration from West to East London by families in search of larger houses at lower prices. When you get off the train from the City and walk home, you're surrounded by thirty-somethings, and they are professionals. They're not workmen. They are not covered in paint like they used to be. They're well turned out, and you can tell they are doing what you might call professional jobs in things like IT or advertising. And these days there are a lot of mothers with pushchairs. They go around in gangs, congregating at coffee shops and sitting on the pavement outside the pubs that are now child-friendly. There's a pub round the corner, and it's like a crèche on a Sunday morning.

The Walthamstow I grew up in was already quite ethnically diverse, with people from the Caribbean and India mainly, but it's now a very mixed environment with new arrivals from all over the world, and that too has changed the face of the place. It's gone from being quite insular to a much more outward-facing society. I think the London Olympics had a part to play in that, too.

The 2012 Games changed the feel of the whole East End of London. It became a completely different place – livelier, friendlier, with more things to do, more restaurants, more nightlife and a new, more welcoming atmosphere in the pubs. The Olympics was quite a moment, when the world started to change, especially for places that got part of the Games, like the Lee Valley White Water Centre, just north of Walthamstow, where they did the canoeing and stuff. Suddenly we had a community again – not like the 1960s when everybody knew everybody – but something new and just as good.

I still walk down Wood Street and think about the shops that were there, and I can get quite depressed about it, but you can see the positives. We now have the Wood Street Deli, the Wood Street Bakery & Cafe, which styles itself as an 'artisanal patisserie/bakery', and there's a wine bar, and you can sit outside and have a glass of red . . . on Wood Street. It's got a friendly feel, and I still feel I belong.

I know I live in the past because that's where I'm happiest. I don't like New Year's Day. Actually, I can't stand it because it's one day further away from everything that's important to me. And I don't like not knowing what's coming. So New Year's Eve and 1 January are non-days.

Nowadays, I walk round Walthamstow with nostalgia for the old times, but I enjoy what is here now. What this means is that Walthamstow – Wilcumestou – is a happier place. I don't mean a happier place for people. I mean for the bricks, the roads and the trees because it has got back for itself a nicer life to exist in and live through.

I can't finish my little tour of my manor without mentioning the magnificent town hall that serves Walthamstow and the wider borough of Waltham Forest. It's a huge symmetrical building with nineteen window bays facing onto Forest Road, designed in the 'stripped classical style', free of almost all ornamentation, and built in Portland stone and topped off with a large copper-clad clock tower.

We used to call it 'Mussolini' because of its resemblance to Italian brutalist architecture of the 1930s. It used to have a big fountain outside with a wall round it and a pond where Dad and I used to sail our model boats. Mum and I used to go past it on the bus, and she would always point out the old Thorpe Coombe maternity hospital which was opposite the town hall. 'That's the room you were born in Markie,' she would say, pointing at an end window as we trundled by.

That part of town is a poignant location for me. In our family, going back years, my mum and dad, and nan and grandad, often used to say to me, 'D'you know what? You should be on the *Antiques Roadshow*, Markie – you're just made for it . . .' It resonated for years. Not that I thought for one moment it would ever come true. But it did in the early summer of 2014, and, by an extraordinary coincidence, I made my second appearance on the show when it visited Walthamstow Town Hall.

I will never forget standing by the old fountain and preparing to do my piece to camera. It was an item about First World War German uniforms and other bits of equipment that a lady's dad had collected in the 1950s while he was a soldier in Germany. She came from Leyton, and our item made the coveted closing slot of the programme that day.

As I stood there gathering my thoughts, I looked up and saw Thorpe Coombe and thought of Mum on the bus and sailing my model boat with Dad. 'Well, Mum and Dad,' I said to myself, 'if this is ever going to work as you have long predicted, this is the day when we'll find out.' Getting the closing slot on that edition felt like scoring a century at Lord's on debut. It really did.

Chapter Six

My dad was my best friend. He was my best mate. We did everything together.

It was amazing because he had this idea – this underlying theory – that whatever we did together I was going to learn something. So I was always going to be enriched by whatever it was that we were going to do.

We didn't just sit there and watch television, for example. We would sit and watch a war film – and we watched a lot of war films – and he would pick bits out of the film that he could tell you more stuff about. So that you learned something about Spitfires or tanks or whatever it might be. Or it might even be about the battle itself – when it took place, where he was when that battle happened, and things like that.

So there was always this constant stream of talking. My dad, Leslie Smith, talked *a lot*. About all sorts of things and whatever it was that I was doing, or what other people were doing – they got the same treatment. It was a conversation, though. He would tell me things, and I would ask him lots of questions, and he'd tell me lots of answers.

In my mind I would think of it as all part of me trying to learn as many things as possible on my journey to being able to look back and do that Smith family thing of saying, 'Well, fifty years ago . . .' So everything I got told and did was part of this bank of stuff that I was going to have like everybody else, and the stuff Dad used to tell me was more ammunition that I could store away.

He was small, only 5ft 6, and there wasn't much of him. But he was in good shape. We are skinny people, the Smiths. My Auntie Bob was 4ft 11, and she could eat three Sunday lunches no problem whatsoever. And she would stay 4ft 11 and size 6 – that's what she was when she died.

Dad was smartly turned out. He wore a shirt and tie, tweed jackets or suits with waistcoats, and polished brown shoes. At weekends he'd let his hair down. Then it would be trousers, a jumper and an open-necked shirt.

He had sharp features but a kind face and a ready smile, and he looked like a ginger-haired version of the late great British film and television actor Peter Cushing. He was bright and the possessor of an incisive and questioning intellect, the sort of person who would never accept anything on the face of it or settle for second best. If something could be improved, he would be thinking – and talking about – how that might be done, and he could engage both sides of his brain. Dad was numerate and he could write.

He was very precise. Everything was well thought through, and he had a reasoned way of telling me about things. He wasn't always laughing and joking; he was a serious person, and though he was never miserable he could get quite grumpy about things that were beyond his control . . . like anything to do with DIY. When it came to mending the car or putting up a shelf, he didn't have a clue. At home we used to say, 'We have a toffee hammer, a hairclip and a screwdriver' – that was our toolkit, and if we couldn't get it done with that, then we'd have to get someone in.

I knew that out of Uncle Vic, Auntie Bob and Nan, Dad was something special. He could play the piano and the trumpet, and he was a voracious reader. Today he'd be one of those kids who would have done an A level at fourteen.

We used to do so much together, like going to the speedway on Friday nights at Hackney Wick stadium on Waterden Road, where we would cheer on our heroes in the Hackney Hawks, or later the Hackney Kestrels. Dad loved it and so did I. A few years back, for my sixtieth birthday, my wife's cousin Tim, and his wife, Sarah, bought me tickets to Poole speedway. I sat there watching the Poole Pirates, loving the roar of the engines and the rich aroma of burning fuel, and I cried because I was there with Dad, sitting at the speedway again.

The sport was in our family. Uncle Vic went to the first speedway meeting ever held in England, at High Beech on the edge of Epping Forest, when 30,000 people turned up and stood inside and outside the track to watch the bikes. In the 1950s, Dad's uncle Ernie was a rider for Poole Pirates. He won races despite having a badly fractured leg after an accident while serving as a despatch rider during the war in North Africa. It was held together by two metal bolts. As a kid, I used to sit on the floor in Auntie Bob's trying to look up his trouser leg to see if he was really some sort of Frankenstein. He wasn't that, but he was certainly one tough guy.

Dad and I got into speedway by default after we went to see Tottenham play Manchester United at White Hart Lane in March 1973. That day, I saw Pat Jennings in goal and Martin Peters in midfield for Spurs, while United's team included Jimmy Rimmer in goal and Brian Kidd and Bobby Charlton up front. It was a draw, but it was the violence outside the ground after the match that made the biggest impression. Afterwards, Dad said he realized there was nothing he could do to protect me if we got caught up in it and decreed, there and then, that it would be the last football match he was ever taking me to.

About a year later a poster caught his eye on his way back from work. 'Hackney Speedway: Make It a Date – Friday at 8'. So we went along and got hooked. The first time was in July 1974, and it was a test match between England and Poland. I thought it was so exciting – the smell, the noise and the speed. I reckon we went every Friday until they stopped racing in Hackney in 1996.

I never bought a motorbike. If anything, watching people like Barry Thomas, Zenon Plech, Finn Thomsen, Laurie Etheridge or Bo Petersen haring around made me not want one. You would see these guys crash at 60 or 70mph into a fence. Mostly they would get straight back up on their bikes, and we were impressed with how tough they were. Dad used to say that Barry Thomas was a sort of Battle of Britain-style rider. In those days there was almost no health and safety, and the riders would wear a 'monkey mask' – a leather face-covering with eyepieces. And Thomas, who rode for Hackney Hawks, would add a scarf tied around his neck that flapped in the breeze like a fighter pilot, and he was very good.

Nowadays, they have squishy air fences round the corners, and they wear suits with lots of protection built into them. It's still bloody dangerous, but safer than back then when the fences were made of chicken wire. The problem was they either went over them, or under them. They would land on the dog track, which had lamp posts around it, and that was dangerous. That's how Vic Harding, a Hackney Hawks rider, got killed in June 1979. And we were there. He got thrown over the fence and hit a lamp post, aged twenty-six.

You go to the speedway, and you see crashes and some of them are not nice, and you think, 'Uh-oh,' and the medics come on and, bless them, the riders get taken off in stretchers. But this one was spectacularly bad. Harding was at the back, and he got some grip on the track from somewhere – it happens occasionally when they find a bit more dirt on the surface and accelerate. He went past the bloke in front and then hit the rider in second, who was Steve Weatherley, an Eastbourne Eagles rider. I mean, really hit him at 65–70mph. The impact threw Harding up in the air and into the lamp post while Weatherley was left paralysed. There was total silence in the stadium. I think we all realized Harding had been killed instantly.

People think speedway is boring. Four riders whizzing around the same old track. But it's like any sport – baseball, for example, which I love. When you know what's going on, it's fascinating. In speedway, you don't watch the leader in any race. You spend your time watching the blokes behind him who are trying to get past each other to get to the front. That's the exciting part. That's the thrill of the thing.

Dad's other big passion was wine, and we would go out and buy a lot of it together. And, because of him, I love wine too. I started drinking it when I was about five years old in a tiny glass, which I would have with roast beef on a Sunday.

His favourite was Pommard, a red burgundy. We would go to Bertie Blyth's shop near the town hall, and he would buy a case of it. One of things I always wanted to do was buy a case of wine like Dad used to, not just a bottle.

When I was going out with my first girlfriend, I took her to an Italian restaurant in Chingford, and I bought a bottle of wine to go with dinner, and it tasted like floor cleaner – awful. That Sunday we were sitting at lunch and Dad had an amazing wine on the go as usual. I said to him, 'How d'you do this, because the stuff I had last night was dreadful and I don't know what to buy?'

'Well, I'll tell you what we'll do,' he said. 'I'll buy a bottle of wine every week for a year, and we'll drink each one. And at the end of the year, I'll tell you which wine you like best.'

So we got to the end of the year, and fifty-two bottles later he said, 'Well, Son, you've got a problem.'

'Oh, why's that?' I replied.

'Well, you only really like Bordeaux; you only like the left bank' – of the Gironde estuary – 'you only really like the Haut-Médoc, so Château Lafite, Château Latour and the Lynch-Bages. You know what that means?'

'No?'

'It means you're going to be poor forever, but you're going to drink some fabulous wine!'

He used to say there are four wines that I had to try before I die – the aforementioned Château Lafite and Château Latour, plus Château d'Yquem and Château Pétrus. The Lafite graced our table at home every now and again, and Dad always bought d'Yquem at Christmas. It tastes like honey with flowers. On my fortieth birthday,

I bought myself a bottle of Latour, which was fantastic. But a Pétrus – regarded by some as the best red wine in the world – was rather harder to get hold of, not least because of the price, at something like £1,000 a bottle (often a lot more than that).

No matter, I decided I would aim at reaching the grand old age of fifty with a glass of Pétrus in my hand. So I set about saving my pennies. When I came home every day over the next ten years, I would chuck my spare change into a couple of brass artillery shell casings that sit in the corner of my study, and gradually I filled them up.

When the time came, I bought this bottle – I think it was about £700. It was the cheapest Pétrus I'd ever seen – and I paid for it with my credit card. Then I came home and counted out the money in the shell casings, and I was about forty quid short. So the bottle cost me about £40 extra, and we had it on Christmas Day on what was Dad's last Christmas.

Dad was Walthamstow through and through. He was born in November 1922 in the front bedroom of 74 Blenheim Road. He met my mother in 1926 when he was four and she was two. Joan Irene Doris Riley lived at 81 Tavistock Avenue, and their back gardens joined together. They met through a hole in the fence.

Mum was an absolute diamond, a lovely little person whom I adored. I didn't call her Mum because I found out one day that on her chequebook it said 'J. I. D. Smith'.

'That's for "J" for Joan and "I" for Irene, Mum, but what's the "D" for?' I asked her.

'Oh no, you don't want to know,' she replied, clearly

wishing whatever it was could stay as her secret forever. But I wasn't going to let go and she knew it.

'Go on Mum . . . what's the "D" for? Dorothy? Deborah? Dawn?'

'No.'

'Oh . . . go on Mum . . .'

'Well, it's Doris,' she said finally, exhaling loudly.

'Really?'

'Yes, Markie boy. But I hate it and please don't use it.'

So, naughty little chap that I was, I called her 'Mrs Doris' from then on. During the war, she worked up near Liverpool Street at the International Tea Company in Mitre Square. Then she worked in the office for Tesco until I came along, and then she stayed at home. She was great. She would let me and Phil get on with it, and like Dad, she had her war stories to tell, including a terrifying moment when she was caught in the open by a German fighter plane.

Mum had a little sister called Brenda, and they were walking along in Walthamstow down by Blackhorse Lane when the fighter appeared from nowhere and opened fire on them with its machine gun. Mum grabbed Brenda and threw her into a doorway as the plane roared over at chimney-top height.

I know this because many years later my friend Gordon came round, and he had a Luftwaffe-issue oxygen mask with him that would normally go with a German pilot's flying helmet and goggles. Gordon had managed to get his hands on something really special because the masks were rare and normally cost about £1,400. He'd got this one somehow or other, and he knew I was both jealous and annoyed that he had one and I didn't.

He put a polystyrene dummy's head covered in a tea towel on the coffee table in the front room and prepared to make the most of it, with a spectacular unveiling.

'Would you like a bacon sandwich and a cup of tea, Gordon?' Mum asked him, before disappearing into the kitchen.

'Yes please, Joan.'

Then off comes the towel and there it is – one of those bloody oxygen-mask things. At which point Mum came back in and stopped in her tracks.

'Oh – my – God!' she enunciated slowly, one word at a time.

'What's wrong, Mum?' I asked.

'D'you know what? That's exactly what the German man looked like who machine-gunned me and Brenda on Black-horse Lane,' she said.

I was stunned and remember thinking, 'Flippin' 'eck! The only reason she knows that is because that is what she saw.'

As a young child, Dad was lucky to survive a period of serious illness, when he was clobbered by the joint attack of scarlet fever and diphtheria. He had to re-learn how to walk, and it took him months to recover under Nan's attentive care. He went to William Morris School in Walthamstow and left in 1936 when he was fourteen, a surprisingly young age considering the career he had in later life.

After school, Dad got a job working for a spice broker in the City near Monument. He always called it the *Piper nigrum* company because they sold black pepper. He was a clerk and an errand boy and would go around the City with messages wearing a posh homburg hat. He bought it on his fifteenth birthday and was wearing it proudly one day on his way through Billingsgate fish market, when a porter threw a cod's head at him. It knocked his hat clean off, and it landed on the fishy mess on the floor.

Always neat, always tidy, Dad was furious and told the porter in his best East End invective where to go before storming off to great roars of laughter from his assailant and his mates. After that, Dad used to joke that you always knew when he was coming towards you because of the faint aroma of a fishing trawler that preceded him.

At the weekends, he attended South West Essex Technical College, where he was doing a three-year apprenticeship on the commodities market in the City when the outbreak of war intervened.

Chapter Seven

Having extricated himself from his responsibilities at Liverpool Street station, Dad was finally on his way to the RAF, still a few months shy of his nineteenth birthday.

His first posting was to Padgate in the suburbs of Warrington in Cheshire where, alongside 300 other recruits, he would begin basic training. My grandad Dick gave him a pep talk before he left home, and my mum went with my nan to the station to see him off. Dad wrote:

> Armed with a great deal of sound advice from my father who was concerned about the safety of my kit and personal belongings – tips from an old soldier used to the petty pilfering that takes place in service life – I left for Euston station accompanied by my mother and my girlfriend, Joan.
>
> The farewell was not the tearful event I had expected. On the contrary, Mum put on an act she had learned during the First World War, and Joan, new to the whole experience, simply looked sweet but pensive. I was the cocky young man off to war – proper war – and I put on an act of bravado. But probably we all felt the same deep down: sad and scared.

Padgate proved a whirlwind of new experiences. Dad found himself in his first servicemen's hut alongside twenty other recruits. He tasted air force cooking for the first time – a concoction of cold fried sausage and hot cooked beetroot, together with a pint mug of strong tea – and he began the laborious process of learning to march on the parade ground. He was also getting to know his fellow recruits and enjoying finally being in the RAF. 'At long last I was a full-time airman,' he remembered.

Dad was a full 5ft 3 when he joined up. Remarkably, he would 'grow' by three and a quarter inches in response to the rigours of physical training. In the meantime, he relied on the RAF tailors to alter the smallest standard-issue uniforms to fit him. 'The storeman found the smallest tunic and greatcoat in stock, and the corporal tailor made swift marks to indicate changes that were needed to give me a "military" look.'

Marching around on the vast parade ground, Dad was unlucky to be given his first reprimand after someone near him responded to the warrant officer's command by muttering an expletive under his breath.

> When we reached the flagpole, we were ordered to halt and turn to face the WO. 'Who said bollocks?' queried the senior NCO. Nobody answered. 'Right, you lot,' he continued, 'you are all on cook-house fatigues for two days starting tonight after supper.' I had been in the air force for less than a week and I was already on two days' jankers – that's service life for you.

As marching discipline developed, other details of air force life had to be mastered. Dad learned how to polish his buttons, his buckle and cap badge without staining his tunic, his hat or his greatcoat. He learned how to respond to a gas attack using a gas mask after being briefly exposed to tear gas. He wrote his will in his paybook, and he learned how to display his kit for inspection.

After a week he was posted, along with 140 fellow trainee Wireless Operator/Air Gunners, to RAF Blackpool where his new accommodation was a seaside guest house. The recruits slept in six bedrooms, four to a room.

Now they began learning the basic steps of drill, first – bizarrely – in socks on the maplewood dancefloor of the Winter Gardens, under the instruction of a Sergeant Sooty, and then on the streets of the town. My father got his first fourpenny short back and sides and attended a lecture by an RAF doctor about the ten quickest ways to pick up any of the several types of venereal disease.

> After hearing what he said I vowed never to kiss another girl, never to go to the toilet with the seat down, never to take a drag from another man's lit cigarette, and never to have sexual intercourse. In short, I equated service life with the celibate life of a monastery, such was the power of sexual education presented in so dramatic a manner.

But this did not stop Dad and his mates from mixing with the WAAFs billeted at Blackpool, who were outnumbered ten to one by the 10,000 airmen posted to the town. 'They were the target of attention of many aircrew cadets, and they were essential companions at the vast dance hall of the Tower Ballroom.'

Blackpool was where Morse code training started. This

was the beginning of a long journey in a discipline that Dad excelled at.

> At the end of the first week, we were marched in our squads to the Tram Sheds at South Shore for our introduction to training in the reception of Morse code. We were each issued with a card carrying the complete code and were given twenty minutes to learn it using 'dah-de-dah' pronunciation. I thought it was rather optimistic of the air force to expect the code to be mastered in such a short space of time, but I was proved wrong. Most of us were 'dah and dit' perfect in twenty minutes.

After that, Dad spent half of most days in those sheds with up to 1,000 other recruits listening to Morse through earphones as the speed inexorably increased from four, to six, then eight, then ten, and finally eleven words per minute. The endless fixation on the code proved destructive to the mental health of some of Dad's fellow recruits.

> The monotonous drone through headphones drove some of the cadets mad. These unfortunate men were placed in the clinic above Feldman's Theatre and disappeared from service life. This may sound uncaring but, in truth, every wireless operator will know how frightening it is to become 'Morse crazy'.

Alongside Morse was training with rifles and bayonets, live shooting at the range, performing 'cold, boring and pointless' guard duty, and learning unarmed combat.

The new year saw Dad posted, along with 120 other cadets, to RAF Yatesbury on Salisbury Plain, where snow lay deep on the ground and the camp consisted of dismal rows of cold wooden huts. But the Wireless Operator training there proved highly effective as the Morse speed went up again, with messages now being received at eighteen words per minute, and sent at twenty-two.

Dad was making progress like the proverbial house on fire, fully bearing out the recruiting officer at Romford's hunch that his learning skills would prove effective. And he excelled not only in the classroom but on Salisbury Plain too, where the recruits trained with machine guns and .38-calibre revolvers, and completed a physical-training programme involving six-mile cross-country runs, which my father found easy, having been a runner at school.

Having passed every hurdle set before him with flying colours, my father then found himself posted to a top-secret outfit near West Drayton on the outskirts of West London. Going there with him was a young man called Willmott, a like-minded soul he had become friends with at Yatesbury.

This was the beginning of a phase in my father's career that was all a bit cloak and dagger, and it was exciting for the young Leslie Smith. When he arrived at No. 1 Signals Depot, he listened intently as the squadron leader set out the programme ahead to the group of twenty-seven Wireless Operator cadets who had been reminded of their obligations under the Official Secrets Act.

> You have been selected to undergo training at this depot in aerial science and the skills needed to assemble wireless telegraphy equipment, receivers and transmitters, and to

operate them using special codes. The short course you will undertake is preliminary to becoming operational in the field in a number of situations, but all of them will involve wireless telegraphy in forested and hilly or mountainous terrain. The work you will do from now on is classified as 'top secret'.

Only nine cadets made it through this rigorous rite of passage, which involved manufacturing and erecting every conceivable type of aerial and creating a range of transmitters from boxed-up parts. Almost inevitably my father was the first to be judged a 'Pass'.

From there, Dad and Willmott were sent to a secret unit in South Wales where they worked on Operation Panda. This was a classified disinformation programme dreamed up by no less a personage than the prime minister himself, Winston Churchill. It involved sending fictitious radio messages about troop and aircraft movements to fool the Germans and deter them from any thoughts they may have about invading Britain from Ireland. Dad loved his time in the rural backwater of Abergavenny and enjoyed being involved in a top-secret project which, he noted, gave him and his colleagues a certain credibility with the locals. 'I enjoyed living the myth that we were "more than we seemed". This approach certainly made us very popular among the girls,' he wrote.

Life in South Wales was followed by another posting to Yatesbury during the miserable winter of 1942–3, and there's an interesting family detail here.

When I married Helen in 1998, we went with Dad to

see Helen's grandma, whose name was Gladys. Now, Gladys Richardson had been in the WAAF, and she and Dad got talking about the war. Gradually, they started to narrow it down until they realized that they were both at Yatesbury during his second posting there. Gladys had been a corporal cook at the camp, and she served the cadets breakfast every morning. If only Dad could have known that the woman serving him bacon and eggs would become the grandmother of the woman who would become his son's wife . . .

Yatesbury Mark II was where the cadets went flying for the first time. Those who were repeatedly airsick were ejected from the course. After waiting for weeks for the weather to improve, Dad finally got airborne in January 1943. He did a series of flights with other cadets in a de Havilland Dominie transport aircraft, and then a couple of 'solos' alone with a pilot in a Percival Proctor. Naturally he took to it like a good 'un.

With that hurdle out of the way, and having been promoted to acting corporal, giving him charge of a flight of forty-three men, north-east Scotland was next on the agenda as Dad headed to RAF Evanton on the shores of the Cromarty Firth. Gunnery training awaited, and he and his fellow cadets spent a few days waiting for a special train to be made available for the long journey ahead. It should have been a routine trip, even if it was wartime . . .

When he first saw the train waiting for them at Chippenham station, Dad's heart sank. It consisted of a small engine and three coaches in which the flight sergeant insisted the men were to travel behind locked doors. It was going to be a slow and uncomfortable twenty-four hours with no avenue of escape in the event of anything going wrong. Naturally, Dad was furious. 'I had to lodge my protest in the strongest of terms with the sergeant.'

After twelve hours, the train pulled into Crewe station, having meandered its way slowly north along the Welsh and English border. 'The flight sergeant unlocked the doors of each coach and ordered us to parade on the platform. There he informed us that we were to be given a fish and chips supper at the Town Hall, courtesy of the mayor. The spontaneous cheer that greeted this news caused a stir even in a crowded Crewe station, and we set off in good spirits.'

Fed and refreshed, the airmen reboarded and continued their journey via the coastal route to Carlisle where, after midnight, the train parked in a siding.

> Apart from the gentle wheeze of the engine, all was quiet, and the men bunked down to sleep. Until, that is, about 1.40 a.m. when our slumbers were most violently disturbed when a slow-moving goods train collided head-on with our stationary special train. There was a loud bang as the two engines met, and then all hell broke loose as they shed their trucks and carriages in different directions.
>
> The first coach of our train was thrown onto its side. The second, where I was, lurched violently to the right, and coach three tilted alarmingly, coming to rest at an angle of about 45 degrees. All three had been derailed, while our engine was locked in a gruesome embrace with the engine of the goods train. They were like two wrestlers, and both of them were on fire.

At the moment of impact, the man sleeping above Dad on the luggage rack landed on top of him. 'I managed to wrestle myself free, and then we helped each other get up. As this collision of bodies was occurring, I heard shattering of glass throughout the train. The same shockwaves caused the woodwork to splinter, and while this was going on the whole train was moving violently. It was all over in a few seconds, but it happened in slow motion in our minds.'

The train then caught fire as the men scrambled to get out of the broken windows. 'The corporal in me prompted me to walk along the bodywork of the upturned coaches to organize the rescue of men who might be trapped in the compartments nearest the burning engine. Some of them had jumped onto the track and made it to the platform, while station staff were dragging men to safety and away from the fire.'

Gradually, the whole flight gathered on the platform, some with bandaged wounds from flying glass, and the flight sergeant called the roll as the fire brigade, police and ambulance crews continued their work. Dad and his charges got the fast train to Inverness at 6.25 a.m., no doubt utterly exhausted and some in shock. Then they took a local train to Evanton, their destination seventeen miles north of Inverness. They got there at 2.30 p.m. The 550-mile journey from Yatesbury had taken thirty-one hours.

They must have looked a sorry bunch when they arrived, with some of the men wearing bandages on their heads or arms and hands. They were met by NCOs from the base and a lone piper, and, as they marched towards their new home, the villagers came out to applaud them.

It was a warm welcome, but my father and his flight

quickly discovered that a Blackburn Botha aircraft had crashed there that morning, killing everyone on board, including four cadets. Dad knew them all from his first posting at Yatesbury, and the news hit him hard.

Chapter Eight

I took the entrance exam for Forest School – a fee-paying public school – where I went after Hyland House Primary, in March 1975.

It was a Friday afternoon, and there was an almighty thunderstorm. I came home and told Mum I had the biggest ever headache. A few weeks later, Dad, who was adamant that I go to the best school possible regardless of the cost, burst into my bedroom one morning.

'Well done, Son,' he said. 'You did it – you passed. You're going to Forest.'

It was all a big thing, and everyone rushed around to tell Auntie Bob and Tom and Nan that I was becoming a Forester. Then the day before my first term started the following September, me and Dad went up to the school. We couldn't get in, but we walked around the back and looked at all the cricket pitches. I still take the doggies up there now and walk around. It's a magical place.

On my first day, aged eleven, I arrived with Dad at Forest Juniors, and we stood under a big oak tree waiting to register. The school motto is *In Pectore Robur*, which means 'Heart of Oak'. It seemed apt to start life at Forest at that particular spot.

You had to give your name, and then they told you what form you were in. I was in 1M. There were lots of kids and lots of dads standing there, and there were two boys who walked up after me. The first one said 'Martin Lewis' when they asked him his name, and they said '1M'. Then the next one walked up and said 'David Foster', and they said '1M' to him too. So they became my buddies.

There was a boy I already knew who was going there called Andrew Gardner. He was also in our class, and he had other friends too. But I stuck with Martin and Dave forever. Well, for seven solid years at Forest, at least. Actually, I have lost track of Martin. The last time I saw him was the day we all discovered that Princess Diana had died. We played golf and then went for a curry. Truth be told, I lost track of Dave Foster, too. I hadn't seen him for about forty years until quite recently, when we went for lunch and it was just like school. We were chatting and he said Forest was quite a tough place and the reason he got through it was because of me and Martin. And I would say the reason I got through it was because of Dave and Martin.

You needed a ring of your own friends because Forest could be a lonely existence if you didn't have compatriots, and those two were a big part of my world. Dave lived at Seven Kings in Ilford. He was thin but tall. He had a lot of blond curly hair and was the brighter one of our group. Not that me and Martin were particularly thick. But when you go to one of those schools, there are a lot of smart people there who are going to end up with scholarships to Oxford to read physics and stuff like that. Dave was a good student, and after Forest he went to Bangor University to read English.

He ended up becoming an insurance broker and running his own company in London.

Martin was this big kid from Wanstead – thick-set with bright red hair, and he had a burn on his wrist underneath where his watchstrap would go. That was from an accident when he was young – he knocked a saucepan over and burned his hand. After school he went into insurance, too.

To start with we were known as 'Foster, Lewis and Smith' because we didn't use first names. It was just surnames. It took me a long time to actually say their names. I certainly wouldn't have sat next to Martin and said, 'Oi, Martin . . .' It would have been, 'Er, Lewis, pass the salt will you.' We were all in the same house – Bardells – until we were split up when we got to senior school in our third year.

Those two were big West Ham fans, and talking and thinking about the Hammers and football occupied a lot of their time, while I would talk speedway – to myself probably. Dave and Martin were not as interested as I was in collecting militaria, but Martin had a friend called Dave Sharp. They had been at primary school together. Dave became a part of our little circle of mates, and he liked collecting stuff from the war, so he became another sort of ally in my world.

Which brings me to Gordon Ramsey (and I don't mean Gordon Ramsay, the chef). I remember meeting him for the first time as if it was yesterday. It was the beginning of the Michaelmas term the following year, so I was starting my second year, and Gordon had arrived as a new boy in the year below.

It was a horrible day – a Thursday afternoon – and it was pouring. You couldn't go outside, and I had taken refuge in the school library where I found a copy of my favourite magazine – *After the Battle*. It was Edition No. 8 and it was about the Battle of the Falaise Pocket when, in August 1944, the Allies surrounded and destroyed German forces in an area centred on the town of Falaise in Normandy.

Now, towards the back of that edition there was a double-page spread with a photomontage showing the military kit that had been cleared up from the Falaise Pocket by a former French Resistance fighter named Alain Roudeix. He had been tasked by the French government to tidy up the battlefield, and, instead of throwing the kit away, he had picked it up and taken it home. The 'Roudeix Collection' consisted of old barns full to the rafters with armoured vehicles, motorbikes, rifles, steel helmets, paratrooper helmets, mortar bombs, fuel cans, SS number plates, gas masks . . . everything I'd ever dreamed about.

Next to the pictures of this stuff was an image of a small boy, aged about nine or ten, standing in one of the barns in the midst of this amazing collection. I had barely noticed him, so intent was I on studying the bits and pieces that Roudeix had accumulated.

Then this kid came over to me in the library and pointed to the picture of the boy.

'You see that kid there,' he said.

'Yes?' I replied suspiciously, because this lad was from the year below and, of course, therefore (normally) to be ignored.

'He's in my class.'

I went, 'No he's not – don't be stupid.'

'He is . . . and I can prove it. D'you wanna meet him?'

I nodded, still wary of a practical joke by someone a year my junior.

'OK, follow me.'

We went outside and walked round to the cricket pavilion where there were two kids sitting on the bench where we used to wait for our turn to bat. It was under a little roof, and they were keeping dry.

'There he is,' said the boy, pointing at Gordon.

I stood staring at him. 'Are you in that magazine, then?' I blurted out.

And Gordon went, 'Yeah.'

'Oh,' I said, shuffling my feet and trying to sound completely unimpressed. 'Really?'

'Yeah,' said Gordon. 'My Dad writes *After the Battle*.'

And that was how it happened. Gordon was sitting next to a guy called Jason Carr, who we called JJ, and, like Gordon, he was a militaria wonk. So all of a sudden I had Gordon, JJ and Dave Sharp, and we started to spend our entire lives talking about all this incredible stuff.

At that time, I was reading non-stop about war and especially eyewitness accounts of the First World War and the trenches. I couldn't get enough of it. But the book that became a really big thing for me was *The Forgotten Soldier*, the classic Second World War autobiography by the Franco-German former infantryman Guy Sajer.

When I first read it, I was about twelve or thirteen. Sajer's mum was French and his dad was German, and he came from Alsace Lorraine. Faced with a choice, he decided to join the German army, aged just three years older than I was at that time. I was in awe of Sajer, first because he was a soldier and second because his book is incredibly gruesome and realistic. It is supposedly a true story, and over the years I must have read it at least twenty times. And, as time goes by, I am no longer in awe of him; I now just want him to go home because he was too young to go through what he did. He shouldn't have been there at seventeen.

The book describes how he joins the Wehrmacht and is employed as a lorry driver in an army service corps-type role. In that capacity he is sent to the Eastern Front in winter, and it's dreadful. His friend gets killed horribly, and then Sajer is asked if he wants to join the elite infantry fighting unit, the Grossdeutschland. The rest of the book is about his appalling life as a soldier, and his account of the German retreat across Russia being chased by the Red Army is hauntingly powerful. Eventually, he was taken prisoner by the Americans and kept in captivity until they reminded him that he was half-French. They told him he could go free if he agreed to join the French army. And in that way, Sajer went from being a beaten German to being a victorious Frenchman in a matter of hours. It's a great book.

Gordon was a little person – smaller than me, but not by much – with a mop of thick brown hair and a fringe above his slightly hooded eyes. He was wearing the junior-school grey uniform and a tartan green scarf which earned him the nickname Rupert the Bear. He had a slight lisp, and he was serious about military things. With his dad writing *After the Battle*, he got to go to places that none of us had ever dreamed of going to, like Alain Roudeix's yard or archaeological digs where crashed German planes or Spitfires were being unearthed. I suppose I was quite impressed that I now knew this person and that I had met his dad, Winston, too.

At that time, Winston was writing a book that would

become the classic work on its subject, entitled *The Battle of Britain: Then and Now*. It detailed every pilot, every squadron and every plane shot down. And as publication drew ever closer in 1980, all we ever talked about was the battle and the kit that the pilots wore in the skies above London. We would have great long discourses about B-Type flying helmets, D-Type cloth oxygen masks and Luxor goggles, and there was, inevitably, a lot of one-upmanship.

Gordon had the special stuff. And we would try to compete. It would be, like, 'Well, I've got two of those' or 'My Dad's got three of 'em' or 'Yeah, well, I will be getting one of those next week, you wait and see'. It was a load of nonsense, really, about how much rubbish we owned, but it was great fun. And Gordon was a bit of a thrill to know, not because he got things that we didn't get, but because his house near Harlow was like a flippin' museum.

Gordon was not interested in medals like I was. But that was no impediment to our shared passion for kit from the war, and one thing he had that I didn't was a German steel helmet. I wanted one like mad, and one day Gordon told me about a shop in Islington called R&R Militaria – and I am pretty sure that that was the first time I ever heard the M-word.

I know I had been to school the day I first went there. Dad came and picked me up, and we went to Islington together. R&R was on Essex Road, and it was run by someone called Rene and someone else whose name probably started with an 'R', but I can't remember who. We went in and it was, oh, *incredible*. And it smelled lovely. There, on this shelf, were lots of helmets, and there were German ones, and they were fantastic, but they were too much money. I think they were about thirty quid each, so quite expensive bits of kit for a schoolboy in 1976 or 1977.

I ended up buying a clip of bullets for a Second World War British .303 rifle. They were spent ones that had been reloaded in their charger, and they cost two quid. When we came out, Dad found he had a parking ticket that cost him a tenner, and he was quite annoyed. He would forever say that clip of bullets cost £12. He really got the hump about it. But then for Christmas that year I got a German steel helmet, which was amazing.

R&R changed hands and became Regimentals, and it was something of a pilgrimage destination for me and Dad. We would go there on a Saturday morning during the school holidays, and then later me and Gordon would go there together. After he left school, Gordon worked with his dad at Plaistow Press where *After the Battle* was printed. Winston carried on writing the magazine until the 195th edition, when he retired and sold it. He's eighty-four now. Gordon has also retired and lives in Suffolk, where he mends clocks.

Dad and I carried on collecting medals, and one milestone I remember from those school days was something I spotted in the window of Hinton's. This was a jeweller's shop next door to Mr Telford's toyshop on Wood Street, and in the window there was a square case full of lots of medals.

One of them was a German Iron Cross from the Second World War, and it was priced at £9. At the time I probably had fifty or sixty Allied medals but no German ones. But I was reading and rereading Guy Sajer, and I decided I wanted that medal. It was something real that I could hold in my hands from *his* war.

I spent the summer holiday saving up. It didn't take too long to reach the target because I was generously compensated for my role as the sole child in the Smith family. Each week I would get contributions from Dad, Auntie Bob and Nan, which together amounted to about a pound. Once I'd got my funds together, I asked Dad one Saturday morning if he would come down to Hinton's to buy this Iron Cross. He did his usual thing of checking I'd learned everything there was to know about this medal before we set off.

'Well, what's an Iron Cross then?'

'Um, I'll tell you what it is,' I told him. 'It's the only German bravery award, and this one is a Second World War one. And you can tell that because it has a swastika on it and it says '1939' at the bottom.'

'And d'you know what class it is, Son?'

'Yes. It's a second-class one because it has a ribbon with it and no pin on the back to attach it to a uniform.'

After a few more questions and a great long spiel from me in response, I passed the test and we headed off down to Wood Street where I bought my first German medal. Very exciting. I paid out the £9 they wanted for it, and we came home with it in a packet and I proudly showed it to everyone.

'Well, Son,' said Dad, 'I think that was very worthwhile research. What's more, I think that Iron Cross is worth at least £10.' And he got his wallet out and fished out a tenner and gave it to me.

The Iron Cross has been around since 1813 during the Napoleonic Wars. I've only seen one of those to hold, once. It predates the Victoria Cross by nearly forty years, and it comes in various classes, mainly second and first. After the earliest ones were issued, the next were dated 1870 for the Franco-Prussian War; then there are the 1914 ones for the First World War, and then 1939 for the Second World War. They still award them to German soldiers today.

Over the years, I collected a lot of German stuff, like pilot badges and logbooks, because I liked aircrew things and me and Gordon were always talking about the Battle of Britain. Apart from RAF stuff from the battle, I collected German kit, including a German flying suit, a German life jacket and a German parachute.

So I had all this stuff, but what started to happen was it suddenly became clear to me that most of it was faked. It was mickey-mouse stuff – all made-up and none of it was real. The Iron Crosses weren't real either. Someone said to me recently that there are now something like 5 million more Iron Crosses in existence than there were at the end of the war, so that gives you an idea.

The other thing that did for me on all of this was that, with most of these items, there was no way of finding out who the people they belonged to were. While it was fantastic to own a pair of genuine Luftwaffe flying goggles, I had no idea who had worn them. So in the end, I had this large collection of uniforms, tin hats, webbing and rifles, and all sorts of other things, but from about 1986, I decided I wanted to focus solely on medals, so I sold it all.

I used to take it in batches to the militaria market in Islington. It was at the end of Camden Passage where there were some shops, and you passed through a doorway and down some steps into a cellar and there were militaria stalls all the way round. Then you went into another basement and there were even more of them.

I would go in and sell stuff while Gordon would still be buying it. The most lucrative sale I did was of a full-size mannequin, decked out in all-original Battle of Britain RAF flying kit – boots, trousers, jacket, gloves, Mae West, B-Type flying helmet, D-Type cloth oxygen mask and Luxors. It had everything, and I sold him for £1,300.

Sadly, I was to discover that my treasured Iron Cross from Hinton's was also a fake. I had started to attend auctions that specialized in medals, and at one of them someone told me how to check if an Iron Cross was genuine. I rushed home to discover that my £9 medal failed at every turn. Very disappointing.

Today, I have three Iron Crosses, all genuine and all from the First World War, two second class and one first class. I keep two in my battlefield bag to show people when I do battlefield tours in northern France. The other one came to me through one of my greatest friends, Paul Murphy, who I met at the London Medal Club and who specializes in buying up medals in France and Belgium, and selling them online.

This one came with the soldier's pay book and the certificate to mark the award to him of the honour. There is also a letter to his mum saying he had been killed but awarded the Iron Cross. It is dated 25 March 1917. His name was Georg Bliss. He was born on 5 November 1886, and he was a member of the 120th (2nd Württemberg) Infantry 'Emperor

Wilhelm, King of Prussia'. He died in the area of Artois near Vimy Ridge, and he is buried at the nearby German cemetery at Neuville-Saint-Vaast.

On my battlefield tours I take people to see his grave and explain who he was.

Chapter Nine

There is no doubt that me, the two Daves, Martin, JJ and Gordon were regarded as quite eccentric at Forest, and we did get the mickey taken every now and again.

The worst moment was when ITV aired an episode of *The Sweeney*, which we all loved, in which DI Jack Regan (aka John Thaw) goes round to a house full of German militaria. He ends up in bed with the woman, who lives there who is wearing a German steel helmet. That took some living down at the senior school at Forest, I can tell you.

I played cricket and was not much good at football and hated hockey. I used to do cross-country running and athletics for my house. But the thing I enjoyed most at Forest – above all else and by some way – was the Combined Cadet Force, or CCF.

This was a massive part of my life, and I loved every minute of it. We were all in it from our first term in the senior school when we were thirteen. I joined on the first day in September 1977. We used to do sport on Wednesdays and Saturdays – football in the Christmas term, hockey at Easter, and cricket and athletics in the summer. But Monday was 'activities day' and you could choose what you wanted to do – either rowing or CCF – and about thirty boys out of the 200 in each year would choose the CCF.

I went in and put my name down without a moment's hesitation. Then I ran to the phone box where I used to ring my parents up at the end of each day to say, 'I'm ready, come and get me.' (They always did this, even though it was probably quicker to walk than getting stuck in Walthamstow rush-hour traffic.)

So I rang that day and my father answered.

'Hello,' I said. 'I've got something to tell you.'

'What's that?'

'I've joined up!'

He went, 'Ah, well done Son!'

And then he told me something his dad had said to him when he joined the RAF. 'Aim at six o'clock of the bull, Son.' In other words, the bottom of the target.

I came home that night, and I was so excited, *so* excited. But there was one thing bothering me. I didn't have my uniform. They hadn't issued it to me yet, and I was beside myself because in two weeks we were going on our first trip, known as a 'Field Day'.

It was to the headquarters of the Royal Green Jackets at Winchester, to which our CCF troop was attached. Both my grandads' regiments, the King's Royal Rifle Corps and the Rifle Brigade, had been based there, and even Henry Dickerson, my great-great-great-grandad, had been there. So this felt like an important place and an important visit to me. I was determined to show up looking the part.

On the Saturday before we were due to go, I got Dad to come with me to school and we went to see our Commanding

Officer, Major Derek Wakeham. He taught geography and he was in the Territorial Army Volunteer Reserve Association. He was as mad as a box of frogs – absolutely barking mad. God, he was odd, but in a fun way. He was known as 'Daddy Wackers', was in his late fifties and was immaculately turned out, apart, that is, from his big beard, which made him look slightly odd as a soldier. Where we had berets, he wore a peaked cap.

So we went to see Daddy Wackers at the armoury where the CCF was based, and Dad explained how important it was for me to have my uniform before I went to Winchester. Miracle of miracles, it was there by Monday morning. I was now the proud owner of my own pair of lightweight green trousers, a properly itchy 1950s-era shirt, a 1950s green woolly jumper, a big pair of black boots, and my blue beret with the Forest School CCF badge on it.

That trip to Winchester was epic. When we got there, we lined up outside the guardroom and came to attention, demonstrating our parade-ground skills after only a few practice sessions at school. The first thing we did was the assault course, including learning how to scale the twelve-foot wall. Then we fired self-loading rifles on the range before taking a break for lunch in the field. Then they took us round the armoury and showed us the German machine guns that had been captured during the Second World War. And then it was time for unarmed combat with an instructor who was a corporal.

Martin was the tallest of my mates, and the corporal picked him out.

'Right, I want a volunteer – you'll do!' he said, pointing at him.

Martin was quite shy and stepped forward reluctantly.
'Name?'
'Martin,' came the whispered reply.
'Martin who? Speak up!'
'Lewis.'
'Right, Lewis, I want you to kick me in the bollocks.'
'What?'
'You heard me. I want you to kick me in the bollocks.'

In response, Martin half-heartedly offered what amounted to a gentle prod.

'No, no, no, no . . . I want you to kick me in the bollocks and mean it,' shouted the corporal.

This time, you could see Martin was riled by this mouthy bloke making a lot of noise in his face and he went for it. But as he lunged forward with his right foot leading, the corporal stepped to one side, grabbed Martin's ankle and flipped him onto the floor. We watched this wondering who was going to be next.

'Right, now we are going to teach you all to do that,' said the corporal.

I looked round for someone to practise with, and there was a kid called Charlie Davies who was even smaller than me – about 4ft 7 – so I chose him and beat the living daylights out of him. Well, sort of. But even the corporal was quite impressed.

While Wackers Wakeham ran the CCF, there was another much older teacher who was a big influence. The Reverend Joe Scott taught History, was also quite eccentric and had been in the Great War. Among his pupils was Richard Holmes who, as the historian Professor Richard

Holmes, wrote widely about war and presented a BBC television programme called *War Walks* in the late 1990s. He was the icon of battlefield touring, and when I got to know him we enjoyed the link we shared through our old History teacher at Forest.

Wakeham and Scott had an interesting take on the pupil–teacher relationship. They were more interested in us learning than them teaching. They would tell us what we were supposed to do, or indicate it, but then let us work out how to do it. They both enjoyed entertaining us with stories about Old Foresters and about objects they had collected.

Scott used to have a cabinet next to him and, every now and again, he would take something out and tell the story of the thing from his cabinet. I loved that, and I installed my own 'cabinet of curiosities' in my house. Its contents – admittedly not added to for some years – include a Ming bowl allegedly from a Chinese shipwreck which I bought through the *Evening Standard*, a framed Penny Black stamp, a poison-dart blowpipe from a holiday on the Amazon, some fossils and a copy of the death certificate of Mary Jane Kelly – Jack the Ripper's fifth victim.

Some of Daddy Wackers' stories about Old Foresters have stayed with me. He told us, for example, about a former schoolboy who had fought in the First World War, and who had brought a hand grenade home with him when he was demobbed. In the 1950s, he became wheelchair-bound, and one evening he rolled himself to the end of Southend Pier, waited until everyone had gone home, and then pulled the pin. When I was fourteen, I thought, 'Oh wow, what a story . . .' But now, having listened to people like Dame

Esther Rantzen arguing for the right to die, I have a much better understanding of why he did it. Wakeham and Scott gave you things to think about like that.

We were cadets and proud members of the cadet platoon in the junior year. We used to march around the tennis courts and up and down the road outside the school. Our first goal was passing the Recruit Course, and when you did that you got rid of your blue beret and got a Royal Green Jacket one instead. We had done the course by Christmas. Major Wakeham would stand there, and we had to march up and down and then do some marching individually. We would march up to him, salute and do all that stuff, and then, at the end of it, we got our green beret. Big moment.

The next goal was something called the Apex Badge. This was a series of skills we had to master – among them a battlecraft course, orienteering and shooting. As part of the Apex tests, we went to Longmoor army camp near Liss in Hampshire where I reached my wits' end one day in the cold and wet.

We were given a map, and we had to pass a test which involved finding a series of points on it. I set off with Dave and Martin. It was March and it was freezing. They gave us Second World War – or certainly National Service-era – capes to keep the rain out, with one huge button at the neck. After about half an hour it started to snow. There was no hint of health and safety – we were a load of kids walking around in the snow, freezing to death, basically. I'm not sure it could be done these days.

My map, which I still have, quickly turned into a papier-mâché ball. We found about five of the points we were looking for and the tins with coloured markers that we had to locate to tick off each target on our cards. But it had all turned to mush, and we ended up sitting in the woods waiting for the lorry to come and pick us up. I sat on a log with my cape pulled over my head, eating a piece of fruitcake, which was our lunch. I also had a banana, which I put on the ground and then someone stood on it. I don't even like bananas, but I was so fed up, I cried.

The next thing I knew, the lorry arrived and everyone was shouting.

'Get on the lorry! Get on the lorry! Oi, Smithy, get on the bloody lorry.'

I tried to climb up, but my cape was getting in the way.

'No,' shouted one of the soldiers who was collecting us. 'Smith, take your bloody cape off first.'

It was so cold, I couldn't get the huge button undone. And there I was, the last one, holding everyone up, fiddling with this stupid button with frozen fingers.

'Come on, Smithy!' they were shouting.

Bless him, it was Martin who came to my rescue. He jumped back down, released me from the cape and pretty much threw me into the back.

Two years into senior school, I got promoted, and it was not long before nan next door – Dad's mum – died. In her final months, she was a very ill lady in the back bedroom, lying there with a picture of Grandad next to her when he was a lance corporal. I went in to see her and, proud as punch, announced I had been promoted.

'I'm now the same as Grandad, Nan – Lance Corporal Smith,' I told her.

She smiled at that and died about a week later.

We were very serious about the CCF. It was our world, and the armoury was our den. We would go there every breaktime and lunchtime. We would sit in that room full of old bits of webbing and our kit, and that was where we talked most of the utter nonsense we used to come out with about the Battle of Britain and German tin hats.

Towards the end of my time at Forest we went to Cumbria, to something called the Warcop Training Area. It was the summer holidays, and the high point of the trip was a twenty-four-hour exercise on the Fells. All of us were there apart from Gordon.

We were on this bleak hillside, firing blanks and throwing thunder-flashes, and it was very exciting. I had full combats on – 1958-pattern webbing and rifle – and I came across this stone wall. I thought, 'This is my Rambo moment – I'm going to jump over this wall and then make my way up behind the enemy.'

So I jumped over it and landed on the carcass of a dead sheep, which pretty much blew up on impact. I was covered in bits of grey-looking stringy stuff. It was stuck on all my buttons and everywhere, really. Eventually, when we had finished, I walked up to Sergeant Bryant of the Royal Green Jackets – an old and scary individual – still covered in the stains and remains of dead sheep.

'What on earth?' he exclaimed in an operatic falsetto.

'Sorry, Sergeant. I landed on a dead sheep . . .'

He went, 'I don't know who to feel more sorry for – me or the sheep.'

Bryant was like a gorilla. He was hairy, small and wide,

and he was brutal. I'm sure he was probably a really nice man. I don't know. I never met him other than being shouted at by him. He *was* a nice man, I suppose. He sort of looked after you. You weren't going to get killed on his watch, but you might get close to it.

One night, we were back at Longmoor on another week-long summer camp. We had finished the course and were coming home the next day. They said that if we were over eighteen we could go down the pub. I was eighteen that year, but not quite that age by the summer. We all went to the local, and we had to be back at a certain time. It was the usual gang, the two Daves, Martin and me, and we played darts and got stuck into a few pints. If Dave Sharp managed to hit the floor with a dart he was doing well. But he wasn't the only one – we were all sozzled because all we needed was a pint or two and we were trashed.

At some point I went to the gents and chose the end urinal on the row. Behind me I heard the door open, and I looked across and it was Sergeant Bryant. I was so terrified, you have no idea. I tried to wee standing to attention. He went to the other end, and I was standing there bolt upright.

He went to me, 'Oi?'

And I said, 'Yes, Sergeant?' And this time it was my turn to sound like a soprano.

He said, 'Listen to me, Smith. I am going to tell you something you're never ever going to forget.'

And I never have. Whenever I go to the loo in the pub this echoes in my mind.

He turned to me – he didn't look at me exactly – he

looked at the wall, and he said, 'Beer . . . you never own it, you only rent it!'

Then he guffawed at his own joke, and so did I.

Looking back, I reckon everybody should do the CCF. It was fantastic. It gave me discipline and a military understanding. It taught us how to work together; it taught us how to give lessons and lead – how to attack something, and how a Bren gun worked. And it got you standing up in front of people and talking about stuff. It certainly served me well in the other things I did.

I would go so far as to say that during my five years at Forest Senior School it was the best thing I was involved in. I loved every second of it – every second – and I finished as a colour sergeant.

In between the CCF stuff at Forest, I got through academically with three A levels, but I had no interest in going to university, despite my father's enthusiasm for it. It didn't set my world ablaze. I wanted to finish studying and get going in the world.

As school came to an end, I started to think about a career, and the job that appealed was working in a museum. I'd actually been thinking of it for years, going back to my early childhood when Mum used to take me to the British Museum to see the Egyptian mummies and things like that. Dad was born at about the same time that they discovered the tomb of Tutankhamun, so we would talk about that, and in 1972 me and Mum went to the Tutankhamun exhibition. Dad didn't make it because of a flare-up of his malaria infection, which he contracted in Burma.

In those days, I wanted to be an Egyptologist. Then

I imagined myself as some sort of general archaeologist, inspired by the talks I had with Gordon Ramsey about Second World War aviation archaeology. By the time I was ready to leave school, I was thinking about trying to work at somewhere like the Imperial War Museum. I always fancied that.

Before I left, I had an interview with the school's careers adviser, and he asked me what I wanted to do. When I didn't say stockbroker and told him I was interested in working in a museum, he seemed to be completely nonplussed and merely grunted. It wasn't exactly the most encouraging response.

Chapter Ten

Life after Forest started with a bang in the summer. It was something that happened on a quiet road in Dorset involving a bright yellow Volkswagen Polo and an old oak tree.

Myself and a few mates had gone on a week's holiday to the home of Stan and Bunty Waterfall, who lived in the village of Leigh, a few miles south of Yeovil. Bunty was my friend Chris Barker's auntie, and we were camping in the garden of their house. In addition to Chris and myself, our group included another friend from school, David Harbottle, plus Jason Carr (aka JJ) and Dave Sharp, who had just passed his driving test.

We had had a great week down there and decided to cap it off with a visit to the Royal Navy Fleet Air Arm Museum at Yeovilton. The Harrier jump-jets based at the airfield there had just returned from the Falklands War, and we were thrilled to see them, complete with kill markings from their sorties against the Argentine Air Force. For our send-off, Bunty was preparing a roast dinner, and we were roaring along in the old yellow Polo to get back in time.

Sharpie was driving with JJ in the front passenger seat. I was behind JJ, with David Harbottle next to me and Chris Barker behind Sharpie. Harbottle had my ghetto blaster on his lap, which would have been belting out something by The Jam (more on that – and them – later). Chris was navigating, and certainly, in the back, none of us were wearing seatbelts.

We got to a point where the road turned quite sharply to the right, but there was also a farm track or driveway that went straight on where the bend started. We were going some – probably 50mph, maybe more – and as we approached the bend Chris shouted, 'Straight on!' Then he quickly corrected himself. 'No, Sharpie, turn right mate!'

The next thing that happened was that Sharpie turned hard right, but he was too late and was asking way too much of the car, fully laden as it was. We had just enough time to realize we had totally lost control on the bend. The Polo seemed to go up at an angle on two wheels – the left two – and then skidded across the tarmac before wrapping itself around the oak tree that stood at the end of the farm track. The screeching noise and the crash as we collided with the tree were horrendous. Then there was total silence.

I had plunged my head through the side window. The seat that Jason was sitting on had come down onto my ankles and squashed them. Dave Harbottle, next to me, had been thrown forward with such force that he broke my ghetto blaster in half with his head. He now had several control knobs stuck in his face and was knocked out. Chris Barker had somehow sailed between the two front seats and escaped injury apart from a sprained thumb. But Jason was in a bad way with a nasty scalp injury, and he was lying unconscious in the front footwell. We could see the crack in his skull where a section of his scalp with hair attached was hanging down. Sharpie, meanwhile, who had been sitting behind a supposedly 'non-collapsible' steering wheel, had collapsed it with his chest, which broke several of his ribs and a collar bone. He had gone through the windscreen and was lying unconscious on the bonnet.

I got out of the window that I had put my head through and ran round to where Dave was lying on the bonnet. There was smoke coming out of the engine underneath him, so I reached in, grabbed the key and turned the ignition off. Thank God the smoke stopped. Then Chris got out of his window. When he saw me, he said, 'Smithy, what's the matter with your leg?'

That's when I looked down and saw that, in addition to the cuts over my face and hands from the broken glass and the skin missing from my ankles, I had a big gouge in my left thigh caused by a bit of metal that had bent inwards when we hit the tree. It looked pretty gruesome – you could see the purple muscle sticking through. In response, I said nothing but just stared in astonishment at the wound. At that point, I more or less gave up and went and sat in the ditch for a few minutes.

We couldn't get Jason out of the car. Dave Sharp eventually came round, and we got him off the bonnet but only back in the car, while Dave Harbottle wandered around with the knobs stuck in his head.

We must have waited there for nearly half an hour before another car finally came along at about 6.00 p.m. They stopped and quickly assessed the situation before driving on to the house at the end of the track to call for an ambulance. It turned up about an hour after we had crashed, and we all went in it together to a local hospital. I'm not even sure which one it was.

We were incredibly lucky. Only Jason was kept in overnight, and the rest of us walking wounded ended up back at Stan and Bunty's place. Dave was very emotional that night and kept saying it was his fault. I told him it most certainly wasn't, and the poor guy burst into tears. The next day his dad, my dad and Chris's dad all drove down to pick us up. A few weeks later, we made a badge which read 'I crunched a Polo in '82'. It was the first thing that had happened to us after leaving school. Not the best of starts.

After that – and for a few years – I was terrified of being a passenger in a car. I didn't mind going in a straight line. It was turning right that I didn't like. When I felt that motion, it always reminded me of those final moments as we skidded across the road in Dorset. I used to have a photograph of the car after the crash, but one of my girlfriends wisely decided to cut it up.

Poor Sharpie died in 2023. He worked as a house-sales conveyancer for a solicitor in Woodford, and he had a heart attack. He'd had a difficult divorce and had become quite lonely and a bit lost. He stayed at my house sometimes, and I made an effort to get him involved in things. I helped get him enrolled as a member of the Maguncor Lodge, the Masonic lodge of the Machine Gun Corps from the First World War. It only meets four times a year, but it gave Dave something to go and do, somewhere where he could have a few beers and talk to blokes and have a bit of a laugh.

The week he died he had been at my house for a lodge meeting in London on the Tuesday, and he went to work the following day, getting up early, making his bed and leaving quietly. We had said 'cheerio' the night before as we always did, but I never saw him again. He died alone in bed the following Friday night at his home near Stansted, and was found by his lovely new girlfriend, Helen, two days later.

I met her at the funeral, and she was in bits, bless her. She had such a positive impact on him. In the weeks before he died, he seemed so much happier because of her – I'd not seen him smiling like that since we were at school. She changed his world.

The funeral was like a Forest reunion. The soundtrack was his beloved Northern Soul plus The Jam, but it was one of the hardest days to endure. Dave was the youngest of our group of friends from Forest, so none of us expected it would be him who would go first.

For some reason, they decided to cut down the big old oak tree me and Dad had stood under on my first day at school. When I went walking there for the first time after it happened, I was so sad to see it gone and picked up two pieces of bark – one for me and one for poor old Dave.

When I go up there with the dogs now – Tilly, our Cavapoo, and Molly, a wolf-like rescue from Marrakesh – something tells me I have to walk the same path me and Dad did together, the day before my first term started, to get the lie of the land.

Walking the dogs up there has become a big thing for me. It's a lovely bit of East London – magnificent trees, and it's a beautiful and peaceful place. Each time I take photographs of the changing season. The hope, one day, is to make a calendar with them. It's a special place for me.

We weren't old enough to see *Quadrophenia* when it first came out in the summer of 1979, and The Who were a big thing for me and my friends.

But The Jam was the band that was talked about a lot when we were at school, and the year before I left we got tickets to see them at The Rainbow at Finsbury Park in North London. That was one rough gig. Total mayhem. I loved it and ended up seeing Paul Weller, Bruce Foxton and Rick Buckler six times before they disbanded a little over a year later.

I couldn't stand mainstream pop and disco – stuff like Bony M., Kool & the Gang and the rest of it – and when the Sex Pistols came along, and after them The Jam, it was brilliant because their music was so different to all that other rubbish. By the time we got going, the Pistols had finished, and I'm not going to say the next best thing was The Jam, but I found their music exciting and interesting, and I got into what Paul Weller was saying about things.

The Jam hit the mark for all of us. We were all into them. They identified as Mods and so did we, and, in the first few years after school, I tried to dress like one. We would head off to shops on Carnaby Street and look for drainpipe trousers, three-button jackets and button-down Ben Sherman shirts, worn with a thin tie and Chelsea boots.

At about that time I started to learn guitar, and all I wanted was to play every single Jam song, along with heavy metal by bands like Judas Priest. Along with The Who, we were into other stuff from the 1960s – Tamla Motown and early Mod bands like The Stones, The Animals and Small Faces. When we had a party, that was the music we played. Chris Barker was always a bit weirder and was into stuff like Flux of Pink Indians, Public Image Ltd, The Clash and The Damned. But for me, it was The Jam.

My favourite track was 'The Butterfly Collector' – Weller's caustic take on groupies – one of the most amazing B-sides ever released. 'Eton Rifles' was another favourite, especially because we had been at a fee-paying school. We never really got the irony that he didn't like us – we thought it was about us and that was enough.

My first girlfriend was into The Jam and the Mod lifestyle, too. I met Theresa Bolden, who lived in Chingford, at the birthday party of a mutual schoolfriend. She had been one of the first girls admitted to the sixth form at Forest. She even had a real Vespa – a bright orange C-reg with all the mirrors. But we never really took to it. We used to ride around the car park trying to get the hang of it, but decided neither of us was going to get ourselves killed trying to look like a Mod on one of those.

The Mod thing, or to be more accurate, the Mod Revival, was about dressing smartly, embracing the modern world, moving away from the final vestiges of wartime austerity, and not looking like a smelly, scruffy-haired biker or Rocker – our sworn enemies. And that, of course, meant that being a Mod was not without its risks, as Theresa and I found out when we headed into town to see the German war film *Das Boot* in the late summer of 1981. It was showing at Leicester Square, and I was wearing my best Mod-style sharp grey suit from Carnaby Cavern. She was in a black-and-white chequered dress.

We got to the cinema about an hour early, and as we emerged from the Tube station I heard a voice behind me.

'Oi, watch out. He's a Mod!'

I instinctively grabbed hold of Theresa's hand and looked round to see about ten or twelve Rockers in their black leather jackets, hair all over the place, bearing down on us.

'We hate Mods,' they were snarling. 'Hate ya . . . come 'ere!'

'Run!' I shouted as the chase began. We sprinted down Charing Cross Road and darted into a bookshop in a side street. We ran into the back and then down some stairs before we realized we were in a sex shop.

Out of breath and terrified, we stood around trying to look like we were interested in their books and magazines. Theresa was only sixteen at the time and 'illegal', but the shop staff didn't seem to care. After about ten minutes we crept back up the stairs only to find the Rockers were still milling around on the pavement outside. At this point the shop owner – bless him – had worked out what was going on and he went to the door.

'What d'you want?' he asked them, holding the handle and leaning out.

'We want to talk to 'im,' they said, pointing at me and Theresa behind the window.

'Well, you're not going to do that in here, so sod off!'

That seemed to do the trick. But we waited about another ten minutes, passing the time of day with the staff, before we plucked up the courage to step outside. Then we made our way round to the cinema where we watched the story of U-96 in the Battle of the Atlantic.

I didn't wear my Mod suit much after that, and in any case, fashion was changing. Big shoulder pads were starting to come in, and that is probably the direction I was heading, Kouros aftershave and all.

Chapter Eleven

Dad's posting to Evanton in Scotland was about learning the black arts of Air Gunnery, as he and his fellow cadets completed a heavy schedule of flying in twin-engined Blackburn Botha bombers. But it took a while for the shock and memories of the train crash on the way up there to fade.

'The usual squad photographs were delayed for two weeks to allow wounds from the crash to heal, and when I sent a copy of my team's photograph home, I was told we looked like a tough, aggressive bunch of men,' Dad wrote. 'It was fair comment. There was a noticeable resolve among us, a grim determination to succeed, and it showed in the expressions on our faces.'

After ground-based training, when the cadets were taught to shoot at moving targets while on the move themselves, the next step was firing a powerful .303 Browning machine gun in the air for the first time. In March 1943, Dad had his first go, somewhere over the North Sea as he took his place in the mid-upper gun turret of a Botha.

To any cadet who enjoyed the smell of cordite, these were exciting times. I awaited instructions as I saw my fellow cadet leave the turret having completed his exercise. And when I was ordered to enter, I went through the drill in the way I had practised on the ground. I eased my way head-first but on my back and, as I did so, the aircraft made a tight turn to port so that when I turned round in the cramped space I was looking into the sea below with no sky in sight. Suddenly, as the aircraft straightened out, both the sky and the horizon came into view and all was well again.

I took my seat and waited for the order to open fire. On command, I let rip a ten-second burst, watching the tracers through the reflector gunsight. Although the bullets were travelling at about 1,000 miles an hour, the tracers seemed to hover at between 500 and 600 yards of their journey into space. Then, at about 700 yards, they bent noticeably leftwards, giving the appearance of a short line of fire just over a quarter of an inch long.

The next step was to practise shooting at other aircraft. These were Westland Lysanders or North American Harvards acting as attacking enemy planes or pulling target drones. The exchanges were captured by a cine camera that was mounted between the two Brownings in Dad's turret.

Flying at 5,000ft, fifteen miles off the coast, I spotted a Lysander on my lefthand side about a mile away. I reported my sighting to the captain, and he maintained a steady course on a northerly bearing awaiting the expected attack. The Lysander made a sweeping approach from the two o'clock high position and, when I judged him to be about 800 yards away, I fired my 'guns', giving the rapidly approaching aircraft three rads deflection in my reflector gunsight. In other words, aiming in front of him on his flightpath. Approaching 160mph, I continued giving him bursts of fire, reducing the deflection until, at 150 yards, I was aiming straight at him. I then prepared for the break-away shot, turning the turret swiftly to starboard, and got in a burst of fire as the aircraft flew over my head.

The Harvard came in next, and Dad duly got in several bursts of fire. 'I had thoroughly enjoyed the dogfights and was confident I had scored two "kills".' His confidence was not misplaced. After reviewing his film, the instructor was pleased. 'I had performed well; and when he replayed the breakaway shot of the Lysander attack, he changed this assessment to "very well". It was obvious that I had the makings of an Air Gunner, a lucky one . . .'

It was during a couple of weeks of leave after Evanton that Dad and Mum got engaged. On a brief home visit, he was afforded what he called the 'royal treatment' by Grandad, who proudly paraded his son – now a sergeant in the RAF – in front of his workmates at the meat depot at Smithfield.

Back on the job, there followed yet more training, this time in airborne radar, and its use in target acquisition on land and at sea, based at RAF Hooton Park in the Wirral. And then it was time for Dad's final assignment before being posted to Catalina flying boats.

He was sent to RAF Carew Cheriton in Pembrokeshire in the late summer of 1943 where he learned the finer skills as a 'master' Wireless Operator/Air Gunner. The flying was in Airspeed Oxfords, twin-engined navigation and radio trainers, and the climax of the course was a simulated mass bombing raid when all twenty-seven Oxfords flew together. It was 3 September 1943 and a day Dad never forgot.

After an early morning church service in a vast hangar to mark the fourth anniversary of the outbreak of war, I was ordered to care for three Air Training Corps cadets on board my Oxford. We were destined to carry out a bombing raid on Aberystwyth in Cardigan Bay as a solo raider. We took off at 0855 hours with the three cadets snuggled in the nose of the aircraft, the Perspex floor panel normally used by the bomb aimer on the 'Ox-Box' giving them a wonderful view of proceedings.

After an hour and a half we were back at base having 'destroyed' strategic installations in Aberystwyth in our low-level attack, much to the delight of our cadets. Without stopping engines, I exchanged pilots, with F/Sgt Braight taking command, and the three cadets still in the nose position. Braight informed me that our orders were to join the mass-flight of twenty-seven Oxfords as No. 2 in the line-up and make an attack twelve miles off the coast of Ireland, south of Cork. We were instructed to take our position in the line-up of aircraft on the perimeter track and prepare for take-off in close order.

With the appropriate signal given, No. 1 aircraft roared into its take-off run, and when it reached the midpoint of the runway, we started our own run, with No. 3 aircraft in swift pursuit. Soon the three aircraft in the first flight had taken up position, creating a V-formation and circling the airfield. Within minutes, all twenty-seven aircraft were airborne and making a massive

V of threes. Taking the lead from No. 1 aircraft and our flight, the whole squadron then moved as one towards the target out to sea.

After 'bombing' the target, Dad's plane turned for home with the crews thoroughly enjoying the impressive sight as the formation headed back towards the Pembrokeshire coast.

We had prepared for a close-order landing after a successful mission. With our flight of three leading the way, we broke away from the formation. As we approached the airfield, the second flight of three were following suit some forty seconds behind us. And this process was to continue flight-by-flight until we were all safely down . . . unfortunately, we never reached that stage.

Below them an Oxford, using the cross-runway, had gone into its take-off run, its crew oblivious to the planes landing above them. Dad never worked out how this could have happened. 'The air above was full of aircraft; the air waves were full of the chat needed to get the large formation of aircraft into landing sequence; the leading aircraft were already in line astern, making their landing runs and visibility was first class. God knows why he opened up his throttles and released his brakes.'

The first aircraft in Dad's flight duly touched down and was then smashed to pieces by the Oxford taking off, killing all aboard both planes instantly, and with the wreckage flying high into the air.

Meanwhile, my aircraft was just about to touch down. Brilliantly, Braight not only aborted the landing, but made a steep climb while carrying out evasive action as we flew into and through the hurtling wreckage of the crashed aircraft. I ordered No. 3 to abort and follow us in an upward climb. As I did so, I saw the wheel and part of the landing gear of one of the stricken aircraft pass my window still on an upward path. I could hear our aircraft being hit by debris as we powered our way to gain height.

The now twenty-six-strong flight was diverted to nearby Templeton, where the crews gathered in the officers' mess.

It was at this point that I was able to attend to the three tearful cadets who had been given a grandstand view of the horror of an air crash which had killed four of their mates who were in the No. 1 aircraft. Braight and I comforted them as much as we could, but I had to ask that they be given medical attention. Of course, Braight and I were also in shock, but we had been fortunate to have been heavily engaged with our duties as the accident happened under our feet, and this activity contained its own medicine.

Two hours later they finally touched down at base. 'It had been a frightening and sobering anniversary for a ghastly war now entering its fifth year.'

By this time – the end of September 1943 – Dad was itching to participate in the war that he had seen so much of on the home front in Walthamstow and in the City, and that he had trained so intensively for in the RAF.

It was two years and seven months after his first interview

Grandad Dick, who changed the family name from Schmidt to Smith in 1914. A lance corporal in the King's Royal Rifle Corps, he was wounded at Loos in September 1915 and again at High Wood on the Somme in 1916.

Walthamstow High Street in the 1960s.

Liverpool Street station, where Dad worked during the Blitz.

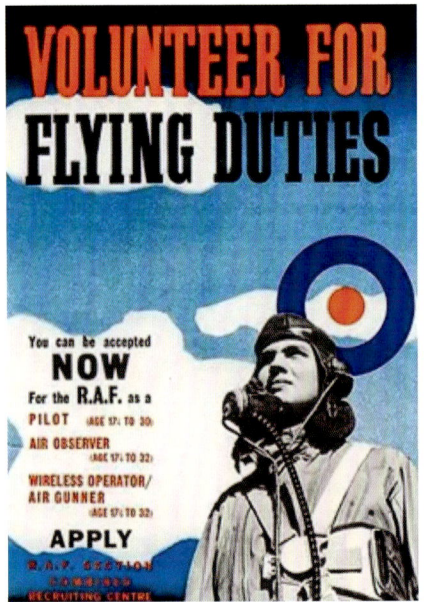

Recruitment poster for RAF duties, including wireless operator air gunners – Dad's role.

Mum's dad, Ted Riley. He was in the Rifle Brigade and Essex Regiment and fought on the Somme in 1918

Dad – a very new recruit at RAF Padgate.

Dad, promoted to flight sergeant, wearing the RAF Air Gunners brevet as seen enlarged. He kept his in the wooden box in the parlour at his mum's.

Dad (left), Harry Shirt and Paddy Thistlethwaite, Red Hills Lake, Madras, March 1945.

A Catalina at RAF Koggala in Ceylon.

Dad (far left) standing next to Harry Shirt, Jimmy Sullivan and Paddy Thistlethwaite, Red Hills Lake, Madras, March 1945.

Dad just returned from his sixth operational sortie. Full flying kit and a parachute. A favourite photo of mine.

Catalina flying over Ceylon.

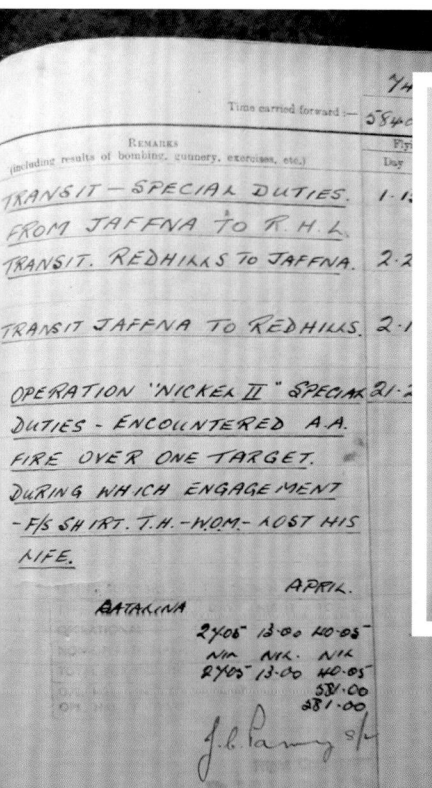

Dad's logbook entry regarding the Death in Action of his best friend Harry Shirt, aged just twenty-two. The photograph of Harry (above) was taken the week before he was killed.

Harry Shirt's funeral, April 1945. My dad is the last man on the right, back row. I'd never seen this photo until Stevan Bennett showed it to me the night we met, and realized our uncanny connection

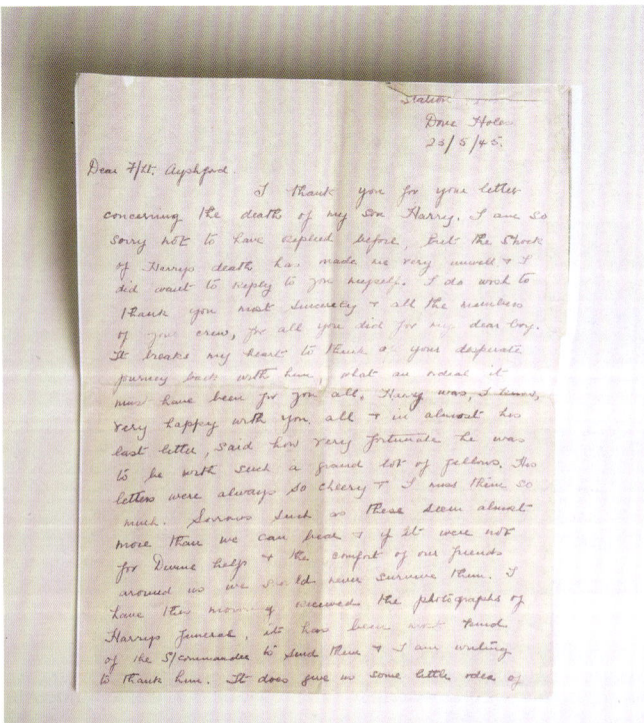

The letter found inside the flying boots, from Harry's mum to John Ayshford which heartbreakingly says 'thank you to you and your crew for looking after my son after he was killed'.

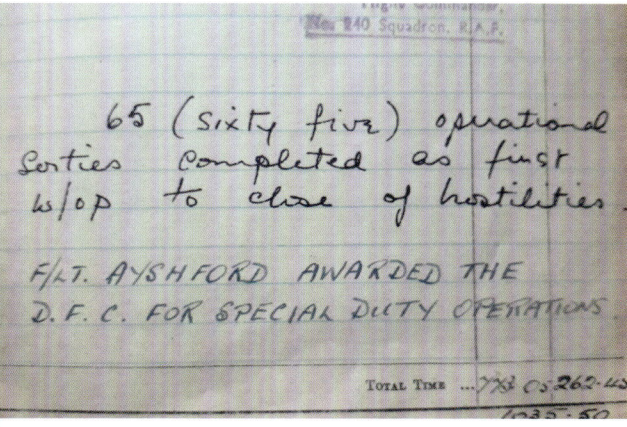

Dad's logbook's last wartime entry. '65 operations completed to end of hostilities'. The entry that he was most proud of.

Me, Mum and Dad outside our house, 1 Fernhill Court, Forest Road, Walthamstow, November 1974.

Me and my best friend, Philip Nobo, summer 1973. I still have the shirt I am wearing!!!

Me in my uniform in the front room at Mum and Dad's in 1991 just after the Gulf War ended. It's now on my mum's sideboard just like Dad's was on his mum's.

With Gordon Ramsey in 1984, on a crashed aircraft dig of a German Junkers 88 at Lator Priory Farm in Essex. The aircraft was shot down on 14 November 1940 on its way to Coventry, killing all the crew.

A sobering moment back in the London Air Ambulance helicopter that saved me in 2003, and caused me to rethink my career direction. I just couldn't bring myself to actually sit on the same stretcher. That was a chilling moment.

at Romford that he found himself posted to Blackpool once again, where he and quite a few other sergeant Wireless Operator/Air Gunners were left to kick their heels waiting for action.

One bright shining light was his love for my mum, and Dad managed to get three days leave from Blackpool in order to get married. When they were engaged, he had gained permission from Mum's parents to marry her 'in the near future' and now, six months later, he and Mum were ready. The service, followed by a small reception at Mum's place, was held on 14 November 1943 at St Mary's Church in Walthamstow before Dad returned to the waiting game in Lancashire.

Then, at the end of November, he was called in by the Adjutant and told that he had been selected to join the crew of a Catalina flying boat operating out of Killadeas on the shores of Lower Lough Erne in Northern Ireland. It seemed that all the skills he had mastered ready to use in bombers would no longer be required.

Dad was given a wonderfully warm reception by the locals in County Fermanagh, and, alongside 180 or so other young recruits to Catalinas, he began to familiarize himself with the rarefied world of flying boats. Used in maritime patrol, convoy escort, anti-submarine warfare and air-sea rescue, the Catalina was the most prolific flying boat of the Second World War, with 3,300 built by Consolidated Aircraft in San Diego. Stretching 63 feet from nose to tail fin, and with a wingspan of 104 feet, they were powered by twin Pratt & Whitney air-cooled radial engines that could produce a maximum speed of nearly 200mph. The Catalina could land on sea or on a runaway using removable wheels, and carried up to five machine guns and 4,000lb of bombs and torpedoes. They had a maximum operational range of over 2,500 statute miles.

Dad and his fellow recruits used an old aircraft moored in a corner of Lough Erne to practise the tricky exercise of climbing aboard from a launch and leaving the aircraft. In between, they crawled all over the cramped and awkward interior. They discovered that a poorly maintained Catalina was a recipe for seasickness because the bottom of the fuselage would act as sump for a horrible mixture of petrol, oil and sea water, and the flying boats would stink. It goes without saying that Dad was determined from the beginning that whatever aircraft he was going to fly would be kept spick and span. By early January 1944, the nucleus of each new Catalina crew was being sorted out and Dad was introduced to the men he would fly with for the rest of the war.

The social mix was interesting. Captain John Ayshford, who had seen operational experience with 210 Squadron on Catalinas, was a twenty-two-year-old public-school boy from Southend. Second Pilot, Flying Officer Don Foster, was from Suffolk and, at the age of twenty-five, had the longest service record, having joined in 1937. He had carried out forty-nine bombing raids as a Wireless Operator/Air Gunner before re-mustering to pilot after three tours of operations.

> The rest of us were sergeants with between one and four years' service. Don Hendrie was the old man of the team at thirty. He had been an Engineer Officer in the Merchant Navy before taking up his wartime flying role as Navigator/Bomb Aimer, having joined the service in

1942 and been trained in Rhodesia. The baby of the crew was Tom Coates, a Fitter Airframes, aka Rigger, who was still eighteen, having joined up not quite a year ago. Tom was also the tallest and the most powerful swimmer.

Initially, Tom was the only Geordie, but that would change when Vic Crawford, First Engineer, joined once the original incumbent left. Paddy Thistlethwaite was a direct entrant to the aircrew role of Engineer and hailed from Lancashire where he had spent his life farming. The signals team consisted of twenty-year-old Harry Shirt from Derbyshire, who had been a direct entrant to the role of Wireless Operator/Air Gunner in early 1943; Jim Sullivan, a Londoner who had joined in 1942 and was nearly twenty-two; and me, the crew's Wireless Operator, who had just turned twenty-one but with three years' service.

In those early weeks of January, the new crewmates spent their days rumbling up and down Lough Erne learning how to control their Catalina on the water.

Most of this taxying was for John Ayshford's benefit, but we all became used to acting as crewmen in a watery environment. We practised the art of catching a buoy, and learning how to deploy and use two massive seadrogues from both the blister gun turrets when mooring up. Quite quickly, we discovered how to move from nose to stern, passing through six bulkheads, through doors similar to those found on submarines. And we found our feet on the exterior of the aircraft, and this was as important to us as the interior. All the gun turrets opened to the breeze, but the front gun was reminiscent of the Great War because it required the gunner to stand with half his body exposed to the slipstream, and all the guns lacked hydraulics, requiring manual effort to move and fire.

A month in, and the day arrived when they got airborne for the first time. This was when Dad discovered how rough the ride on a Catalina could be, especially the landings when Ayshford would execute a 'stall-in' approach. With this technique, the tail of the Catalina would hit the water first, and then the fuselage would bounce and bump as the nose came down and the speed decreased. The crew had to be ready for the first impacts and then the final thump as the plane became a boat again.

> We made twelve take-offs and landings on our first day in the air, some of them of the 'stall-in' variety. We would wedge ourselves in, between two hard parts of the fuselage, with hands cupping neck, chin buried in chest, ready to take the strain each time the aircraft hit the water. The stall-in landings were painful no matter how well the crewman had prepared. After a dozen of those landings, we were all carrying memories of violence if not physical bruises. Nevertheless, we were deeply impressed with the skill of our skipper. He managed the exercise with confidence and only much later confided in us that he had never done it before during his many hours as a second pilot. He fooled us but still gained and deserved our vote of confidence as a man we could follow with pleasure.

Stall-in landings were one thing on Lough Erne; they were quite another out to sea in a near-gale, and it was not long before they were doing just that near the deserted island of Ailsa Craig on the Firth of Clyde. 'We did twelve stall-in landings on a wild sea. The first was awesome and they didn't get any easier.'

The crew executed long six-hour flying exercises in readiness for going operational, and Dad perfected the role of on-board photographer when they used the Catalina for bombing. This was certainly not for the faint-hearted, and the first time he did this they had an instructor on board.

> At last we were ready for bombing, with two missiles to be let loose on each attack. Two of my crewmates were appointed by the instructor to hold my legs as I leaned out of the port gun blister as far as I could go with the heavy Williamson F24 camera strapped to my chest. Once I was in position, with the special intercom working and helmet on, the order for the attack was given.

Bombing practice was clearly risky for Dad, but he and his crew were lucky they had not been doing it a few months earlier. Several aircraft based at Killadeas were lost, together with their crews, when faulty depth charges exploded above the surface, bringing the planes down. In light of this, Dad and his crew used small bombs to practise these skills while the fault in the depth charges was investigated.

By the end of February, they were ready for their first operational flight. It was the first of five anti-submarine patrols over the Atlantic when Ayshford's Catalina accompanied

Allied convoys making their way to Britain from the United States, while also searching for German U-boats. These were long flights covering hundreds of miles of ocean with the aircraft armed with (now safe-to-deploy) depth charges – three under each wing. Dad took off armed each time, with all sorts of special frequencies and call-signs and ready to identify his aircraft to shipping using flares and Aldis-lamp Morse.

The first was a 300-mile flight towards Iceland, but with regular detours to conduct box-searches or with elongated zigzags en route. Dad and the rest of the crew were amazed to see such busy shipping lanes in the North Atlantic, unaware that they were witnessing the build-up to D-Day. There was a real buzz of anticipation as the crew prepared.

> We were fully prepared to attack any U-boat that chose to show itself or even just its snorkel. This activity was far superior to exercises: this was the real thing, and by the time we turned onto our home leg we were getting into the swing of operational flying. We weren't bombing Berlin, but we were on a determined 'search and kill' mission, and the adrenaline pumped through our veins.

Two days later they were sent out on a second patrol, this time centred 200 miles south of the first, when they escorted a number of ships sailing alone.

> We didn't locate any enemy activity, but then neither did we lose a ship. When I wrote home that evening, my confidence on a high, I could only reflect with my family that it was three years ago on this day that I had spent

more than nine hours trying to join the RAF Volunteer Reserve. Now I was beginning to feel like a real veteran at long last.

After another patrol when the Catalina accompanied a convoy with dozens of ships for five hours, their next operational sortie was their first at night.

It was more hectic than the daytime ones and placed a heavy strain on the radio operators and the men on gun-watch. We again provided escort to part of a convoy approaching British waters, but I found the gloom of the Atlantic unfriendly – I couldn't really see the vessels to which I was sending my crisp Aldis messages, no matter how bright they appeared in the darkness.

After being posted to Oban on the Scottish west coast, the crew conducted its longest operational flight, accompanying a very special ship with a precious cargo.

When we met our target 200 miles out to sea we could understand why we had been pressed to give her escort. She was the RMS *Queen Mary* sailing at full speed alone on a violent sea. On board were thousands of American GIs with their equipment, a vital component of the D-Day force being assembled in Britain. I had great pleasure exchanging signals with this 85,000-ton beauty of a ship.

She ploughed through giant waves as if they didn't exist, and I had never seen a vessel travel so fast, in excess of 25 knots. In accordance with procedure, we stayed half a mile away as we did a crawling oval sweep around her. Our radar worked perfectly. The *Queen* showed up as a sizeable blip, but we were searching for snorkels or other parts of U-boats which would be visible on screen.

That sortie was followed by a night-time sweep of the island waters off the west coast of Scotland. It ended in tragedy.

We were to fly with another Catalina crew in tandem with take-off at 0230. This was our ninth operational flight and one that made the BBC morning news, as we were to find out on our return to Oban after five and a half hours of flying. Alva Lidell, one of the most recognizable voices on the BBC during the war, announced that two of our aircraft had conducted a reconnaissance of North Atlantic waters and that 'one of our aircraft failed to return'. It was not the sort of news anybody wanted to hear, and it was very poignant for us when we were told that our companion aircraft was the one referred to by Lidell. She had crashed into a mountain in the Inner Hebrides, killing all nine airmen on board. We had enjoyed a pre-operational breakfast with them only the day before. It was very sad, and it dawned on all of us that we had enjoyed a lucky escape.

In Oban, the crew received the posting that would dominate the rest of their and Dad's war. It was to 240 Squadron in South East Asia Command, based at Red Hills Lake at Madras on the east coast of India, and they would start by flying their own Catalina out to the Far East.

They went via a long hop to Gibraltar, then to Djerba in Tunisia, and then over Tripoli and across the Gulf of Sidra to Benghazi. After taking off early in the morning, Dad took a photo of Benghazi for 'old times' sake'.

> And then we headed through the pages of recent military history as we flew the coastal road through the battlefields of Tobruk, Sidi Barrani, Marsa Matruh and El Alamein, where I took pictures from low level.
> Although the Battle of El Alamein had taken place nineteen months earlier in October 1942, the scene of the massive confrontation between the Germans and the Allies was frozen in time thanks to the dry air of the desert. The thousands of shell holes were still showing in a pock-marked pattern and in sharp relief, covering ridged sand dunes and flat plains of desert land. The wreckage of tanks and lorries scattered the scene, which was embroidered with rusting barbed wire.

After stopping at Kasfareet on the western side of the Suez Canal on the shore of the Great Bitter Lake, the crew hitched a ride on an RAF lorry for the sixty-mile journey to Cairo where they spent three days behaving like tourists. They got mugged 'like any other group of sprog servicemen', and Dad and Harry Shirt – now firmly his best mate in the crew – got collared in the bazaar and taken to the Blue Mosque to have their fortunes told in the sand. 'Harry was told that he wouldn't see the end of the war, and I was informed that I would peg-out at the age of fifty-four. We realized we had been trapped into breaking the servicemen's code, which spells out why fortune-tellers are to be shunned, no matter where.'

Next stop was Lake Habbaniyah on the banks of the

Euphrates, about fifty-five miles west of Baghdad, where Dad recovered from an attack of dysentery he had contracted in Egypt. Then on to Bahrain, and then through the gulf to Korangi Creek in Karachi. At that stopover, Ayshford was waylaid by jaundice and they nearly lost Tom Coates when he fell overboard while cleaning the fuselage with a scrubbing brush and a bucket.

The first goal of this long journey east was to deliver the Catalina to RAF Koggala on the southern tip of Ceylon (now Sri Lanka), and they eventually moored it up there on 21 June, after a journey from Oban that had taken just short of a month and involved sixty-five hours of flying.

Jungle life at Koggala proved a challenge, complete with deadly snakes that had killed seventeen of the RAF personnel who had built the base. Add to that an attack of coral poisoning, after Dad got knocked over by a breaking wave on the reef while swimming, and the crew having all their wages stolen from Dad's room while he was trying to sleep his fever off, and it was an eventful stay.

After three weeks, they departed and made their way by sea, road and rail to their final destination with 240 Squadron at Red Hills Lake in India. They got there exactly fifty days after leaving Scotland.

Chapter Twelve

Everyone else apart from my friend Martin had disappeared to university, so all that was left in Walthamstow were me and him. Then, all of a sudden, he said, 'I've got a job.'

'Wow, blimey, that's good,' I thought. 'Riches – £69 a week.'

So off I went trying to find a job of my own. I didn't know what I was going to do. I still wanted to work in a museum. Actually, the Imperial War Museum, no less. And I quite liked the idea of being a soldier perhaps. But I thought I had better do something – anything – and I found this job as a clerk at the Department of Health and Social Security, aka the DHSS, and it paid the magic number of sixty-nine quid.

It was based in Leytonstone, just down the road from Walthamstow, and I hated it. I was a Giro writer. Every week people got a payment for sickness or invalidity benefit, and it came in the form of a Giro cheque. My job was to take a big pile of blank cheques and write them out, all day long, every day. It was dreadful, the worst kind of back-office job imaginable.

Within about two weeks, I went before a panel to be assessed for promotion. I told them I wanted to work in a museum, and that I was working on the principle that if I did my current job in the Civil Service, I would eventually be able to do that. I explained that my idea was to sort of move across.

It was a revelation and a plan that was met with not one word of encouragement. In fact, they told me it would never happen. But I did get promoted. I went from being a Casual Clerical Assistant to a Clerical Officer. Instead of being a Giro writer I had become a Giro rater. Now my job involved the slightly more interesting task of working out what each person should get so the Giro writers knew what numbers to write on the cheques.

I worked in Leytonstone for several years. It was the worst job the world has ever seen. I was desperate to get out of it, pretty much at any cost. But the problem was that once I had done it for a year or so I was stuck. I wasn't getting paid much money compared to other people, but it was enough to survive on, and I came to rely on it. I couldn't afford to risk it coming to an end and having no job to go to.

But I still dreamed of museum life, and after a couple of years I signed up for a twelve-week course in archaeology in Walthamstow. It was held on Tuesday nights in part of a school on Forest Road, and it was not much more than an introduction to the principles of archaeology – how you found stuff and how you recorded it.

At the beginning they said, 'Has anyone done any archaeology?'

I said 'yes'. What I actually said was, 'Yes, I've done some aviation archaeology.'

The bloke in charge got completely the wrong end of the stick. He took that to mean I had been involved in a new idea at the time, which involved flying over places in small planes and identifying crop circles or the layout of ancient earthworks.

'No, not flying in planes. What I mean is digging up stuff from the Second World War. Like bits of Spitfires from the Battle of Britain and things like that,' I told him.

He wasn't terribly impressed. He seemed to think what I was talking about was not archaeology, which is interesting given that 'battlefield' or 'conflict' archaeology is now a popular discipline in our universities.

At the time they were digging up Billingsgate Fish Market, and someone on the course was working there, so we got regular updates on what was being found.

We went on field trips to High Beech in Epping Forest, to look at Iron Age forts, and to the site of a church in Stratford in East London that was being demolished near where the Olympic stadium now is. There was a crypt under the church, and they were taking out the coffins. We found out what the bodies were like and how some were found with jewellery on and that sort of thing. At the end you got a certificate. It was an interesting course, and it made me want to work in the museum world even more.

In my spare time, medals and militaria collecting was still the big thing. And me and Gordon would get together every week. Gordon had been going to the battlefields in France with his dad for many years by then, and his stories about them – about the fact that there were tin hats everywhere, or so he said – were eating away at me.

I had to go there, and one day I said to myself, 'Right, I'm going to do this. I'm going to go to the Somme,' which seemed like the ultimate battlefield, if you were going to pick one.

The trouble was I didn't want to go on my own. For some reason Gordon wasn't available on the first trip, so I said to a couple of guys I worked with that I was 'going to the battlefields of the First World War', and they both decided to come along. One was called Ian, and the other Roy. I think they had heard me going on and on about this kind of thing and it had piqued their curiosity. 'It sounds like fun, Smithy, I'm in,' said Ian, as Roy stood next to him nodding.

I was beyond excited. I worked out how to get there. Car to Dover. Car on ferry. Drive to Arras. Then to Bapaume, then the Somme. Yellow stickers on the headlights, and all that.

I went to the militaria shops in Islington and told everyone I was going to the Somme, and one of the proprietors mentioned a Madame Brouillet who lived in the small village of Pozières.

'She runs a B&B. You can stay there, Smithy,' he said.

Well, that was handy. So we had the accommodation sorted.

It was a Thursday in the first week of June 1986, and I was twenty-two. I was packing up the car outside the house, with Dad standing there winding me up.

'Ah, Son . . . you're going on a big mission tomorrow,' he said. 'Driving on the wrong side of the road. Eating strange French food. Ha, ha, ha . . . Oh . . . dangerous stuff, my boy!'

He was treating it like a flight over enemy territory like he always did, bless him. And there was I, determined to finally go and do this.

I wanted to stand on a trench line, and I wanted to find something from the war. I had heard so much about this place, where the trenches were still there and the barbed wire was still there, and it was exactly the same as it was.

When I was at Forest I'd got hold of a book called *Old Soldiers Never Die* – the classic Great War memoir by Frank Richards. He was a private in the Royal Welsh Fusiliers who had fought on the Somme and almost everywhere else on the Western Front – and it was another one that I read and reread. After that, I barely looked at another book that was not about the First World War. So to go to the Somme a few weeks before the seventieth anniversary of the battle on 1 July was a huge thing.

We set off for Dover in my white Vauxhall Cavalier early on Friday 6 June, the anniversary of D-Day. On the boat, I remember thinking how cool it was that I was going to France for the first time on that date. Nowadays, you drive down fast roads to Arras and the Somme valley, but at that time you had to wiggle your way there.

Eventually, after several hours in the car, and arguing over the map and which way we should go, we got to the town of Bapaume. This sits at the north-east corner of the battlefield, and, from there, we turned onto the D929 that cuts right through the centre of the Somme towards the town of Albert.

Heading south-west, off to the right were the villages of Courcelette and Pozières – our destination for the night – while, to the left, I saw, for the first time in my life, the signpost to High Wood – the Bois des Fourcaux. So I drove down there, and I said to Ian and Roy, 'Right, this is where we are going to start.'

I knew about High Wood. I had read about it in a book called *The Hell They Called High Wood* by Terry Norman, and it meant something special to me because I knew Grandad had been wounded there. So I drove down there and stopped by the side of the wood and got out. I was standing on the Somme for the first time. This was the place where more than 1 million men were killed or wounded in five bloody months in 1916, and which is dotted with more than 640 cemeteries.

What I didn't know was that that first field I stood in – where I got out of the car – was almost exactly where Grandad Dick was blown up seventy years earlier. I was standing only a few hundred yards from where he and his battalion of the King's Royal Rifle Corps had attacked the Switch Line trench that ran between High Wood and Delville Wood in 1916. It was the place where Dick and his machine-gunner were hit by a German shell after going over the top, with Grandad suffering a wound to his wrist and his gunner being blown to pieces. I had no idea of it at the time, as I stood there staring at the trees, and only worked it out many years later.

All the woods on the Somme are privately owned, and when the war finished the owners came back and put fences around them and then left them. They didn't do anything to them. The rumour was that none of the trenches had been filled in, and all the stuff was still there. But you weren't supposed to go in, not least because you might come across a wild boar or be shot by a hunting party.

With us that day we had a metal detector, which was illegal on those battlefields because of the danger you might blow yourself up. After our visit to High Wood, we made our way a bit further south to Trônes Wood. This was the site of more desperate fighting in 1916, where thousands of men on both sides were killed or wounded. I had no idea where the trenches were, nor the significance of that place as we looked for a gap in the fence where the logging lorries went in and started to walk down a path between the trees.

I had the detector ready, and almost immediately it went off. I dug into the earth with a small spade I had brought along and found a piece of shrapnel. I could have fainted. I was so excited. We went a bit further and it beeped again. This time we found a big knife which I reckoned was probably something to do with forestry work, not the First World War. So my big – and very hopefully carried – empty bag I had with me was still empty. Another beep, and we found another piece of shrapnel and, not far from it, a silvery thing which, after cleaning it off, I reckoned might be a flare cartridge. It was made of brassy aluminium, so it did not set off the detector.

We were beginning to think that two pieces of shrapnel and a spent flare cartridge was our lot for the day, when Ian said he was going off for a pee. A minute or two later he came back.

'Are these any good?' he said, standing and staring at me with two round metal things in his hands.

'Where the on earth did you find them?' I shrieked as I ran over to look at them.

He'd only stumbled across two British steel helmets, stuff that would have been worn by Tommies on this battlefield in 1916. I couldn't believe it, despite what Gordon had always said.

We walked back to where he had found them.

'There,' he said, pointing at the shape of a shell hole along the front of the wood.

They had been lying on the surface and were rusty, with green moss growing on them. One had a bullet hole through it. We put them in our bag and got back in the car. I thought, 'It's not going to get any better than that, is it?'

That evening we drove into Pozières, which by August 1916 had been reduced to rubble. We found the bar owned by Madame Brouillet. Her husband had only one arm. The place was tiny and our room, which we shared between the three of us, was in the eaves. It was very authentic with a sharply sloping roof.

We slept on iron bedsteads with feather pillows and blankets, and for nine francs each we got breakfast too. We didn't speak French, and they didn't know much English, so I'm sure our halting exchanges with the proprietor sounded a bit like scenes from the TV sitcom *'Allo 'Allo!*

The next day we were up early ready to drive the thirty-five-mile Circuit de Souvenir, a signposted tour of the entire battlefield. We went to the Newfoundland Memorial Park near Beaumont-Hamel where soldiers in the Royal Newfoundland Regiment suffered horrendous losses; to the Hawthorn Ridge Crater where a German frontline position was blown to smithereens at the start of the battle; and to the Memorial to the Missing at Thiepval designed by Sir Edwin Lutyens, which has the names of 73,412 men on it who have no known graves. Then we drove home stunned, it would be fair to say, by what we had seen.

Right from the start I had been thinking this place was

amazing. It wasn't like it is today. Now there's nothing on the battlefield to find. In those days you could find stuff all the time. Everywhere. The mark of the First World War was everywhere you looked. Barbed wire by the side of the road, shrapnel balls, nose cones off shells, even a cap badge if you were lucky. They were the Holy Grail for collectors like me. You could find all sorts of things.

To me, it was a magical place that I had to go back to – there was no way that was going to be the only trip I did to the Somme or the other battlefields of the First World War. I was going to return again, and again, and again, because I was in awe of a place that I had read about, talked about and heard about, and now I was there. These were the fields where my grandads had put their lives on the line.

And so I used to go back with Gordon because he was as keen on doing this as I was. It meant I always had this one 'oppo' to go with, and I didn't have to bore anyone to death trying to persuade them to come with me. And I read, and read, and read. I got maps, and I started to work out where bits of the battle and the trenches were, and things like that.

As that progressed, it got to the point when I had become so familiar with the place that what I wanted to do then was to take other people to show them. I wanted other people to understand what this place was like, and that really was the burning desire – to take people to a place that almost felt like home to me. Of course, the one person I would have loved to take was Dad. But he wouldn't come.

'I don't want to see it,' he would say. 'I don't want to know.' I think he found the idea too distressing, and perhaps he worried about triggering his own memories of war.

He couldn't come with me, and he never came on a battlefield tour.

If there's one place that I have to go back to – need to go back to every time I visit the Somme – it's the Sunken Lane at Beaumont-Hamel. It's where Geoffrey Malins – a cameraman employed by the War Office – famously filmed the opening attack on 1 July 1916 in what became the most watched piece of film in the history of British cinema.

It gets me every time – that he was there that day when 19,240 British men were killed and more than 38,000 others wounded – and he was filming it, including the moment they went over the top. In the grainy black-and-white images, you see those guys come out of the trench on the side of the hill, and they run along, rifles in hand, helmets at jaunty angles, and then they start to fall over. Then they try to run towards the road, and more of them fall down dead. And they really are dead. It's not playing. It's real.

The Sunken Lane was a geographical feature, a farm track, and the British army was going to attack from it towards the German line, which was about 180 yards away. They got about 90 yards – then didn't get any further than that. The Sunken Lane is still there, and it looks almost exactly the same as it did the day those men were in it when Malins was filming them.

The 1st Battalion, Lancashire Fusiliers had just come back from Gallipoli. When they were waiting to go over the top, with bayonets fixed, you can see them talking to each other. And in 2009 the Imperial War Museum asked a lip-reader to see if she could work out what they were saying. She quickly guessed that they were not educated men by the way their mouths were forming as they spoke. At one point a Tommy operating a mortar says to his second lieutenant, 'I hope we're in the right place this time because, if not, I'm going to bomb 'em all and then bugger off.'

It's classic bravado before battle, but it's their faces that tell the real story. They are the faces of petrified young men. And from when Malins filmed them, they probably had about twenty minutes left to live, twenty minutes until the whistle blew and they went over the top into the teeth of enemy machine-gun fire. That lane and their cemetery, which is ninety paces away from their trench, is where I go every time.

I must have been to the Somme and other battlefields in northern France with Gordon about fifty times over a twelve-year period. I've been there hundreds of times altogether. At some point, the idea came to me to collect a medal or some other item of militaria for someone killed on every day of the First World War, and we started with 1 July 1916. The recipient of my medal for that day was William Buchan, and his name is on the Memorial to the Missing of the Somme at Thiepval. I wanted to visit all of the people whose medals I collected, so Gordon and I went to Thiepval and photographed his inscription to put with his medal.

As time went by, I would take with me a list of all the cemeteries I wanted to visit to try to find the men whose medals I had most recently acquired. And that is how we gradually varied our visits from the Somme to other battlefields, like Ypres and the cemeteries around Loos and Passchendaele.

I started to understand more about how the battlefields worked, and more about where the frontlines were, by having those medals and finding out where the men who were awarded them were buried, which was quite hard in the days before the internet. Often, I would work backwards, establishing what battle a soldier was in and then trying to find out not only where he was buried, but where the fighting was that he was involved in.

Over the years I started to join the battlefields together – the Somme, Arras, Fromelles. But what took a long time was to work out that if, for instance, you were looking at the Battle of Passchendaele, how did that link up with the Battle of Cambrai? Or the Battle of Festubert? And how does that affect the Battle of Loos? It took a long time to get the chronology into my head and understand how the movement across the battlefields worked. It probably took me twenty years to be able to stand anywhere on that landscape and say, 'The British are here, the Germans are there.' That might sound simple, but it's not. It's really quite hard to work out because each battleground is a big place. The Somme, for example, might look very small on a map, but when you're actually standing there it is huge. So to work out where a trench line turned, or where the Germans went over the top – that took a long time.

One of those trips with Gordon was to photograph the names of two brothers whose memorial plaques I had bought from a medal dealer in Islington. They have consecutive service numbers – 1329 and 1330 – and they were killed on the same day – 5 May 1915. Their names are on the Menin Gate Memorial to the Missing at Ypres in Belgium, and Gordon and I found them there and photographed them in 1987.

They were nineteen-year-old Arthur Fairburn and his twenty-five-year-old brother William, and they were killed while serving with the 6th Battalion, King's Liverpool Regiment during the Second Battle of Ypres. Their names are also to be found on the war memorial in Alexandra Park on Coronation Road in Great Crosby on Merseyside.

At some point, their families must have sold the plaques. Gordon and I tried to find out where they had died, and I'm pretty sure it was to the north-east of Ypres, near a village called St Juliaan. They may have been killed by chlorine gas that was being used in the Ypres Salient by the Germans for the first time in the war, but most likely it would have been shellfire. They were either blown to bits, which is why they are on the Menin Gate, or they are still buried in the field where they fell.

Matching their medals with their inscription on the monument, and finding out where they were from and where they died, was an exercise that I will never tire of, or take lightly.

You can only imagine what their family must have felt when they were informed what had happened that day in May 1915 . . . and for years afterwards.

Chapter Thirteen

After a few years calculating the value of Giro cheques, I took an exam in a library in Pimlico organized by the Civil Service Commissioning Board with the intention of being posted to the Ministry of Defence. Instead of trying to work for a museum, this was going to be my escape route, or so I thought. You had to pass and get into the top 5–10 per cent to qualify for a move to the MoD, and I narrowly failed to achieve that. I was gutted not to have made it.

In the meantime, I completed a move from the DHSS office in Leytonstone to a new job with the Social Security Medical Appeals Tribunal, which was based in an office on Tottenham Court Road in Central London. What we were looking at were people who had complained about the way they were treated by the 'system'. They'd either not received sickness or invalidity benefits they believed they deserved, or, if they had, they hadn't been paid enough.

My role was as clerk of the court. Sometimes I took notes of proceedings – I invented my own shorthand for that – but mainly my job was to make sure those appearing before the three-member panel, which was normally led by a lawyer of some description, knew what to do and where to go. I would meet them outside the room and explain who I was, who the panel was and what was going to happen. Then we would go in. I would sit there. The panel would ask various questions. The hearing would come to an end. And then I would usher them out again and make sure a recording, or my notes of the verdict, was properly typed up afterwards.

I know I said my first two jobs at the DHSS were boring. Well, this one was barely any better. It was so dull. Possibly its only saving grace was that we used to move about all over the place, which broke up the monotony. The venue might be a town hall or a church hall where you might hear ten cases and then move on the next day. In London, we would go to my local town hall in Walthamstow or the church hall at Wood Green. The ones further afield included places like Peterborough, King's Lynn, Cambridge or Watford where I used to volunteer to fill in for clerks who were off sick or on holiday.

Of course, I was always talking to everybody about military things, and at Watford I met a guy called Mr Bird who was one of the two lay people on the panel that day. He was in his seventies, so military age from the Second World War, and we got talking during the lunch break.

'I was in a tank,' he said, after we had been chatting for a few minutes in a general way about D-Day.

'Were you? Tell me about it,' I said.

'Well, I was at Dunkirk, and I got shot.'

'Oh no, did you actually?'

'Yes,' he said. 'Through here,' he added, rolling up his sleeve to reveal a scar on his left forearm. 'The tank got blown up and we got out, and I was running away and the bullet went through here,' he said, clamping his right hand over the old wound.

Then he told me what the medics at a dressing station did to him to prevent the onset of potentially fatal 'gas-gangrene'. It involved driving an armourer's rod into and out of the wound with a piece of disinfectant gauze shoved onto the end of it. It sounded horrific.

'The medic got hold of my arm,' he explained, 'and he pushed the rod through the hole and then pulled it out, and I fainted right there – just crashed to the floor.'

After he got better, Mr Bird was posted to North Africa where his tank was properly hit by a German artillery round. The shockwave broke both his legs right at the top by his pelvis, and that was him, finished for the war.

Then he told me about his father's service in the Great War. Mr Bird Senior had been in the Cambridgeshire Regiment, and one day a shell landed close to his trench. He was blown into the air and came down in no man's land. When they found him and brought him back in, he was in a state of shock but otherwise uninjured. The main thing was what he was wearing – or not wearing. All his clothes, save for his shirt collar and his boots, had been blown off him. He was completely naked. Incredible.

We had such a great chat together. The next time the tribunal came to Watford, I saw him again, and he said, 'Oh, Mr Smith, I've got something for you.' He rummaged in his briefcase and produced his dad's medals, his cap badge and his Signaller's badge. He insisted I have them and, naturally, I've still got them and still treasure them. That was *so* nice of him.

As a young medal collector, there was one thing that had been bugging me for a while. There was an organization – and it's still going – called the Orders and Medals Research Society (OMRS). This august body, which was formed in 1942, exists to promote general interest in the study of orders, decorations and medals, and I always felt being a member of it was like a badge of credibility as a collector. But in those days, I was so unsure of myself. The joining process and finding out whether I would be considered for membership used to absolutely terrify me.

You had to get an application form and have it signed by two people who were already members. On the form you had to say what medals you collected. And that was the problem. I mainly collected medals from my two grandads' regiments, the King's Royal Rifle Corps and the Rifle Brigade, and from the RAF because Dad served in it. Did that make me a proper collector?

I used to meet people at medal fairs who were OMRS members, and who would tell me about their collecting and make me feel like an absolute beginner. You would hear people say – and I'm only slightly exaggerating – 'I only collect the Bedfordshire Regiment, and, of them, I only collect 6th Battalion, A Company, 12th Platoon . . . er . . . 6th Section.'

'Blimey!' I would think. 'How on earth do you do that? How do they even know about regiments to that level of detail? And more to the point, where would you ever find your next medal?'

I was still going to Islington on Saturdays, and there was a bloke there called Dave who sold medals, and another guy called Stephen Wheeler who was also a medal dealer. After hearing me out on the subject of the OMRS, Dave said he would sign my application form, and Steve was happy to second it. So I filled it all out and stated that I collected the King's Royal Rifle Corps, the Rifle Brigade and the RAF. I genuinely thought that if they came a-knocking at my door to check, I would have those medals to prove it. So I sent it in, said a little prayer, and was astonished to see that, almost by return, my membership card had arrived, no questions asked. I was OMRS member No. 4129.

Over the years, my early insecurities have gradually melted away. What you find is that the guys who say they collect this platoon from that company of the Bedfords, or people killed on Tuesdays when it was raining, often don't have any medals that fit the bill quite yet. It's talk. They are often collectors of things that are almost impossible to find, which has the added bonus of saving them from spending money having to buy them. I know one chap who only collects medals awarded to military bandsmen. When I offered him some that I happened to have one day, I discovered they were for soldiers playing the wrong instruments. Hilarious.

But collecting is never easy. I would go with Dad to medal fairs, looking for medals from my chosen specialities, and find nothing, or medals that were far too expensive. And that is how I came to my idea of collecting a medal for a soldier killed on every day of the First World War. After starting with medals from 1 July 1916, it grew to the whole of July, then one for every big battle of the war, and finally one for every day of the whole conflict.

Buying medals was one thing. Finding out about the people they had been awarded to, other than where they were killed, was much harder. You had to write a letter enclosing one pound to the Commonwealth War Graves Commission to access their records. So if you sent enquiries about ten medals, that was ten quid, money that you could spend on more medals, so there was a moment when I had to decide. Another option was to visit the Guildhall Library where the registers were held, just off Gresham Street in the City. I did that and tried to find out as much as I could.

The game-changer came when I joined the MoD (about which more later). The library there had thousands of books about each regiment and each battalion. They had personal stories of people, catalogued by battalions and regiments, and they had a complete list of 'Soldiers Died' in the First World War. So all of a sudden I had this massive resource where I could go and spend my lunchtime with the three medals I had bought that weekend. The next thing that came along was the internet, and the moment the Commonwealth War Graves Commission put their database online in 1998. Suddenly there was a whole world of information available at the click of a mouse.

The way my First World War project works is I use a five-year diary to cover all 1,553 days of the war, and I fill in the details of the recipient of medals for each day as I collect them, and then research them. For the medals where I have had some success in finding out more about the person involved, I usually end up with a small folder or bag containing the medals and various bits and pieces that I have managed to find – copies of service records, letters or newspaper articles, or other items that may be pertinent.

So whenever I go anywhere, when it comes to the First World War I am usually looking for medals from particular days – days that I haven't got – and one of my biggest outlays in the early days of the project was a medal for someone who's now been with me for years.

His name is Herbert Mackness. And one day, in a shop off Trafalgar Square run by a guy called Ray Holditch, I found a framed picture of him which came with his medals – the 1914–15 Star, the British War Medal and the Victory Medal. This little piece of history was expensive because Herbert was Australian, and because there was a picture and I could see him. The price was £125, a vast sum of money in 1990, and probably sixty quid more than I'd ever paid for a medal at that point. But I bought him because he died on a day that I didn't have.

The medals came with the Memorial Scroll that was sent to the families of soldiers killed in the war. It reads:

> He whom this scroll commemorates was numbered among those who, at the call of King and country, left all that was dear to them, endured hardness, faced danger, and finally passed out of the sight of men by the path of duty and self-sacrifice, giving up their own lives that others might live in freedom. Let those who come after see to it that his name be not forgotten.

Like all the people whose medals I have, I was determined that Herbert would not be forgotten. I asked Ray where he had come across him, and he told me the medals had come from a house clearance in Southend-on-Sea in Essex. In those days you could write to the Australian authorities, and for a fee – in Australian dollars – they would send you a set of service papers. From those documents, I discovered that Herbert's sister, Miss Edith Mackness, was living at an address in Rainham in Essex, not far from Southend, and that his medals and effects were sent to her on his death.

Herbert had been born in Stepney in East London in 1887. At some point, he had emigrated to Australia where he had worked as a labourer. He was in the 32nd Battalion, Australian Infantry, which was raised as part of the Australian 8th Brigade at Mitcham on the outskirts of Adelaide in August 1915. Herbert didn't go to Gallipoli, but in November 1915 he sailed from Australia, initially to Alexandria in Egypt. From there he boarded His Majesty's Transport Ship *Transylvania*, which took him to Marseilles where he landed on 23 June 1916. The ship was sunk a year later in the Gulf of Genoa by a German submarine, with the loss of 402 soldiers and 12 crew.

Herbert's picture reveals a strong-featured young man looking confidently ahead, and it was no surprise to discover that he was disciplined for insubordination during his brief army career. His service papers summarize this as follows: 'Mackness refused to obey a lawful command given by his superior officer when ordered to move off with a fatigue party. He stepped out and refused to go. Awarded 20 days Field Punishment No. 2.'

This young man had less than a month to live after arriving in Marseilles. The next we know of him, he is posted as Missing in Action on 20 July at the Battle of Fromelles to the north-east of the Somme, close to the Belgian border. This was the first big battle fought by Australian troops on the Western Front, and it was a total and unmitigated disaster. It was supposed to be a diversionary attack to distract the

Germans from what was happening on the Somme, where an offensive by the British army was planned. But the German machine-gunners at Fromelles were ready, having largely been unaffected by a seven-hour preparatory bombardment of their positions. The bombardment had the additional, negative effect of removing any element of surprise about what was about to happen.

When the troops of the 5th Australian Division and 61st British Division attacked on the evening of the 19 July, the outcome was hideous. Over two days, the Australians suffered 5,533 casualties – either killed, wounded or reported missing in what was the worst defeat in their military history – while the British figure was 1,547.

As Sergeant Jimmy Downing, an Australian survivor, put it, 'Hundreds were mown down in the flicker of an eyelid, like great rows of teeth knocked from a comb . . . men were cut in two by streams of bullets . . . it was all over in five minutes.' German casualties, meanwhile, were just over 1,000 men. Despite the temporary occupation of small sections of their trenches by the Australians during the fighting, the Germans were back in place when the battle was over.

Hundreds of Australian soldiers were never found after what was an entirely futile engagement, Herbert among them. Then, in 2009, new aerial photographs of the battlefield identified a series of what looked like burial pits by some trees at a place called Pheasant Wood at Fromelles. This prompted a major operation to exhume the remains of over 300 Australian and British soldiers who had been buried by the Germans after the battle to ward off the spread of disease. Using DNA extracted from the skeletons, and then matching that with DNA from families in Australia and elsewhere who had relatives still missing at Fromelles, some of these soldiers were finally identified before being re-buried in a new cemetery at the site. I followed this closely, and every time they found another set of remains, I hoped it was going to be Herbert. But he continues to be missing, and so the story – his story – never ends.

I remember the day that Gordon and I went to Fromelles for the first time and to the VC Corner Australian Cemetery to find Herbert's name. It was a Sunday afternoon, it was getting dark, and it was wet and cold. We got out and walked up through this weird little burial ground, and there he was on the wall at the back. I took a photo and felt that sense of completing a circle. But really the circle never ends because it was after that visit that they found the burial sites at Pheasant Wood.

And so there was, and is, always the hope that one day someone will find him and that his name will get taken off the wall of the missing, and I will go there again and see his grave. In the meantime, I've sent Herbert's photograph, and photographs of his medals, to the museum at Fromelles so that he is part of their story.

Herbert occupies 20 July 1916 in my First World War collection. For Christmas Day 1914, I have the medals of Private Edmund Griffiths of the 2nd Battalion, East Lancashire Regiment, who was killed at the age of twenty-two. I bought his medals from a dealer in London, and I have his 1914 Star and his Victory medal, but his British War Medal is missing. This is often the case because it was made of an ounce of silver, and less well-off families would sell them for cash.

Edmund was born in Blackburn in 1892 and joined the regiment in 1914. He went to France as part of 24th Brigade, landing at Le Havre on 6 November 1914. I have never been able to pin down exactly how, or where, he was killed, and like Herbert his body was never found. His name is on the memorial at Le Touret near Béthune which commemorates 13,479 British soldiers who died in that sector of the Western Front before 25 September 1915 and who have no known grave.

Edmund's three medals were sent to his widow who lived in dire poverty in Blackburn. But the story doesn't end there. After his death, Edmund's little brother, who lived with him and his wife, also joined up and, at the age of eighteen, followed his sibling's fateful footsteps to France.

His destiny was to be shot through the head by a sniper, causing a severe brain injury. His sister-in-law then looked after him for the rest of her life until she died in 1945. At that point, the younger brother was committed to an asylum and died the following year. The sad story of the Griffiths family and the way the Great War devastated their lives is one of many like it that I have collected.

I can choose stories from so many days – 862, in fact, of the 1,553 that made up the war. The person and medals I have for 23 April 1917 are particularly special. He was a chap called Eric Arthur Welch who was born in London in November 1894 but was living with his parents in Lancaster when the war broke out. He was educated at Lancaster Royal Grammar School and then became an apprentice engineer with a firm in Bedford, and later with the lorry builders Atkinson & Co. in Preston.

With the onset of the war, Eric volunteered and served in the ranks before being promoted to second lieutenant in the 10th Reserve Battalion, King's Own (Royal Lancaster Regiment). But after being transferred to the 7th Battalion, he grew restless with the relative inactivity of his postings and successfully applied for a transfer to the Royal Flying Corps, the forerunner of the RAF.

This was quite a leap, and soon Eric was undergoing pilot training and was posted to 53 Squadron. From there he was transferred to 16 Squadron, which had been formed in France at St Omer in February 1915, before moving to an airfield at La Gorgue, about twenty miles west of Lille. The squadron was deployed on offensive patrol and reconnaissance duties over northern France throughout the war.

It was only a matter of days after his transfer to La Gorgue that Eric's B.E.2 single-engine two-seater biplane was shot to pieces by a German plane over Maricourt on the Somme just after midday on 23 April. Eric was twenty-three years old, and he is buried in the Petit-Vimy British Cemetery at Vimy. His mission that day was to overfly German positions, observe the fall of shot of British artillery, and then report back on their accuracy or otherwise. Killed with him was his twenty-two-year-old Observer, Sergeant Amos George Tollervey, who is buried next to his pilot. I have Eric's 1914–20 British War Medal and his 1914–19 Victory medal.

That might have been it as far as my research on Eric went, until I came across a combat report for 23 April by the legendary German ace Baron Manfred von Richthofen. He described coming across a B.E. two-seater on the German side of the lines over Maricourt but was unable to identify it as it broke up in mid-air. It seems Eric never saw the Red Baron coming. 'I observed an artillery flyer and approached him unnoticed,' wrote the celebrated German pilot, who would himself be killed almost exactly a year later over the Somme. '[I] shot at him from the closest range until his left wing came off. The machine broke to pieces and fell near Maricourt.'

In some cases, with my medals-to-a-man-killed-for-every-day project, I have settled for things that can be linked to an individual other than medals, when medals cannot be found. These could be dog-tags, (blood-stained) paybooks, walking sticks, the cardboard boxes medals came in, Christmas gift tins sent to soldiers, or letters. This is the case, for example, for 19 August 1917, for which I have a letter home from Second Lieutenant John Basil Smith who served in the Royal Warwickshire Regiment.

Basil died on that day, after being wounded a day earlier and twelve days after writing to his mother for the last time.

7 August 1917

Dear Mother

Very many thanks for the letter. I am very sorry to say I have been too busy to answer any, and now this will be my last letter from the Base. I am leaving for the firing line tomorrow morning about 1130 and my address will be 2nd Lt J. Basil Smith, 14th Royal Warwicks Regiment, BEF, France. I hope to be able to write to you again soon. There will probably be some more news. All the Warwicks have had an awful time.

The Birmingham battalions have been on the Somme lately, and I hope they move before [long]. I have only heard I am leaving tomorrow so you must excuse more now. I want to get my share of the war over and come back to England for good.

Well, goodbye for the present. Hoping to see you all in the near future. Love to all the others, Daddy, Elsie and Barbara.

Yours ever,

Your ever loving Basil

It's so sad, like so many of these sorts of letters home from the front. Using the magic of the internet, I subsequently found a local newspaper cutting about Basil, from which I discovered that he was the only son of Councillor and Mrs A. E. Smith of The Quarry, Warwick.

He had been educated at Arden House School, Henley-in-Arden, and Cheltenham College, and had gone into training at the outbreak of the war before receiving his commission in 1915. The article about their son's death appeared in the same edition of the paper that announced Councillor and Mrs Smith's silver wedding anniversary. Basil was one of twenty-six former pupils from Arden House who died in the First World War, and his name can be found on a memorial at the site of the school, now Warwickshire College.

A little later, I tracked down the unit war diary written in the trenches that recorded what happened to Basil. The Warwicks were at a place called Farbus, or what was left of it, during the Battle of Arras. The diary records that on 18 August Basil was wounded by 'German bullets fired at an aeroplane'.

It seems he was fatally injured, probably in the head, by spent rounds. We can be certain that Basil was very unlucky to die in that way.

Chapter Fourteen

Collecting is one thing I do. Being a guide to battlefields is another. It was really a natural progression from my own interest in the First World War, and indeed other conflicts, to share that with others.

To start with, I would take people in ones and twos in my own car, and we would spend three days on the Somme, or at Ypres, Verdun or Arnhem. Then I created Over the Top with Smudger's Battlefield Tours ('Smudger' being a nickname people use for 'Smith'), and then I merged it with a company run by my friend Peter Wapshott to create Barbed Wire Tours Ltd. This was a proper business, with tours being advertised in magazines and so on, and small minibuses or coaches of people involved.

What I quickly realized with the First World War is that people struggle to understand the scale of it. It's different from the Second World War, and they only get that when they go to the battlefields. I try to equate the numbers – the casualties on a particular day – to modern-day football crowds to help people grasp the reality of it. So we are talking, in the first hour of the battle on the Somme, everybody in Wembley Stadium being killed or wounded. Then people start to get the idea.

I always feel there is such a lot of information to get across, especially when you have people for only two and a half days, and especially when you see how much they want to learn while they are there.

What I try to do is not point into the distance and say something like, 'Over there are the trenches.' What we do is go and stand in them, so that when we come out of a trench, or walk across a beach, we are following in the footsteps of the soldiers who came before us. And because I take some of my medals with me and discuss each one in turn, the people on the tour don't have thousands of names on a wall to stare at when we get to a memorial or a cemetery. They can look for one name. There might be a picture too, like in the case of Herbert Mackness. And you'd be surprised how many people have taken him off me and held his picture next to his name at the VC Corner Cemetery at Fromelles. Then they have their picture taken with him, so that they can remember someone they regard as *their* man lost in the war.

In my way of doing a battlefield tour, the emphasis is not about the grand plans of generals at corps or division level. Of course, you need some understanding of the overall picture, but almost everyone who comes on these trips is the great-grandson or great-granddaughter of a corporal or a private, not a general. So I do it the other way round. We start with the concept of what it was like being a private, and I take five people who fought in a particular engagement, use their medals to help tell their stories, and then eventually bring in the bigger stuff. By the time we get to the end of that section of the tour, they have understood what happened to those five ordinary people and how their contribution fitted into the larger picture of the whole battle.

People often ask how I deal with the sadness of these places, going back so often. Because they are sad places. For me, there's a mix of emotions. Over the years, I have felt the anger that we all experience when we learn about the First World War, and the emotional side of coming to terms with what happened on the Western Front, but the feeling of being privileged to be there has never left me. In fact, it has only grown over the years.

When I am with a group of people, and I am walking along to the next place I am going to talk about, I have moments to myself. They will be chatting away and taking photos, and in those moments I am back in those other days, and I do say to those whose graves we are visiting, 'Hello boys, I'm here again. Nice to see you.' Stuff like that. Whenever I go to those places, and whoever I take with me, that feeling of excitement and being honoured to be there never leaves me. I still feel it, whether it's a beach, a bridge, a trench line, a cemetery, it doesn't matter – I'm still just as inspired by those places as I ever was.

When you tell people the stories of the medals, and the people who were awarded them, and how many of them got killed, you see the impact it has. But I always say I am not there to be sad on their behalf. I am there to tell them what happened. When you explain that 800 men went over and only twelve came back, that gets to people. They have never been to that place before or read about it, and now they are standing on that field. When you say, 'This is where it happened; this is where they went over,' it stops them in their tracks. For me it is about telling those stories, so that those men are not forgotten.

I come up with themes for each tour. The one I do for the Duke of Wellington's greatest victory I call 'Waterloo: Welcome to Hell, Gentlemen'. No one actually said that as far as I know, but it neatly sums up what was a pretty grim battle. Waterloo is an incredible place because it is almost exactly the same today as it was when they fought there more than 200 years ago.

Looking at it as Napoleon would have seen it, you have the Charleroi–Brussels road and, at the bottom of the hill, there is the farmyard of La Belle-Alliance. Over to your right in the trees is the farmyard of Papelotte. Then up the same road about a kilometre and a half away is La Haye Sainte farm, and then over to the left, past the Lion's Mound that commemorates the Prince of Orange, there is the farmyard of Hougoumont.

Waterloo is a great one for getting people out of the bus and standing where the soldiers stood and understanding how events unfolded. Some years ago, I took the London Fire Brigade Retired Members Association to Waterloo, and there were fifty-four of them all together, ranging in age from sixty to over eighty years old. We got out of the bus and stood on the road by the Belle-Alliance. I explained where the French gun line was, and how, in the first part of the day, three columns of French soldiers came up the slope to the right of La Haye Sainte farm towards the British line. In those days, there was a holly-bush hedge along the top of the ridge, and the British infantry were lying down on the other side of the slope, waiting.

I talk about the chaos, because the guns were firing and the air was filled with smoke. And I explain that those who were there, and who saw anything that day, said that all you could see were the tops of the bearskins and the glint of the bayonets of the French as they came up through the corn and through the smoke. Then, as they reached the top, the order was given in the British ranks: 'Stand up, prepare and fire!'

The French columns were hit by something like 8,000 musket balls. In those columns, the young soldiers were in the middle so they couldn't run away, while the veterans were on the outside. Two things were wrong with that concept. One, only the front and side ranks could fire, and two, in the confusion and noise, no one could say 'stop' or 'turn left', so the column was like a machine that moved relentlessly forward.

In this case, the front ranks hit the holly, and it was like marching into barbed wire. They got stuck, and the British opened fire at the same time, blowing them to pieces. The rear of the French formation had no idea what was happening, and those soldiers carried on up the slope, crushing those in front of them. It was carnage, and then the British charged, led by the Royal Scots Greys, in a scene captured in the iconic 1881 oil painting by Lady Elizabeth Butler.

Even those who have read extensively about Waterloo never seem to quite realize how steep the slope is where the French came up, and when they see it they are stunned. With the Fire Brigade veterans, I got them to stand along the top of the ridge so they were looking down at where the French would be approaching. Then I handed out musket balls to everybody so they could feel and sense their weight and start to imagine the damage they would do at a range of twenty feet. Then I told them to kneel down, and at that point they could see nothing but the Belle-Alliance farm in the distance. That's when they understood how this engagement unfolded. When I said 'Stand up', one or two of them struggled and even fell over, bless them. 'Oh, bugger the bloody French,' said one. 'I can't even stand up on my own two feet, let alone fight them.'

Another classic setting to get people out, standing in the right place, is Omaha Beach on the Normandy coastline. It's the one I use as the climax of a three-day Second World War D-Day tour that includes visits to Pegasus Bridge, Ranville War Cemetery where 2,236 Commonwealth soldiers are interred, the German cemetery at La Cambe, and Sword and Gold Beaches.

At Omaha, German troops of the 352nd Infantry Division were in the cliffs overlooking the shore, armed with small arms, mortars, artillery and machine guns. When you get people down – and it's quite a long walk – onto the beach itself and to the water's edge, and then turn them around, that's when what the Americans faced that day hits them. It's like, 'Oh my God, that is the most enormous thing these people had to attack – it's huge.'

The idea is to get them to stand exactly where the troops staggered ashore – if they had survived that far – and then walk up to where they fell trying to make it across the beach. It leaves an indelible impression so that whenever they see, hear or read about that battle again, they know they have been there and can remember exactly what they saw and what they felt.

After days like that, the atmosphere is electric in the

group. You've got fifty blokes and ladies who've been out all day, all soaked, all covered in whatnot, and the noise at dinner is incredible. They are talking ten to the dozen about the battle, about the soldiers and about the settings. That's when you know you got through to them because they've become invested in what we've done.

At the end of those tours, I always say to everybody as we come off the boat back to Blighty – we don't call it England – I want you to remember a couple of things. The next time you see a grainy black-and-white film about some boys in the trenches, I want you to remember just for that second that you were there and you know what they did. And the other thing I want you to remember is that we have done something that so many of them never got to do – we came home.

Talking of the trenches, I still do a tour on the Somme about the Accrington Pals, the men of the 11th Battalion, East Lancashire Regiment who were raised from places like Accrington, Chorley, Burnley and Blackburn. It's called 'Two Years in the Making, Ten Minutes in the Destroying: The Story of the Pals on the Somme'.

The idea of the Pals began in Lancashire when the Earl of Derby suggested that men were more likely to enlist if they thought they would be doing so alongside their friends. It proved an effective recruiting tool, and by the end of 1914 there were Pals battalions all over Britain.

On the morning of 1 July 1916, the Pals were tasked to go over the top and advance on the fortified village of Serre. So what I do is take my group to the Sheffield Memorial Park at the scene of the attack, where the trenches and shell holes from the battle have been preserved and where there is a memorial to the Accrington Pals. We stand in the trenches at the bottom of a little slope called Railway Hollow and then spread out and start walking up the incline in an extended line, as the Pals had done on that fateful Saturday morning. I usually say to people, 'Keep walking until you get to the top and you can see the bottom of the trees in the village of Serre, and then put your hand up.'

They walk slowly up the field, and when they reach the top where the cemetery is, you start to see them putting their hands up. What they don't know is that I have timed the walk, and generally hands start going up after about nine minutes, which is about how long it took the Pals to get to the top, and by which time almost all of them were dead or wounded.

It's an amazing experience – it's not merely being on the battlefield – you are walking the line of the attack, or should I say the massacre, and you're there with them. And as people move ahead, I remind them that German machine guns are opening fire, shellfire is coming down from behind the German lines, and there are shells going over the top from their own side.

To help bring it to life, I tell them about the story of a twenty-one-year-old Signaller who took part in the attack that day, named Private Orrell Taylor Duerden. As absurd as it may seem now, soldiers in those engagements were often required by their generals – in this case General Sir Henry Rawlinson, who commanded the 4th Army of the British Expeditionary Force on the Western Front – to dodge the hail of bullets while carrying the wherewithal to convert captured German trenches into new lines of defence. So they didn't go over the top only with rifles in their hands, but carrying shovels, pickaxes, bits of corrugated iron, and a lot more besides.

Young Orrell and his friend and fellow Signaller in Z Company, Corporal Hale, went over carrying telephone wire so that field communications could immediately be established with the captured trenches. We know what happened next because there is a report in the local Accrington newspaper of an interview with Corporal Hale, conducted a few weeks after the battle. He explained that after they had gone about 100 yards, a shell exploded in front of them, knocking Hale to the ground. In the noise and chaos around them, Orrell asked him if he was hit, and he told his friend, 'No! I'm OK.' He got up and they continued.

'We could see the lads dropping all round, and we remarked that it was marvellous how we were being missed,' said Hale.

They got as far as the German lines, where Hale was hit in the hand by a bullet. They jumped into a trench and Orrell helped him bandage the wound. Then he said to Hale, who had not noticed his friend was also wounded, 'Will you take this piece of shrapnel out of my head?' The young signaller had been hit in the temple by a small projectile, and Hale removed it. They agreed it wasn't a serious injury, and Orrell joked that his friend was so lucky to have received a classic 'Blighty' – a wound that would see him returned home. The trench then got hit by a shell which smothered them in dirt, and then, in a touchingly English way, Orrell and Hale shook hands and said goodbye to each other. Hale began to make his way back to a dressing station behind the lines, while Orrell went forward. He was never seen again.

Orrell's regimental number was 17870. He had been a weaver before the war, and his father, James, was the President of the Accrington Weavers' Union. His mother, Eliza, never came to terms with his death and always wore a pendant with his picture on it in the hope that she would see him again. She believed he might have lost his mind and ended up in a German prison camp because his body – like those of thousands of men on the Western Front – was never found. His most likely fate was that he was blown to pieces and that his remains are still in that field.

Orrell means a lot to me. Some years ago, I came across his memorial plaque on a dealer's list, but I didn't have enough money to buy it. Instead, Gordon bought it, and we both started investigating his story. We discovered that Orrell wasn't on any memorial whatsoever. So we wrote to the Commonwealth War Graves Commission, making the case for his inclusion, and in response they added his name to the Thiepval Memorial to the Missing of the Somme. It can be found on the Addenda Panel, Pier and Face 5D. I feel quite proud that me and Gordon found him and put him up there.

When the hands of my battlefield tour group go up at the top of that slope above Serre, I tell people that they are standing roughly where Orrell was last seen, and it hits them. Suddenly we are not thinking of hundreds of people dying, but one young man from Accrington in Lancashire, a person and a character who was someone's son and brother and who died in that field while still only twenty-one.

On one of my early tours in the days when it was still ones and twos in my own car – in this case a Ford Escort called

'Norman' – I took my mum's cousins Peter and John Foulkes to the Somme. Their uncle, Charles Clarence Foulkes, is one of the missing on Thiepval. He was killed near the village of Longueval in front of Delville Wood on 14 July 1916. They were mad keen to go, and I was more than happy to take them.

We did the bit at Serre with the Pals, and then we went back along the line towards Beaumont-Hamel where there is a big ridge called The Redan, which was where there was a group of British frontline trenches in 1916. There is a little cemetery there with a crucifix in front of it where the farmers used to pile up shells and hand grenades for collection by bomb disposal teams. It was always quite fun to show people what the French call the 'Iron Harvest'.

That day, I stopped as I always did to see if there was anything interesting there, and I noticed the field next to it had been ploughed. I said to John and Peter that we could have a quick look to see if we might find anything.

We had made little headway into the plough – maybe twenty-five feet – when we started to find the base plates of Mills bombs, or hand grenades. When the grenades go bang and spread shrapnel all over the place, the base plate is left behind and drops to the ground, usually bent and deformed. We started to find these things and then bits of the casing that had exploded away from them.

In among all this, we then started to find white porcelain marble balls with a hole in them. These were from German stick grenades. These had a hollowed-out wooden handle with a line of string inside which went through the centre of the porcelain ball and then had a knot stopper at the end.

German soldiers would unscrew a cap at the bottom of the handle, and the marble ball would then drop down with the string attached. They would grab the ball and pull it to ignite the grenade before throwing it.

So we were finding the base plugs of Mills bombs and the porcelain balls and screw-off caps of stick grenades. We found about twelve caps and six or seven bits of stick grenade and began to realize we had stumbled upon a hand-grenade battle from 1916. It was frozen in time in that tiny little bit of field, and it was quite something. You could walk a little further and there was nothing to be found, and that was where the British line was.

We reckoned this exchange must have happened in no man's land, and what we had come across was probably an incident when the British saw a German patrol coming, and they had thrown hand grenades at each other. And there it was, laid out in front of us. We took bits of our battle home, and John still talks of that day and our discovery, even though it was many years ago.

Sometimes on my tours I have recruited my guests to help me find people on memorials, and that was the case with a great-uncle of one of my expert colleagues on the *Antiques Roadshow*, Hilary Kay. We were filming a *Roadshow* First World War special episode at Étaples Military Cemetery near Boulogne, and Hilary and I were chatting among the headstones about the war when she told me about her two great-uncles. They were German and they had both been killed on the Western Front, but Hilary knew almost nothing else about them. She did not know where or when they had died, and she asked me whether I could help her find them. The only thing she had were their names. I said I would see what I could do.

I wrote to the German equivalent of the Commonwealth War Graves Commission – the Volksbund Deutsche Kriegsgräberfürsorge – and they wrote back and said they could look for them for a small fee, which I paid. Not long afterwards, a letter arrived that said that in the case of one of Hilary's relatives they had no record. But the other one – whose name was Walter Königsberger – was buried in a German cemetery north-east of Ypres, near a town in Belgium called Roeselare.

On my next tour, I had a minibus full of people, and on the last day I said to everyone that we were going to go to this place to see if we could find Walter for Hilary. It was a pretty miserable overcast day as we drove to the little hamlet of Hooglede in Flanders. There we found a large German cemetery on the edge of the village laid out on flat ground behind neat stone walls and dotted with large oaks. Instead of headstones that you see in British cemeteries, the Germans had used stone plaques arranged in neat rows divided by strips of heather and interspersed with groups of small stone crosses. Each plaque commemorated two soldiers.

On that autumnal day, with leaves on the ground all around us, the cemetery was totally silent, and it felt rather dark and foreboding even in broad daylight. We walked the neat stone pathways with everyone spread out, keeping an eye on the plaques on each side, until someone raised their voice in the trees to say, 'I've got him!' Then we gathered around a simple black stone rectangle which marked the resting place of Hermann Rose, who died on 31 August 1917, and Walter Königsberger, who lost his life on the same day.

I made a little speech saying that we were there for my friend on the *Antiques Roadshow*, and then I called Hilary.

'You'll never guess where we are,' I said.

'Oh no, where?' she replied.

I said that we were with Walter and that there were fourteen of us all together in the cemetery at Hooglede.

'We've found him for you, and I'll send you some photos in a minute, and the next time I see you I'll tell you all about it,' I told her.

And that's when Hilary said, 'Ah, Uncle Walter, all those years the footsteps walked past, and today they stopped just for you.'

That was something very special, and I think we all shed a tear for him, trying to imagine what kind of person he might have been, and trying to reconcile that with that simple black stone memorial at our feet.

Chapter Fifteen

I never gave up on my plan to move across the Civil Service from the DHSS and the Social Security Medical Appeals Tribunal to the Ministry of Defence. Having failed to make the grade the first time, I took the exam for a second time in June 1989 at a place in Great Portland Street.

I can't remember that much about it except one question, which was about cats. It involved a cat's home with five rooms, each a different colour, and five named cats who would only stay in certain coloured rooms, but also had individual preferences – not colour-related – about which room they would stay in. You had to work out which cat went where.

It was enough to drive you mad. I think the idea was to test your lateral-thinking ability or logical reasoning. Whatever it was, this time I managed to solve enough problems in the exam to reach the magic number to qualify for a transfer to the MoD, and I was more than ready for it after nearly eight years with the DHSS.

I was called for an initial interview at a place in Whitehall next to the Old Admiralty Building. On the way there I bought a copy of *The Times*, and I read a story in the foreign-news pages about relations between Poland and Russia and industrial action in Russia as the Soviet regime continued its disintegration.

The chairman of the panel was a big jovial man sitting with two other people. He ran through my educational record – O levels, A levels and so on.

'Well done, Mr Smith,' he said.

'Oh, thank you,' I replied.

'Been reading the paper this morning, have we?'

'Er, yes, as a matter of fact I have.'

'Oh, jolly good . . . anything catch your eye?'

'Well, yes, actually, the events in Moscow and relations between Russia and Poland.' I then free-associated knowledgeably on the subject for a minute or two.

'Ah, very good, very good, Mr Smith,' he intervened.

'Well,' he added, looking left and right at his two colleagues who nodded in turn, 'that all seems rather encouraging doesn't it. Well done, Mr Smith, and goodbye. You will be hearing from us shortly.'

And that was it. About two weeks later a letter arrived that informed me I had passed the commissioning board interview and would now receive a posting to the MoD. I was very excited. But then I spent several months waiting for someone to post me somewhere. It was about October when I received a summons to another interview, after which I was told I was being posted to MoD Main Building to work in the Air Movements Branch. It was called S9 (Air).

This was a big moment after so many years of working at the DHSS. I remember thinking as I made my way to my new place of work for the first time, 'I've done it. I'm here, I'm in it. Finally!'

And all those people who all the way along had said, 'Oh, you can never transfer, you can't do that, you'll never do it, you'll never get there.'

'Well,' I thought, 'sod them. I *have* done it.' My father was so proud of me. It was good stuff in his mind, and I would come home each evening and tell him what I was doing, and he loved hearing about it.

Our role in S9 (Air) was to buy and sell space on aircraft, and we also did payments for search-and-rescue helicopter missions. The rules were that if you took someone from a place of danger to a place of safety in an RAF Sea King, that was free. But if you took someone from a place of safety to another place of safety – like a hospital transfer – then the RAF charged the health authority involved.

I ran the section with a woman called Jane Darby, and we spent our days doing helicopter payments, buying seats for military people on civilian aircraft, or buying freight space for military stuff on civilian aircraft. During the build-up to the First Gulf War in late 1990, all six of us in the office moved over to freight full time. For all the hours that God gave us, we bought space or chartered civilian aircraft to take people and stuff to the Gulf.

During the war itself, I worked with something called D Mov Ops RAF. This meant moving from civilian aircraft to exclusively military stuff. We were tasked with organizing military aircraft to the Gulf, and one element of this was helping to arrange the transport of SAS soldiers to the region. I had the job of sorting out their arrival in places like Riyadh in Saudi Arabia. They would come in on freight aircraft, but because their movements were secret, they did not appear on any manifest, and they were not officially in the country. I would organize people who would know they were coming, who would get them off the aircraft and 'disappear' them into the airbase.

It was during the Gulf War that our routine in Main Building was rudely interrupted one morning. On 7 February 1991, I was sitting at my desk in Room 1381 on the first floor of the vast neoclassical edifice designed by E. Vincent Harris, when there was an enormous bang.

We had thick white-nylon blast curtains in the office, and as I heard the noise I turned round to look behind me where the window was. As I did so, I saw the window bow in and the blast curtain blew in over the top of Sarah, one of my colleagues. And then it went back again. She was sitting there with her Mars Bar, about to dip it into her tea, when all this happened. Bless her, she was still holding her Mars Bar but had thrown her tea all over herself and her desk.

The first big bang was followed by two more, and we also heard three thuds as the charges exploded on the other side of the road. Even though we were sitting in Whitehall, I guessed immediately that it was mortar fire we were hearing from the way the bangs were followed by the thuds. I went over to Sarah and asked her if she was all right, to which she replied, 'Yes, but I've spilt my tea.'

I think I said something along the lines of, 'Bugger your tea.'

I then moved everyone away from the windows, which looked out over North Door and the Old War Office Building, and then the phone rang. It was a routine enquiry about booking flights.

'I'm sorry,' I said, 'we can't deal with this now. I think we may have just come under attack with mortars, so I'm going to go, if you don't mind . . .'

I put the phone down and then looked out of the window. We could see a white Ford Transit van burning at the junction of Horse Guards Avenue and Whitehall, and quickly we put it all together. It had to be the IRA and one of their most audacious operations of the Troubles.

We discovered later that they had managed to fire three 140lb mortar shells at Downing Street, where John Major's Cabinet was meeting behind bomb-proof windows. The IRA used a homemade mortar platform that fired through a hole in the roof of the van, and then a pre-set incendiary device immediately destroyed the vehicle afterwards. One shell landed in the back garden of Downing Street, thirty yards from the Cabinet Office, leaving a crater several feet deep, and the other two overshot and landed on Mountbatten Green nearby. Four people suffered minor injuries including two police officers.

In Main Building the sirens went off, and we were evacuated downstairs to one of the bunkers in the basement. It was very exciting – great fun, in fact. But then we spent a long time sitting around doing nothing until they finally let us go home via the South Door, from where we could walk along the Embankment to Westminster station.

Looking back, it feels weird thinking about what went on that day, and that a terrorist organization would attempt to blow up the seat of the British government in that way. And they got pretty close to doing so. But at the time we all lived with the ever-present danger that the IRA would try something spectacular on mainland Britain, as they tried to force a breakthrough in their bitter struggle for Irish unity.

I loved my work with D Mov Ops, some of which I did from RAF Akrotiri in Cyprus. I was made for it. Just being on call, being efficient and delivering what was required on deadline. But when the war came to an end, it got rather dull again, and towards the end of 1992 I asked for a new posting. I went along to the MoD careers people, and the guy there started by talking about another boring job, which I turned down.

'There's something else that might interest you, though,' he said invitingly.

'Oh good,' I replied. 'What's that?'

'Well,' he said, 'I can't tell you what it is, I'm afraid.'

And that was exactly what he said, and all he said. So I thought about it, and it sounded exciting. I mean, he couldn't even describe what it was so it would have to be something secretive, and that meant fun, didn't it?

'OK,' I told him confidently. 'I'd like to apply.'

'Good. I think you might enjoy it,' he said, smiling conspiratorially.

He told me I would have to fill in various forms – there were quite a lot of them – and then they would carry out security checks, and that this would take time. I told him I was happy to go through the process and see where we got to.

You had to nominate three people who had known you for more than twenty years, and whom they could interview. Family members were not allowed. I chose Phil, Brian who ran the barber's shop in Walthamstow, and Brian who had married one of my mum's cousins. He was a stockbroker.

Each of them got interviewed at length. They were with Brian the barber for about an hour, with Phil for about an hour and a half, and with the other Brian for about an hour.

In a subsequent vetting interview, the guy on the other side of the desk knew not only that my father had been in the Royal Air Force but reeled off his service number too. He also knew Grandad's number and that he had been in the King's Royal Rifle Corps, and that my other grandad had been in the Rifle Brigade and then, from 1919, the Essex Regiment.

But what they were most interested in was me telling them anything that I could be blackmailed about. They wanted to know about my bank account, how much I owed in any loans or mortgage payments, whether I was interested in pornography, and anything else they could think of that suggested I might be easily 'bought' by a foreign intelligence service.

I sat through a series of interviews, progressing from 'Developed Vetting' to 'Enhanced Positive Vetting', each one a five-hour session, until eventually I was informed that I had passed. I was warned that within six weeks of starting my new job I would have been photographed by every intelligence agency in the world.

I was posted to something called Defence Intelligence 13, where I worked throughout the 1990s, mainly on secret operations, the details of which remain classified. Suffice it to say I absolutely loved my job, and after a childhood of war games and then collecting militaria, I was in my element and very proud of the role I played.

I loved the cloak-and-dagger aspect of it, and when friends

asked what I did, I used the old joke about having to kill them if I let them in on my secrets. At other times, I would tell people I designed fishtanks. Although I was brought up in a family of storytellers, and I love that aspect of what I do on old battlefields and on television, I had no problems at all about keeping my day job to myself. I had signed so many pieces of paper, and my work environment was so rigorous in the way it ensured we observed the letter of the security protocols we worked under, that the idea of breaking confidences was simply out of the question.

While most of my job in this period remains under wraps, one element I can talk about was my role in the deployment of UK forces to Kosovo in 1999. This was part of NATO's intervention to stop Serbian forces overrunning the former Serbian province and ethnically cleansing and terrorizing Kosovo Albanians. Following a NATO bombing campaign against the Serbs, the Yugoslav army began withdrawing from Kosovo, and the first elements of what became known as KFOR – the 50,000-strong NATO-led Kosovo Force – were deployed in June.

I volunteered to be part of the UK contingent about two weeks after the initial deployment in October 1999. I was the Intelligence Officer in a management group based at Command HQ, and our job was to pull in information from all the different services involved in the Kosovo intervention and use it to inform operational decision-making.

We were based in the capital, working in a concrete underground basement and sleeping in bunkbeds down a corridor. It was fairly rudimentary, but it was the real thing, and it was great. We worked twelve-hour shifts – 8.00 a.m. to

8.00 p.m. – and it was busy, so much so that the days would fly by. I would sit at a long table, at the head of which was a colonel. On my left was a guy from the army, on my right the Logistics Corps, then opposite me the Royal Navy, and next to him the RAF.

My job was to interrogate the army, the air force, the navy and logistics throughout the day, and to receive signals from all sorts of people on the ground in Kosovo and then write an intelligence report or summary at the end of every day. That would go out at 6.00 p.m. to headquarters staff, or I would brief people directly, including occasionally senior ministers.

There was a lot of running around and shouting and going off to different briefings and assimilating video briefings coming in from London. At times we would predict things that were going to happen, and, when they happened as we had foreseen, our response was all the more effective. I was there for months, and I remember the signal landing on my desk that said hostilities had ceased, which I thought was quite cool. I wanted to keep it, but that bunker was so secret there was no way I could ever do that.

When I finished in Kosovo and returned to the Old War Office Building in London – we used to call it 'OWOB' – I received a commendation from the Deputy Chief, Defence Intelligence for my contribution, which I am very proud of. The wages I'd saved while I was away, meanwhile, were instantly used by my then girlfriend, Helen, to buy a new set of curtains for the front room. Every time I close them, I think of my time in that bunker in Kosovo.

In my time as an Intelligence Officer, I heard real bullets

being fired, and I heard real artillery shells and real mortars land. It was what was always going to happen in my life because I volunteered to do all this stuff. I couldn't not go because my father had done his bit, and so I did the same.

In our bunker there was a big whiteboard on which anything and everything that was important to our deployment was recorded. The board was just behind where I sat, maybe a foot and a half, no more. All troop deployments, aircraft movements, ships – everything was on that whiteboard. So you could look at it and immediately know who was where, and what was what, and when.

One day an air commodore came to visit us. He came in at one end of the bunker, and we all stood up.

'Morning, everyone. Do carry on, sit down, sit down,' he said in typically jovial, visiting-senior-officer style.

He walked up to the top of the table, and he and the colonel stood chatting for a while. Then the colonel introduced the bloke from the air force, and the bloke from the Royal Navy, and then the bloke from the army sitting next to me. As they were doing this, the colonel and the air commodore were making their way along the table behind me.

When it was my turn, the colonel said, 'And this is the Intelligence Officer, Mark Smith.'

I replied jauntily, 'Hello, sir.' We chatted for a few seconds, and then he spoke to the person at the end of the table who was 'Petrol, Oil and Lubricants', and then he was off.

It was usually the same group of people on each shift, so around that table we knew each other pretty well. As the colonel and the air commodore disappeared, the bloke opposite me from the RAF, who was wearing a Breitling watch from his days in the Red Arrows, looked up. And then he looked at me and blurted out, 'Oh, for flip's sake!'

I went, 'What?'

He went, 'Ah . . . look behind you, Smithy.'

I turned round to see that the air commodore had wiped a large swathe through the middle of the whiteboard with his jacket while squeezing by behind me. The result was that much of the detail about what we were doing in Kosovo that we had so carefully accumulated had disappeared. It was heart-breaking. It took us about four days to reassemble that Kosovo jigsaw as it had been, and I am sure the good air commodore was none the wiser.

Kosovo was intense, and it was a great project to be part of. Generally, when you do an office job in the MoD you are a tiny little cog in an enormous wheel. But for once, you did a job like that, and you *were* the wheel. Whatever you did was going to make a difference to the people there or our troops, and make a difference instantly. It meant that, instead of just doing stuff, you did stuff that genuinely had a purpose, and you could see how things changed from day to day, as what you reported on changed.

After I returned from Kosovo, I looked for a new role and a promotion and ended up back in Main Building in early 2000 after my time in the Old War Office Building. This time I was on the ground floor, working for something called D Fin (Pol), or Director Finance Policy. Some elements of this would prove an almost Kafkaesque waste of time.

The purpose of this little unit – there were four of us in one large room – was overseeing and ensuring the financial regularity of MoD funds. It was our job to look at all sorts of requests for military deployments and satisfy ourselves that they were good value for taxpayers' money, and then approve them or not as the case may be. It might, for example, be a request by a charity for a local army unit to help move a restored steam engine. Was this a proper use of public funds? How much time would it take? How much local publicity would it garner? Was it worth it?

After a few months of trying to adjudicate on these things, I devised what I called the *Sun* test. The idea was that, before we said yes to any of these requests, we should sit down and imagine what the front page of the *Sun* would look like on the following morning. It was a good way of working out how idiotic we might look if we made the wrong decision.

Another part of our job covered what was termed Military Aid to the Civil Community and Military Aid to the Civil Powers. The former was when everything floods and the army is called in; the latter was when there was a riot and the army is called in. Our role was to approve those deployments.

This was definitely the weirdest office I ever worked in. It was run by a woman who had been in the MoD probably since the Crimean War. She wouldn't let us talk to each other during the working day. You had to sit there in silence, and she wouldn't turn the lights on. You worked under your angle-poise lamp. It was like being in the first year of senior school. She used to sit opposite me but, instead of talking to me, she would send me emails.

One morning her reign of misery came to an abrupt end when she walked in, undid the lock on her personal cupboard, opened the door and stood inside. Then she threw the contents of her filing tray – and the wooden tray itself – across the room. It smashed into the wall near where I was sitting, and her papers went everywhere. She never said a word and simply turned round and walked out. We never saw her again. In her absence, I got an acting promotion to her job.

By far the most pointless part of D Fin (Pol) – even if it could be enormous fun – was our role in something catchily called the Nato Training Group Financial Sub-Group. This was a branch of the alliance that ran conferences twice a year and regular meetings in 'Partner for Peace' countries to help them change their financial accounting systems from old Eastern Bloc practices to Nato standards. The countries involved – which ranged from places like Austria to Romania, Azerbaijan to Lithuania, Latvia to Estonia – regarded these get-togethers in their capitals as excuses for a massive bender funded by our respective Ministry of Defences.

It was always a five-day trip, and the format was always the same. Arrive on the Monday and go to an official reception. Conference all day Tuesday, followed by a night out and a booze-up. Cultural day on Wednesday, when we would be taken somewhere 'special'. This ranged from rug-buying expeditions to visiting special tourist projects, like a bizarre replica of the Southfork Ranch from the American soap opera *Dallas* . . . in Romania. We went to nightclubs with stage shows put on especially for us. In Austria, where I chaired regular, and generally futile, meetings of an international sub-group, we visited the War Museum of Military History in Vienna – the Heeresgeschichtliches Museum. A genuine highlight was the opportunity to sit in the car that Archduke Franz Ferdinand was in when he was assassinated. Thursday was more conference time, followed by a closing-reception booze-up. Then Friday morning, it was wash up and leave.

During four years making these regular trips alongside my immediate boss, Roger Paxton, I drank and ate for Britain – everything from boiled sturgeon to roast brown bear to pickled lamb's tongue, eyeballs, testicles and brains. On the alcohol front, consumption was often a matter of being polite – in other words, being seen to drink everything that was put in front of you, regardless of how many times your glass was refilled.

The problem with all this wonderful travelling and foreign hospitality was that it achieved almost nothing. There was little progress on our underlying objectives, and no one seemed capable of taking decisions that moved things along. Being someone who likes to make my mind up about things, I found it incredibly frustrating.

Towards the end of my four years in the job, I turned up at a meeting in London that was held regularly to assess progress, and I took with me the agenda for the first of those meetings I had attended four years earlier. When it came to 'any other business', I pointed out that the agenda that day was identical to the one four years earlier and that almost nothing had been achieved in the interim.

'I would just like to put on record that this whole job that I have done for the last four years is the biggest waste of time that I have ever lived through,' I told them.

Of course, I was politely informed that I simply couldn't

say that sort of thing, and it would not be put on the record. I knew then that I had reached the end of the road with D Fin (Pol), and something would have to change.

While all this was going on, one indisputably brilliant thing that happened was that I married Helen Dunstan on the anniversary of D-Day in 1998. That was two years after I met her and realized that life without her would be a pretty empty world.

We met at a local line-dancing evening not far from home when Helen, then twenty-five, was running an art gallery in nearby Buckhurst Hill. We got talking and discovered we shared many common interests. Helen had missed the previous line-dancing evening because, I learned, she had been on a battlefield tour to the Somme.

She told me about her brother, Edward, who collects militaria, and we arranged for them both to come round to see my medal collection. It was a sort of non-date that turned into Helen and I going out together for a pizza, and we have never looked back.

Helen is a leading dealer in nineteenth- and twentieth-century British decorative arts. She now has a dealership in Somerset where you'll find both British nineteenth-century designs and antique textiles sourced during her travels around the world.

Although she spent her early years in Kenya, where her father was working as a civil engineer designing large dams, she was brought up in Devon and went to school there before attending Aberystwyth University. She took a joint honours in the History of Art and History, and then went on to complete an MA at Essex University, Colchester, in Museology.

Helen's a like-minded soul and the perfect foil for me – we both understand what it is to be a collector, and people do mention sometimes that our house in Walthamstow, not far from where I was born and raised, is full of various kinds of weird and wonderful stuff.

Chapter Sixteen

Life on the east coast of India, on the shores of Red Hills Lake, a reservoir that supplied water to Madras, was a whole new ball game for my father and his crewmates.

At the home of 240 Squadron, they had to contend with often severe weather conditions in which to fly during the Monsoon, while, on the ground, the British airmen quickly succumbed to illness and disease.

Dad contracted Dengue fever within a few days of arriving in India and then endured a horrible experience while being treated at St George's Fort Military Hospital in Madras.

In a desperate state, drifting in and out of consciousness and being offered precious little nursing help, he had staggered to the ward kitchen to get some water. On returning to his sodden bed, he lay down and then remembered a bag of boiled sweets sitting on his nightstand. Perhaps they might give him some sustenance. They had been given to him earlier that day by a well-meaning hospital visitor – he described her as a 'titled woman'.

> The bag felt odd. I couldn't sit up and I couldn't see, but I could feel it. I realized that I had put my fingers into a mass of inch-long ants, each armed with vicious

pincers. I received a few painful nips from the ones that had climbed up my fingers and hand before I summoned the last vestige of energy I possessed to hurl the bag of sweets and the little animals in it into the centre of the ward. But I had no way of dealing with the ants that had already entered my mosquito net and bed space . . .

Dad fell into a deep sleep only to wake up and discover there were still ants in his bed.

I realized that my hand, arm and both legs carried blotches of congealed blood – my blood – and that I was still sharing my bed with ten or more ants that were growing in size with my imagination. I went mad. With incredible energy, I killed every ant in sight, and because I couldn't reach a few that were in the top of the net, I pulled it from its fittings and threw the lot into the centre of the ward. A few minutes later, a male nurse appeared. 'So you're better, then,' he proclaimed like some great philosopher, as he surveyed the net on the floor.

Though he did recover from the fever, a few weeks later Dad found himself in the Military Hospital in Bangalore after being airlifted there with pneumonia. He beat that too.

The crew spent the final months of 1944 supporting the Allied war effort in Burma where the 14th Army was starting to enjoy hard-won success against the Japanese under the leadership of Lord Mountbatten. By this time, John Ayshford and his team were among the most experienced and accomplished Catalina crews in the RAF. They conducted scores of lengthy sorties across the Bay of Bengal, often in atrocious weather, many of them providing convoy protection for Allied ships bringing reinforcements and supplies destined for the troops fighting in the Burmese jungle. On one occasion they hunted for a Japanese submarine that had earlier been spotted by an Allied bomber, but without success.

By the new year – January 1945 – Dad's crew had completed hundreds of hours of operational flying and been earmarked to join an elite collection of nine Catalina crews in the Far East carrying out secret 'Special Duties Operations'. Now their missions over Japanese-held territory included delivering or picking up agents, which involved risky landings in hostile settings, photographic reconnaissance of possible landing sites for Allied troops, and dropping propaganda leaflets over enemy-held towns and cities.

Having officially 'volunteered' for Special Duties in early March, they were tasked on 13 March 1945 with their first covert mission. It was one of two flights in his RAF career that left a lifelong mark on my father.

They sat down for their pre-operational 'breakfast' at Red Hills Lake at midnight on the 12th, so as to be fully kitted out and ready for their briefing at 0130 hours in the Special Duties Operations Room. As they entered the complex that housed the room, they noticed it was being guarded by members of the RAF regiment.

> We entered nervously, unsure of what to expect. But inside we met the smiling faces of a bevy of officers including the squadron CO, Gavin Robinson, and the camp CO, a group captain. They made us welcome, sat

us down facing a curtained wall map, and then cheerfully set about the task of briefing us for our mission.

The ceremony of pulling the curtain back reminded me of the unveiling of a plaque by some dignitary at a village fête, but what it told us was not so appealing. The cord indicating the route we were to take stretched for miles to North Andaman Island off the Burmese coast on the western edge of the Andaman Sea, and then to the Gulf of Martaban, which looks like the crotch of Burma and contains the notoriously dangerous town of Moulmein [now Mawlamyine]. The route did a loop in this area and then travelled southwards along the Tenasserim coast [the narrow coastal region of southern Burma] before retracing its steps, and then onto a homeward trajectory. Thankfully, according to the Met officer, we would meet fine weather throughout the journey which was expected to take 25–6 hours and amount to a flight well in excess of 3,000 miles.

The prime objective was an air-sea rescue mission for the crew of a B-24 Liberator, Y/354, a four-engined bomber that had been shot down while on an operation against Japanese forces somewhere in the Gulf of Martaban. The secondary objective was a photographic reconnaissance of the coastline south of this area. Dad and his crew would be flying at 50 to 100 feet for most of the hours of daylight above Japanese forces occupying this important area. Their captain on this occasion would be Squadron Leader Colin Parry, flight commander of 240 Squadron, but John Ayshford was also on board, as co-captain.

After taking off just as dawn was breaking, the Catalina flew as planned at between 1,000 and 2,000 feet to the northern tip of the Andaman Islands.

Then we descended to 50 feet to get underneath Japanese radar and stayed at this altitude for the next fifteen hours, more or less. We charged into the Andaman Sea in bright sunshine and made for Moulmein, with all turrets manned and a close watch being made for our friends from Y/354. I opened a radio watch on the frequency used by the hand-cranked radio transmitter in all RAF dinghies, and which carried an SOS message automatically.

Dad was intently focused on trying to pick up a signal from the downed aviators as the Catalina flew search patterns above waters which were busy with shipping.

Suddenly I heard the faintest of signals on my emergency frequency. Within seconds, I swung the direction-finding loop into action, and, as the skipper made some course changes at my request, I gained a bearing from a signal that barely reached strength one on the nine-point scale. We proceeded to execute a standard search pattern on and about the bearing I had given and carried out this manoeuvre for two hours, flying at between 50 and 200 feet.

Three times Dad picked up faint signals from what they presumed was a dinghy, but they never managed to make contact. 'We all tried desperately hard to make a sighting so that we could land and rescue men who were in dire straits in hostile territory. But we were unsuccessful. At 1300 hours Parry called off the search, indicating that we had another task to perform, and we set off southwards along the coast.'

The exhausted crew arrived back at Red Hills Lake, twenty-six hours and ten minutes after their departure the day before. It had been their longest flight to date. The failure to locate the downed airmen would come to haunt Dad, though at the time he and his fellow crewmates were more intent on celebrating a successful return from their first Special Duties mission.

Six busy weeks later, the crew prepared for a sortie codenamed 'Nickel II'. It would be a groundbreaking mission for 240 Squadron – the first time a flying boat would be used to drop leaflets over enemy-held bases on Sumatra. It would prove a tumultuous moment for Dad, an experience that he never came to terms with, one that he talked about incessantly with me, and it was on his mind until the day he died.

This was an arduous mission involving leaflet drops over forty-one targets in northern Sumatra, beginning and ending with two long transit flights across the Bay of Bengal. The planned flight time was thirty-six hours.

> We journeyed to our aircraft, J/240, and found it stacked with leaflets, dropper baskets, and our rations. The leaflets were in Japanese and featured a map of Europe, with the Germans being squeezed on all sides as Berlin was under threat and their inevitable defeat imminent. The message to the Japs ended tersely. 'It's your turn next!'

Ayshford flew them east to the Nicobar Islands and then turned south-east towards the northern tip of Sumatra.

They made landfall flying at low level in moonlight and then looked for the coastal railway line to help them find the first of their nominated targets. Dad fitted the leaflet dropper to the starboard turret and gun mounting, and the leaflets were stacked by Vic Crawford in the tail compartment. They were ready to deliver some air mail to the Japanese soldiers below.

We approached the first target at a height of 700 feet, and I had a marvellous view of the scene below as I leaned out of the turret to load the dropper-bag. The full moon was powering its reflected light from the port side, unaffected by cloud interference. I told the skipper that I was ready to drop on command, and within two minutes I was ordered to do so. I had to lean out of the blister to operate the dropper, and, as I pulled the rope handles to accomplish my task, half my body was in the slipstream. The leaflets spewed into the air correctly, and I watched their slow descent from my half-in/half-out position.

After four more successful drops, Dad was preparing for a sixth one over a sizeable Japanese-held town.

As I leaned out of the turret to hold the rope handles of the dropper bag, Harry Shirt tapped me on the shoulder and bawled in my ear words to the effect that it was now my turn to be on radio watch and his to be on leaflet-dropping duties. We changed places, grinning at each other as we did so, and I made my way forward to the operator's seat.

Harry then peppered targets six to ten before Don Hendrie came on the intercom to let them know that target eleven was a large harbour town and they would be over it in two minutes.

Harry filled the dropper and we all waited. The aircraft climbed to 700 feet as we approached the harbour area, and was travelling at 105mph. The town we were overflying was called Lhokseumawe and was recorded as containing personnel from the Japanese navy. Four bundles of leaflets had been allocated to them.

Harry leaned out of the blister to make his drop on cue, but, as he pulled on the handles of the dropper and started the process of spewing the leaflets into the air, the Japanese opened fire with heavy machine guns and light anti-aircraft guns. It was 2217 local time when all hell broke loose aboard J/240.

During the first burst of machine-gun fire, aimed at the starboard blister, Harry was hit by a heavy-calibre bullet. He was knocked backwards into the body of the aircraft and into the arms of Crawford. Soon afterwards, Crawford was hit by a bullet that seared his stomach, but he didn't feel it because he was too preoccupied with Harry's condition. Flight Sergeant Ray Read was also hit by a machine-gun bullet in his stomach as the aircraft started to take violent evasive action by diving to sea level and then turning to port.

Ignoring his own wound, Vic Crawford, aided by Jim Sullivan who had been manning the port gun, set about giving Harry first aid using the kit carried in the bunks compartment. They applied dressings and administered morphine and gently carried Harry to the starboard bunk where they made him as comfortable as possible, trying all the time to block the wound in his side. I cannot speak too highly of the humane and courageous work Crawford and Sullivan did during this moment of crisis among the crew. They were magnificent.

In my compartment, Hendrie had been standing at his nav table in his normal stooped, casual position, working on his charts, when a large bullet hole appeared 'somewhere near Singapore', according to his later description of the event. When I heard the thumps of bullets and shells hitting the aircraft, I sat on my legs to get them out of them way and then noticed – like Hendrie – that I had large bullet holes in my immediate vicinity.

We had taken evasive action soon after the guns had opened up at us, but as we flew over some small warships moored in the harbour, they too opened fire with heavy anti-aircraft guns and made us swerve to starboard again. Robinson ordered the despatch of all remaining leaflets, and only then did we head out to sea, gaining altitude as we did so. I was ordered to send a message to Colombo in code indicating that we had been hit, had suffered a casualty and were now heading for Kyaukpyu.

Kyaukpyu was a Burmese coastal town on Ramree Island in western Burma that had recently been taken by US Office of Strategic Services personnel. Having reported that his best friend had been seriously wounded, Dad then contacted Kyaukpyu again to request medical assistance for Harry when they arrived. 'At this point I left my seat and clambered to Harry's side, kneeling on the catwalk. I told him I had arranged medical attention for him, and, as we held hands in the dark, he squeezed my fingers and asked me to get him something to drink.'

It was shortly after Dad returned to Harry's side that the young man from Derbyshire died. Dad was almost certainly in shock at this point and was struggling to come to terms with what had happened. 'I returned to my desk trying hard to convince myself that what I had just witnessed was Harry dropping off to sleep. I had to believe that was the position as I continued my radio watch.'

The Catalina landed at Kyaukpyu soon after dawn and moored to a buoy previously used by the Japanese.

> Coates, Sullivan and Thistlethwaite had plugged the numerous bullet holes in our hull and sides prior to landing, so there was no danger we would sink. A launch approached, made fast to our port side, and took ashore the two officers initially. Soon the rest of the crew were taken ashore, but I refused to leave until the promised doctor had attended to Harry.
>
> Five minutes later an American medic arrived, took a swift look at Harry, and then grabbed me by the shoulders. He informed me that Harry was dead, had been so for some hours, and that I had done all I could to save his life. Now, he said, it was time for me to go ashore with him to save myself from the effects of the night's events and be with my crewmates.

That morning, there was a debate about what the crew should do next. As they discussed their options, Dad made

Woolwich Barracks, where I was interviewed for the Royal Artillery Museum job in October 2003.

My favourite place – on a battlefield tour on the Somme, this time in 1998.

At Arromanches by an original landing craft, Normandy tour June 1999.

Looking through the aperture of the gun layer's position in one of the gun emplacements at the preserved German gun battery at Longues-sur-Mere, Normandy.

With Alain Roudeix, June 1999.

Crashed Spitfire display in a Normandy museum when we visited on the eightieth anniversary of D-Day, 6th June 2024.

Me and Edward Dunstan – having made it into the much dreamed about Alain Roudeix's barn, June 199

Alain Roudeix's barn – an incredible day meeting the man himself.

Visiting the Tiger tank at Vimoutiers near Falaise, Normandy the actual tank as seen on the front cover of *After the Battle*, edition no. 8.

Our wedding day. Helen and I just outside the church in Devon where we were married on the 6 June 1998.

With my great friend and Barbed Wire Tours colleague Peter Whapshott on a tour to the Western Front in 201

On a battlefield in Normandy.

A battlefield tour to the Somme for the battle's 100th anniversary, re-creating Geoffrey Malin's 1916 film clip in the Sunken Lane at Beaumont-Hamel.

Filming the *Antiques Roadshow* at Colchester in 2024.

With *Antiques Roadshow*'s presenter Fiona Bruce.

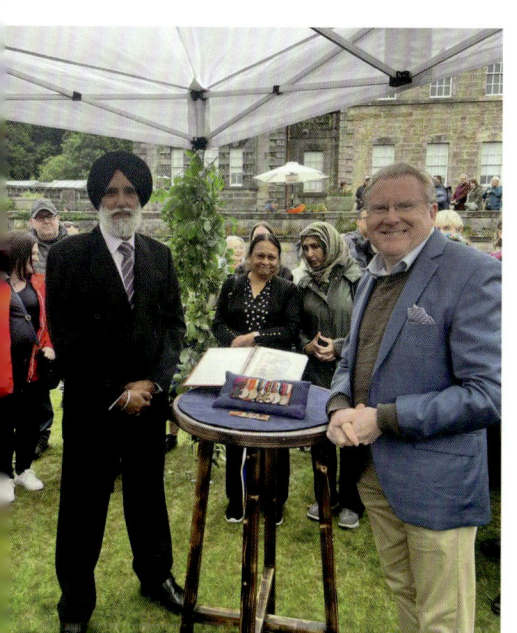

Filming the Victoria Cross awarded to Naik (Corporal) Gian Singh at Pollok Country Park, Glasgow in 2023. His son was so lovely. When I said the VC was worth a quarter of a million pounds, he simply said 'It's just my Dad.'

The flying boots belonging to Flt Lt John Ayshford DFC that contained the letter from Hilda Shirt – Harry's Mum.

Climbing aboard the Catalina at Duxford for the flight over London in May 2025. I am following Steve Foster, the son of Dad's second pilot, Don Foster. 'The first time in eighty years Smith and Foster are going to fly in a Catalina together.'

The Catalina at Duxford ready for take off. The flight made me even prouder of Dad for what he and his crew accomplished.

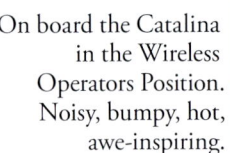

On board the Catalina in the Wireless Operators Position. Noisy, bumpy, hot, awe-inspiring.

The end of my long journey. The moment I stood next to Harry for the first time. I said 'Hello Harry. You don't know me, but I have come on behalf of Les.'

1695129 Flight Sergeant T. H. Shirt. Wireless Operator/Air Gunner. Royal Air Force. Died 26 April 1945. Age 22. 'Always Remembered'.

Christmas Day 1981, Auntie Bob, Hilda, Doll, Barry and Dad.
My eighteenth birthday just before the war stories started.

The poster of medals 1793–1973.
Dad said 'We will collect all of them.'
I eventually acquired the last medal
47 years after we started!

Dad on his sixtieth birthday, 6 November 1982

clear to his senior officers that he and the crew wanted to take Harry back to Madras for burial and not leave him on Ramree Island. In the end they got their wish, and after refuelling the aircraft, they prepared for the long flight home.

> The horrible reality of Harry's death hit us with sledgehammer force as we boarded the aircraft to find our friend draped in a cloth lying on the starboard bunk. Once again, our American hosts had handled matters with a show of empathy and respect. They were a first-class bunch of tough men.
>
> We took off from that frontline base and headed to Red Hills Lake, hundreds of miles away. On landing, we moored to a buoy near the pier so that the medical staff could offload Harry's body. I watched this from the launch I shared with the two officers and Hendrie, on our way to the debriefing.

Operation Nickel II had taken thirty-three hours and twenty minutes – Dad's longest flight to date. That alone should have been a cause for celebration, but Harry's death cast a long shadow, and now he and his crewmates had a funeral with full military honours to organize. But first they had to get airborne again. In an old tradition that went back to the First World War and the Flying Corps that predated the RAF, it was always the practice that a shot-down survivor was immediately sent flying again so that his nerves 'could be kept steady'. In 240 Squadron the same policy was applied in the wake of Harry's death.

Dad's crew plus Peter Trotman, taking the place of Harry, completed a thirteen-hour flight to the Andaman Islands and back the day before the funeral. They did it in the same plane, now patched up, but on their return they were informed that J/240 was to be scrapped. In its place they were given Catalina F/240, an 'old battle-horse' with a long record of operations on Special Duties.

> More important than the shuffling of aircraft for our operational use was the funeral of Harry Shirt on 4 May at St Mary's Cemetery in Madras city at 2.00 p.m. Aided by our boy Sarmi – a fourteen-year-old Tamil servant who attended to us throughout our posting at Red Hills Lake – and as sad as we were through the loss of a dear friend, we dressed in correct military style for this emotionally charged service.

Dad and the crew travelled to the cemetery in air force lorries and then stood in a single line at the foot of Harry's open grave as the ceremony began.

> It was very moving. We had all witnessed funerals with full military honours earlier in our careers, but we had never been involved in one as chief mourners. We knew what was expected of us as we paid our respects and said our farewells to a cherished comrade.
>
> I noticed that the priest had posted a small wooden cross on the grave at the end of the service and was surprised to read that Harry Shirt was credited with being a member of the 'Royal Air Force Regiment'. I took steps to ensure that his correct title and squadron would be displayed when the supposed security reasons had faded into oblivion. This was done eventually, and today the

grave carries the correct designation of Flight Sergeant T. H. Shirt, aged twenty-two at the time of his death.

While the war in Europe was building to its climax with the race to Berlin and the final destruction of the Third Reich, there was no end in sight in the Far East. Like many who were serving out there, Dad felt just as forgotten in the RAF in India as the 14th Army famously did in Burma. He had been at Red Hills Lake for almost exactly a year.

Many of us had received letters from home hinting that we were enjoying life in the sun, and these were painful in their total ignorance of the reality that we faced. The philosophy of the Japanese, twisted and warped in our eyes, promoted an attitude to the war and to fighting that conflicted sharply with our own perceptions. And news of the atrocities carried out by a vile enemy, particularly on prisoners of war, did nothing to lessen the utter revulsion we had for the Japanese race as a whole.

The terrors of the Monsoon, the heat and the rain, were little understood by the British public, and there was a total lack of empathy for service personnel who endured these conditions with a typical acceptance of their environment in sound service tradition. Even worse was the feeling that people 'back home' hadn't a clue about tropical illnesses. They suffered from colds and an occasional bout of influenza in Britain: we had 'monthly trots', the shivers of malaria and numerous other fevers, plus the debilitating effects of simply being in the wrong place vis-à-vis our environmental upbringing. Most of us became grotesquely skinny lightweights which belied the fact that we were, by and large, well fed and cared for medically.

It was against this general background that we viewed the uplifting news from the European battleground during the spring of 1945, with the death of Hitler at the end of April and then Victory in Europe Day four days after Harry's funeral. But the immediate problem facing every serviceman in the South East Asia Command centred on the question: 'What happens to me in the interim?' For me, the war went on and seemed to have no end in sight.

There would be no let up for Dad and his crew as they continued with secret missions while dealing with what he called the 'backlash of shock' in the wake of Harry's death. This took the form of crew members suffering a variety of illnesses and one, Jim Sullivan, being hospitalized with nervous exhaustion.

The flying was intense, with landings in enemy-held territory to infiltrate agents and pick up their exhausted and emaciated predecessors, and in Rangoon during the Allied invasion of the Burmese capital. In deteriorating and often dangerous monsoon weather, they pioneered parachute drops of agents and freight into Japanese-held territory, and by the end of July, Dad had notched up more than 1,000 hours in Catalinas.

You can tell that, like the other members of Ayshford's crew, my father was getting to the end of his tether as the war in the Far East dragged on.

As I rested after the latest operation, I took stock of my position. The achievement of reaching 1,000 hours flown was more symbolic than meaningful in RAF terms, although at that point in time only a small number of men had reached this milestone in a flying career. I felt that I had been very lucky to have survived this far, and that it was time to call it a day. However, as a realist, I knew that as a member of the senior crew on Squadron and SD Flight, my experience was in short supply as the war entered a stage when the Japanese were on the run.

Shortly afterwards, Dad and his crew completed the first ever drop of three agents – they were British soldiers – into Japanese-held territory from a Catalina. They were preparing for another similar operation when the news of the atomic bomb attacks on Hiroshima and then Nagasaki brought the war to a close. On 18 August 1945 – three days after Victory over Japan Day – Dad was promoted to warrant officer and declared 'tour-expired' by his squadron leader. His war was over.

Dad left the RAF in September 1946 and got a job working for BOAC (British Overseas Airways Corporation) as an economist, which he didn't particularly enjoy.

It was while he was with the airline, and not long after he joined the company, that something happened which underlined how much the war had taken out of him. He was having lunch one day when he collapsed, his head crashing into his bowl of soup in front of him. He was rushed to hospital and assessed. He told me what happened next.

'What happened?' the doctor asked him.

'I've no idea,' Dad replied. 'Absolutely no clue what happened there.'

Then the doctor asked him what he did during the war, and Dad told him about his RAF career.

'How long did you do that for?'

'Oh, about three years and 1,000 hours,' he said.

'And how many sorties did you carry out?'

'Sixty-five.'

'Right,' said the doctor. 'You've been living on adrenalin for three and a bit years, Mr Smith, and today the adrenalin has stopped. That's why you collapsed into your soup. The first thing you need is some proper rest.' And he was signed off work to help him recover.

The career that appealed to him, with his ever-curious intellect and ability to explain things (whether you wanted them explained or not), was teaching. Dad did a teacher-training course and got a job as an English and then History teacher at George Gascoigne Secondary Modern School in Queen's Road, Walthamstow.

By 1953, he was headmaster of Markhouse Road Secondary Modern, also in Walthamstow, and used to joke that he was the youngest headmaster in England. He stayed there until 1967, having a profound effect on a generation of youngsters who, to this day, come up to me at the end of talks to say they were taught by him and how lovely he was.

It's hilarious for me because everywhere I go in Walthamstow I still come across his former pupils. The local firemen, policemen, staff in the post office, all include his former pupils. 'Oh, I was taught by your dad – he was the business,' they tell me. It's a great credit to him because not all of us like all our former teachers that much . . .

After Markhouse Road, Dad became a Reader at

Goldsmiths College in New Cross, part of the University of London. He was a lecturer in Education, and he wrote several books at that time. They included a History textbook that millions of children in Britain would have used called *The British People, 1902–1975*, which he co-authored with Peter Mauger.

In the 1960s and 1970s, Dad started to get invitations to talk at other universities, and he travelled all over Europe and then to America giving lectures on Education theory and practice. I remember him going to Sweden because he brought me home one of those little badges that you sew onto your rucksack to say you'd been there. Very proud of that, I was.

Dad retired in 1989, aged sixty-seven, but was still very active and increasingly preoccupied with his war. We would talk endlessly about it, and he dwelled on Harry's death and on his and his crew's failure to find those downed airmen in the Bay of Bengal. As the years went by and the whole subject of trauma became more of a thing, it began to dawn on me that Dad himself was suffering a kind of trauma. He would live and re-live Harry's final moments, as if trying to expunge them from his mind, and, poor chap, he never quite managed to do that.

Chapter Seventeen

My last few months employed in Whitehall were spent mainly at home in bed recovering from something that happened outside the Thatched House pub on Leytonstone High Road. It was a close encounter with the afterlife that changed my whole worldview.

I had come back from what would turn out to be my last foreign trip with D Fin (Pol). It was to the German army staff college at Hamburg, where I delivered what I'm sure was an utterly compelling lecture on the step-change at the MoD from cash accounting to the accruals method.

I have to admit, it was a slightly weird experience talking about the technicalities of recording expenditure incurred in one accounting period but not paid until a future one, while standing in front of a life-size portrait of Field Marshal Erwin Rommel.

That weekend, I thought I'd relax by going to Alexandra Palace where Helen and one of our greatest friends, Annalise Bush, were running a stall at an antiques fair. There might be the odd medal for sale, you never know. So I drove over there and walked round the fair with Annalise, and, having seen enough, decided at about 3.00 p.m. to make my way home. I bought a burger outside and then jumped into my car – by then a silver, two-door sporty thing made by Hyundai – and headed back towards Walthamstow. It was raining, and I was looking for a cash machine on the way because we were going out for dinner the following Tuesday.

Eventually, I spotted a Turkish supermarket on the high street with a sign in the window advertising free cash withdrawals. Opposite there was a long cobbled section that ran parallel to the main thoroughfare where you could park. I pulled in and got out, closed the door and then opened it again to get my jumper. I leaned in and grabbed it and shut the driver's door for the second time. Then I walked round behind the car on the cobbles, ready to cross the road. I was standing, waiting. It was wet, but otherwise a perfectly normal afternoon in summer.

I never saw what happened next, save for a vague sense of movement to my right. I certainly had no memory of a red Ford Mondeo coming at me – on the cobbly bit where you park, not the road – at about 40mph. And I had no memory of the impact, as the car smashed into me, sending me face-first into the windscreen, then high in the air above it before landing behind it on the main road itself.

It was driven, we later discovered, by a Kosovan illegal immigrant who was wanted for deportation. It was not his car, he had no driver's licence, the car wasn't taxed, it had no MOT, and the police reckoned he was on his phone as he left the carriageway and swerved into me. He did so at a speed that left me unconscious, lying in the road, and requiring the kiss of life from a policewoman to restart my heart.

I had hit the car with enough force to write it off. My head was split open above my eyebrows, I had broken both my cheekbones, my nose, both my eye-sockets, my left arm and four ribs on the left side of my chest. I had a nasty scalp wound on the back of my head, and I had smashed my knees together with enough force to cause severe bruising from my feet to my hips. The police called for the air ambulance, and I was airlifted to the Royal London Hospital at Whitechapel, where I was admitted to the major trauma unit.

For Helen this was a more traumatic experience than for me. A police officer had gone round to our house that afternoon and, finding no one in, had spoken to our longtime next-door neighbours and great friends, Darren and Isobel Vandenburg. He told them that the man who lived at our address had been involved in a fatal road traffic accident, news that spread panic.

Isobel called Helen over and over again until she finally answered while still at the fair. Helen and Annalise immediately downed tools – their neighbouring stallholders volunteered to pack up for them – and tried to make their way to Whitechapel, thinking I was either dead or dying.

They got as far as Tottenham police station in dreadful traffic, arriving in a state of shock and pleading for help to get to the hospital. Two police officers then drove them – blue lights flashing – to the Royal London, where they arrived to find Helen's brother, Edward, who was an orthopaedic registrar at the hospital, already there. He had incurred about three speeding tickets on his way, having been alerted by Helen.

'He's alive,' Edward told them, as they stood in the corridor outside the trauma unit where, seconds later, I whizzed by on a trolley looking somewhat battered. I had

had another heart seizure in the helicopter, and in the trauma unit there were seven emergencies before I stabilized. Poor Helen was left to watch the numbers on the machines and shout for help each time they went below prescribed limits.

All I remember of those first hours was speaking my name, hearing the word 'helicopter', and saying or thinking to myself, 'I like helicopters.' Then it's a jumble of fragments – a voice behind my head that kept talking and talking and me trying to answer. Then clarity for a few seconds, as I drifted in and out of consciousness.

'Your CT scan has come back. You're OK, so we are going to take this collar off,' I heard someone say.

'Thank heavens for that,' I thought – or possibly said aloud – as they pulled me up into a sitting position from the spine board that I had come in on.

'Oh, the back of his head's come off,' I heard someone say, as the nurse lifted me with his hands under my armpits. He was referring to the loose flap of skin on the back of my skull where it had hit the road and that would have to be glued back on.

After the excellent treatment I received in the trauma unit, I was moved to a major-injuries ward. I spent five days there in a bit of a daze before they allowed me home on condition that I was monitored on a twenty-four-hour basis for the following week. My sister-in-law, Lizzy Dunstan, who is a nurse, insisted I use a wheelchair on the morning I left.

I came back in Annalise's car, and they put me in the back bedroom. Helen, Annalise and several other amazing friends – among them Darren from next door, another neighbour and close friend Abe Raidan, and Siobhan Tyrrell and her wife Roisin McKeniry – duly sat with me. I would doze off and then wake to find someone new sitting at the end of my bed each time.

It took four months to recover fully, and even then I emerged into normal life wary of walking on busy streets or anywhere near cars. But the accident had a more profound impact than a natural reaction to the danger of being run over.

I remember lying in that bedroom on a beautiful summer's day, looking out of the window. I could see the leaves in the trees, the movement in them and the blue sky behind them, and I remember thinking, 'This is a really quick journey we're all on. It's minutes rather than years. It's so fast – you cannot afford to waste any more of it. You cannot get annoyed with things for no reason. There's no point. And there is an incredible thing that you've got – which is being able to walk around and talk to people, because it should have stopped that day in Leytonstone. That should have been the end.' And then I thought, 'We're going to change now, Mark. We're going to go off, and we're going to do different things, and we're only going to do nice things, and if we want to do something we're just going to go and do it.'

This became the thought, almost the lesson, of what had happened to me. Above all, it underlined how much I needed another job. I *had* to do something else, and I genuinely knew I simply could not do D Fin (Pol) any longer.

Returning to the office part-time, it felt pretty weird in all respects. I still couldn't feel much on the left-hand side of my face and my left arm – full feeling has never returned in those areas – and coming back to D Fin (Pol) was never going to cut it.

There was a young woman in our department – a follower of the Zoroastrian religion, as it happened – who was looking to get promoted, crossing between designated bands in the Civil Service, which is never easy. And because I sat on the panel to assess these applications, she asked me how she should go about it.

Officially, we were sworn to secrecy about what we would be looking for at interview, but I never believed that was necessary. So I helped her prepare and fill out the forms. After our meeting, she left the *JOB* – the *Job Opportunity Bulletin* – that contained details of hundreds of Civil Service roles based in London, Britain and all over the world, lying on my desk.

I opened it and flicked through to the pages relevant to my rank. Having been promoted to acting head of DFin (Pol), I had subsequently been invited to apply for my own job and got it. The first job on the list, in my substantive rank, was Director of the Royal Artillery Museum, Woolwich. To be considered, you had to have served in the Royal Artillery, you had to have a Master's degree in Museum Studies, you had to have finance experience and you had to have a background in project management.

It left me with an all-too-familiar sinking feeling because I had seen this post advertised a few years before. I hadn't applied for it then because I had not been in the Royal Artillery, and nor had I a degree in Museum Studies. But this time I thought it sounded so cool, and I couldn't get it out of my mind. I'd always wanted to work in a museum, and this felt like my opportunity at last. I read through it again and thought, 'What have I got to lose? I've simply got to apply.

They can say no if they want. But sod it, I'm going to fill out the form anyway.'

So I filled it in, ticked the two boxes for finance and project management experience that I qualified for, and got my boss Roger to fill in his bit and posted it. I was fully expecting to hear back after about a month from someone who would tell me that they were 'terribly sorry' but my experience did not fulfil the requirements of the job. What happened was that a week later I got a letter inviting me to an interview at the Royal Artillery Officers' Mess at Woolwich Barracks. 'Crumbs!' I thought. 'Who knows, I could be on to something here.'

I duly appeared on the appointed day, and they were running late. The mess was housed in an impressive building with the longest Georgian facade in Europe, set in front of a vast parade ground. As you walked in, the door was guarded by two small cannons. Inside, the walls were adorned with oil paintings of officers and battle scenes and drum banners. I was ushered into a small room where they sat me down with a cup of tea. And there I waited until someone came along and said, 'Would you like to join us now?'

I was admitted to a suitably ornate library or reading room where a panel chaired by the regimental colonel, Simon Hutchinson, sat behind a polished desk in uniform. I sat opposite him with the window behind me. Alongside Hutchinson were two others, one of whom was from the Imperial War Museum, the other a civilian museum expert of some kind. Behind them sat Brigadier Ken Timbers, one of the founders of the museum.

Now, the evening before the interview, I had called Peter

Cormack, an old friend who was Keeper of the William Morris Gallery in Walthamstow, and whose brother was the Collections Manager for the Royal Air Force Museum at Hendon. I had a feeling he might be able to help.

'What sort of museum-y questions might I get tomorrow?' I asked Peter.

'Well, they might talk about conservation and collection management and things like that,' he said. 'But that's the sort of thing you know about because of your medal collecting. So if you tell them what you do on that score, you'll be fine.'

'OK. Anything else?'

'Yes,' he said, 'if you get a chance, throw in AMOT.'

'What's that?'

'It's the Army Museums Ogilby Trust. It was set up by Colonel Robert Ogilby in 1954 to help promote the regimental history of the army and now supplies military museums with grants. It's a key player in how these things are run.'

'Oh, OK,' I said before launching into a battery of questions as Peter filled in the chasm-like gaps in my knowledge of how military museums are run.

The other thing I had done before the interview was go to the Royal Artillery Museum itself and buy a ticket at the door. It was huge. I'd heard about it and I'd seen posters advertising it as an attraction on the London Underground, but I'd never been there.

The museum was housed in a large old ammunition factory from the 1880s that was part of the Royal Arsenal at Woolwich, where three separate collections within the Royal Artillery – the guns, the medals and the uniforms – were brought together. Inside were hundreds of cannons, guns of all kinds, aeroplanes, rockets, uniforms and medals that I later discovered were part of a collection of more than 3 million exhibits. There was a bit they called the Field of Fire, a show that started with a film about the history of artillery. Then you would go into a room with four enormous screens, with tanks and guns around the outside. The place filled with smoke, and the floor shook as the guns fired and the music played, telling the story of artillery from the Second World War through to the First Gulf War. I thought that bit was quite spectacular.

The museum was massive, but it was cold, quite dark, and the thing I couldn't help noticing was that there was no one else there. I got the feeling that all was not quite as it should be with the Royal Artillery Museum.

At the interview, I told them something of what I knew about the Royal Artillery, explaining that I had been collecting medals from gunners for years. I spoke about the history and the way the Royal Artillery had until 1924 been divided into three arms – the Royal Field Artillery, the Royal Horse Artillery and the Royal Garrison Artillery. And I spoke about the differences between batteries and regiments and that sort of thing, and how I researched my medals.

We talked about conservation, and I told them about the archaeology course that I had done in Walthamstow. Then the chap from the Imperial War Museum asked me about AMOT.

'What can you tell me about it,' he said, looking intently at me.

'Ah, you mean the Army Museums Ogilby Trust?' I replied, before launching into a rehash of everything Peter had shared with me the night before.

'Oh, very good, very good, Mr Smith,' came the response, but really it was skin-of-the-teeth stuff.

The next day, still in the long recovery phase after my accident, I was feeling awful after the exertion of going to Woolwich for the interview. I was in bed after lunch when the phone rang.

'Hello, Mark. This is Colonel Hutchinson here.'

'Oh, hello,' I said, trying not to sound surprised to be hearing from him so soon.

'I've got some good news and some bad news for you,' he went on.

'Go on, then,' I replied. 'What's the good news?'

'You've got the job.'

'Well, umm, wow . . . that's great to hear,' I said. 'Thank you very much. So what's the bad news, then?'

'Well,' he said, 'the museum's really not doing very well, and it could be shut by Christmas.'

I would find out a lot more about what the problems were in due course. At the time, I said to the colonel that I would like to think about things and get back to him. Inside, though, I was still excited about this opportunity, even if it might go up in smoke before I got my feet under the desk. The big issue I could see was getting there and back each day – across East London from Walthamstow to Woolwich.

I went back to the office, which was now in St Giles Court, while Main Building was being refurbished, and there was a big map of London on the wall. I stuck a pin in where we lived in Walthamstow and another one at Woolwich for the museum, and then I looked, and I looked, and I looked, trying to work out whether I could face that car journey twice every day. I knew the traffic could be horrendous in that part of London on a typical weekday, and it was by far the biggest consideration in my mind as I tried to work out whether or not to accept the job offer.

I had a chat with Dad about it. Sitting in his chair, he reminded me that he had done a similar commute in his days working at Goldsmiths in New Cross, so even though the traffic had got worse since the 1970s, it was still doable.

'But you know, Son, this is what you've always wanted, and it's a good job,' he said. 'You'll be working in a museum and a military establishment at that. Even if you've got to sit in a bit of traffic, it's got to be worth it, hasn't it?'

He was right. It was the job I wanted, not just a way out of DFin (Pol) but a step towards my real passion in life as a collector of medals and militaria. The funny thing is, had I not been run over, I feel sure I would have turned the job down over worries about the commute and about the future of the museum. But in the new world that I was living in, with my determination to do what I wanted to do and follow my heart a little more than my head, I thought, 'You know what? Let's give it a go. Let's just give it a go.'

It was time to leave Whitehall and start a new adventure in Woolwich, and I couldn't wait to get stuck in. And in case I ever forgot or ignored the lesson I learned during my recovery, I wrote a 'note to self' in my digital calendar. It repeats every year on 11 May, the day I was run over.

It says *ostium aperatrum* – open the door – the day the door opened.

Chapter Eighteen

After my first day at the museum – 19 January 2004 – I was very excited, and that night I drove round to Mum and Dad's house to tell them all about it. After explaining what I had been up to at Woolwich, I noticed that Dad had been unusually quiet.

Eventually he said, 'Ah, Son, that's fantastic, really well done.' Then he told me he had been to the doctor that day.

'Oh yeah?' I said.

'Yes,' he said. 'It's nearly time to close the hangar door, I'm afraid.'

It didn't properly register at the time what he was telling me, but from then on the clock ran down to the day he died the following July.

As the weeks went by, and winter turned to spring, he was doing less and less and was going off to Whipps Cross Hospital for regular check-ups, and we could all see he was getting weaker. He had come round for Christmas that year but had ended up sitting alone in the front room for long periods because he was worn out most of the time.

He did make it to the museum once. It was not long before he died, and he was there the day Dame Vera Lynn came to visit when we opened a new exhibition. At one point, the soundtrack at the museum was playing Neville Chamberlain's address to the nation from Downing Street on the eve of war on 3 September 1939. 'As no such undertaking has been given,' we heard Chamberlain gravely intone, in reference to British demands that Germany withdraw its troops from Poland, 'this country is at war with Germany.' Then came the line when Chamberlain explained what a 'bitter blow' this was to him after his 'long struggle' to win peace had failed.

At that point I heard my father mutter under his breath, 'Yeah, it gave me the hump as well!' That was a very funny moment.

It was in preparation for one of his hospital visits that he collapsed and crumpled on to the floor in the hallway at his home. I was there, ready to go with him and Mum, and I couldn't get him back on his feet. We called an ambulance, and they carried him out. I will never forget the cruel and clinical attitude of the doctor into whose care he was taken at Whipps Cross. There was no time for compassion. Dad had had a new X-ray of his chest, and his lung cancer was the size of a tennis ball.

'That's it,' he told me, pointing it out on the image. 'And this isn't going to end well. It doesn't look good at all.'

'Yeah, but he's a brave lad,' I told him. 'He's survived a lot worse than this, I can tell you. What I'm going to do is buy him some tickets for the Olympics in 2012, and we'll go together. That will give him something to live for.'

I was doing my level best to put a positive gloss on a miserable situation, and, of course, I was expecting the doctor to agree with me and say, 'What a lovely idea.' But he didn't. He said nothing. And I sat there, in the silence, staring at the X-ray and thinking, 'Oh dear...'

A couple of days later, I went to see Dad, and he was in a strange mood. He was talking about aeroplanes and being an airman again – he wasn't with us any more in London. He was back in early 1945, on board Catalina J/240 over the Gulf of Martaban, rolling around in dreadful monsoon weather at night, searching for the crashed Liberator flight crew in their dinghy.

'I haven't got that second call from him,' he kept saying, re-living those moments in the air sixty years earlier. Then he would point at the bed opposite.

'You see that bloke over there,' he told me. 'He was a pilot.'

'Oh yeah?' I replied.

'Yeah, he was a flyer too, but he flew different things to me.'

Then I would hear snapshots of the old war stories I knew so well, and he talked again about Harry, but more about the attack and the damage to the aircraft than Harry's death.

On one of my last visits, during a moment when he was more lucid, I pressed him for more detail on the story that had haunted him for so long.

'You tell me about Harry all the time, Dad...'

'Yes, Son.'

'Well, for example, was it dark when it happened?'

'Oh yeah, it was pitch-black.'

So I said, 'Well, how long did the attack last for?'

And he said, 'Oh, maybe nine seconds...'

That's when it really hit me – that for fifty or sixty years, it was those nine seconds – *nine seconds* – that had defined his whole life since the war. Those nine seconds were the baggage he had carried with him, and that he had talked about almost every day.

It was his lifelong smoking habit that got him in the end. Dad had started when he was about eight and smoked all the time – forty a day, every day. He did try to stop every now and again but never made much headway. One of those times we had gone to play golf up at High Beech, where we wouldn't have to walk very far for nine holes.

'I've got a patch on, and I'm giving up now,' he had informed me confidently as we strode on to the first tee. But by the time we got to the second hole, he was effing and blinding all over the place, and I was laughing because he was swearing so much.

By the ninth fairway, this well-dressed professor had reverted into an East End barrow boy, giving it the full treatment – 'These useless patches. What a pile of rubbish.' And so on...

I was, like, 'Dad, calm down, you can do this.'

But he was having none of it, and the swearing continued until we got back to the car... where we discovered the offending patch lying in the boot. It had fallen off before we had even started.

'Sod it!' shouted Dad as he grabbed his fags from the passenger door and started chain-smoking about ten cigarettes while I put the clubs back in the boot.

A few days after my last visit to Whipps Cross, I had arranged a night out for my staff at the museum. We went to the India Club, the iconic restaurant on the Strand where I was a member and which closed recently after seventy years.

After a delicious curry, we adjourned to the Coal Hole pub down the road, and I was chatting away in there when something said to me, 'Look at your watch.' It was ten minutes to ten. When I got home, I walked through the front door and Helen came out of the front room to greet me.

'We've lost Dad,' she said.

He had died at ten to ten. And that was it, really. The funeral was at the City of London Cemetery where about 125 people attended, many of them former pupils or staff of his. The eulogy was given by Derek Steward, who Dad taught and who later became one of his staff at Markhouse Road School. I couldn't bear to hear it and went outside . . .

His life was over, and my life with him was over. We all have dads, and they all have a unique presence in our lives, for good or for ill. I know I was one of the lucky ones to have him, and my mum, who died three years later. I had a father whose influence on me was all-pervasive but entirely positive and loving. He gave so much, telling me the stories of his life and his war and enjoying watching me grow up. OK, he never stopped talking, but it was often either useful or fun listening to what he had to say, and he never talked down to me. We were always on a level, and that's why I said he was my best mate . . . not many people can say that about their dads.

Chapter Nineteen

From my first day to the day I finished there – twelve years later – I never went to work again once I started at the museum. I only ever left the house to play. That's all I ever did.

I was like a kid at Christmas, surrounded by 3 million things that I was interested in and passionate about – everything from ancient cannons from Wellington's day to field artillery and self-propelled guns from the Second World War, modern anti-aircraft systems, missiles and missile launchers, medals, uniforms, an incredible library about artillery in warfare, and a million photos to boot.

Simon Hutchinson had warned me in advance that the museum was in trouble – people weren't going to it, and it wasn't generating enough money. As Museum Director, I would lead the collections team looking after the exhibits, and it was our job to turn this around.

Except that I wasn't the director. I arrived that January morning in 2004 to discover I had been downgraded to Museum 'Curator'. I took it on the chin. I was in for a penny, in for a pound, and I didn't care much what I was called.

I managed to start on the wrong foot from day one, when I questioned the wisdom of the new name for the museum – 'Firepower'. This had been arrived at with advice from an expensive branding consultancy, but it struck me as impractical. If you were looking up the Royal Artillery Museum, you were not likely to search for it under 'F', I pointed out, and it should be something simpler and more direct that would be easier to find. This did not go down well, and I found myself in front of Simon Hutchinson again.

'I hear you don't like the name of the museum, Mark,' he said. 'It was chosen by a panel of people who know what they are doing in the museum world, so we are not going to change it now. Look,' he went on, 'if you are going to continue like this, we shall have to part company with you, and we don't want to do that.'

Still, there was still plenty to look forward to in my new role, and I had no plans to go anywhere else. Another thing Simon told me that week was that my continued presence in Woolwich was dependent on me getting a Master's degree in Museum Studies, which struck me as quite fun. I found a course at University College London which I qualified for, through having completed paramedic training at the MoD to degree level.

It was a one-day-a-week, two-year course. I didn't enjoy it much, partly because I was about twenty-five years older than everyone else, and while most of my fellow students seemed to be interested in the museum world they had no area of expertise or anything they were particularly excited about. The course taught you how to catalogue things and stuff like that, but I'd already been at the museum for a year by then, and I'd been cataloguing my medals since I was seven, so this wasn't a huge leap. They also taught us about funding a museum, but I'd already done the finance bit at the MoD, so there wasn't much new there either.

At the end, we had to write a dissertation. Mine was entitled 'How to Portray Conflict in a Museum Environment'. What it boiled down to was this: how do you portray what war is really like through exhibits? For example, a gun standing in an exhibition hall is an inanimate object. But when you see guns in action, first of all they stink because of all the cordite and other explosives, and second, they are usually covered in muck, with grass and mud and all sorts of rubbish all over them. And when you stand in a trench and your feet are soaking wet and it's freezing cold, how do you get that across to someone in a nice warm museum? Or the question might be: do you actually *want* to make a museum more realistic, and can you do that?

I think I ended up by saying that the best you can do is give people an idea. That you need to work hard at providing triggers for the senses, using audio and visual aids. But you can never come up with what it's really like because you can't fully replicate the characteristics of guns in war – the smell, the deafening roar and the massive explosive impact of modern artillery.

In my day job, though, I took my cue from that bit of work. I got someone to build me a shell case for a 25-pounder field gun. Instead of a primer at the bottom of the case, we incorporated a 9mm blank round. It meant we could load the gun, and you could get kids to fire it. There was a pretty big bang, and it was good fun. We would get them to stand in all of the places of a gun detachment with a real soldier shouting commands at them. They would fire the gun, and then all move round and then fire it again. There was no recoil, but it did smell, which was great.

We also had a living-history team who were a lot of little old men – some of the many volunteers I had working with my team. They each wore bits of uniform – not all the same uniform, and not all complete outfits – but they tried hard, bless them. They used to wheel out a 2-pounder anti-tank gun, and we had some shell cases for it that could take a .303 blank, and they fired that outside because it made a properly big bang. They used to go into action with it and fire five rounds, all standing round with various boots on. The whole thing had a rather quaint Home Guard feel, and the kids enjoyed it.

I loved that place from the day the then retired Brigadier Ken Timbers – one of the founders of the museum, and whose baby it was – showed me around. Ken is a charming man and one of the foremost specialists on the history of the Royal Artillery. We did a tour of Gunnery Hall after lunch one day, and he told me about every single gun, how they worked, how you 'lay' a gun – the process of aiming an artillery piece – what gunpowder is made of, how cannonballs work, how shells work, everything. And I remembered every word he said because what he did that afternoon was incredible. He brought it to life, so that by the time I finished the tour with him I could fire those guns. They had been quite concerned that, as the new curator, I had not been an artilleryman, but that afternoon Ken Timbers taught me how to be one.

His tour formed the basis of my own walk-round that I used to do for people. I would do a specialist 'Curator's Tour' for small parties, or devote a whole day to a twenty-strong visiting group from the Orders and Medals Research Society, when we would go through the entire collection of 12,000 medals. I also used to do a 'Behind the Scenes Tour' where I would take people to the storerooms, and we would go through some of the stuff we didn't have on show at the time.

It was all part of our efforts in the collections team to keep the museum alive. They included the various exhibitions that we launched. The first was the opening, shortly after I arrived, of a new Cold War Gallery that had been developed by my predecessor. This featured a chronological display from 1945 to the present day, with postwar guns and images of significant events like the fall of the Berlin Wall. This was the one that Vera Lynn came to, and so did Dad.

Another one was 'Out of the Dark' to celebrate the 200th anniversary of the museum, with 200 rarely seen objects set out in a trail around the museum. Then we did 'Real People, Real Lives', where each visitor would be handed a card at the entrance giving them the details of a particular individual. It could be a gunner at Waterloo or someone manning an anti-aircraft battery during the Blitz. As they went round the museum, they would gradually discover what happened to the person they had become. And we did a 'National Service' exhibition for which we had no budget, so I helped pay for that one out of my own salary.

The trouble with 'Firepower' was not just its name. It went far deeper than that. The museum had been paid for with a Heritage Lottery grant and matched funding from other sources, but Woolwich was a poor location, with access only by train from London Bridge. Worse, the entire surroundings of the museum had been turned into a building site as the old military structures were repurposed as flats and homes. The net result was that ticket receipts were not matching expectations and money was tight.

The saddest part of this story is that in the final months of the museum's life in 2016, through the hard work we had put in, we had found a way for the business to make a small profit for the first time. But it was shut down as they were finishing the new Elizabeth Line station on the London Underground a few hundred yards from the museum. When it did close, almost the entire collection went into storage amid ambitious plans to rehouse it in a new development at Larkhill in Wiltshire, the home of the Royal School of Artillery. But, as of eight years later, that plan has yet to come to fruition.

By the time I resigned from the museum in January 2017, a few days before it closed, I was nevertheless able to look back and see the positives. Me and my team had loved our role, and I had made lifelong friends out of some of the great people I worked with, not least our librarian, Paul Evans, my No. 2, who I promoted to become Head of Library and Archives. An uncompromising northerner with naval heritage, Paul was as robust an individual as you could ask for. He had no qualms about saying it as it was, whoever he was speaking to, or their rank. Les Smith was our Collections Manager who looked after the guns. He is another outstanding individual, as is Steve Hookins, a writer and historian who was a key part of the curatorial team. Our Registrar, Marc Sheriff, was, and still is, the world's greatest authority on cloth badges. Not forgetting Wendy Mortledge, my Office Manager and assistant, who was beyond fantastically efficient.

While I am at it, there is one other individual I should mention. She was not on my staff, but she became a fixture at Woolwich in my time and we all loved her. She was a small, thin woman called Mrs Coppersmut. We never found out her first name, and she was a medium. She came to the museum at least once a week if not more because, as she put it, she liked to talk to the ghosts.

She'd turn up in the morning and walk around. We gave her a free pass because she was always there and she used to work with us as a volunteer too. She used to say there was a spiritual presence in one of the main corridors – a corridor that my dog refused to walk down. According to her there was someone standing at the end. Over in Building 41, the Cold War gallery, she would stop and say 'listen'. And we would hear – or did we? – footsteps walk slowly across the ceiling above us. She was a fun lady, Mrs Coppersmut.

I had learned some useful skills at Woolwich, not least how to give a guided tour from Ken Timbers which, along with the many talks I gave at the museum, would lead me into after-dinner speaking. As a result of my speeches, I have been able to raise thousands of pounds in donations for several charities, among them the Commonwealth War Graves Foundation, the Special Boat Service Association and the London Air Ambulance. I had also developed my battlefield-tour experience at the museum, having established a contract between Woolwich and the Army Foundation College in Harrogate. Alongside Steve Hookins, Peter Wapshott and his brother-in-law Phil, we would take young soldiers around the battlefields during week-long visits to Normandy on a tour called 'The Realities of War'. Any money raised would go to the museum. The soldiers would come out in batches of 300, and we became proficient at moving them round from one 'pitch' to another. Those days were good fun.

The other thing I learned – or got used to doing – at Woolwich was speaking on radio and television. My very first TV appearance came early on in my time there, when I was interviewed for a programme called *Deep Wreck Mysteries* made by Canadian television for the History Channel. The idea was that there was always some unexplained element to be speculated upon about a wreck they would send divers to with the cameras. In this case, it was a First World War vessel, the British Hospital Ship *Rewa*. It was sunk off Hartland Point in Devon in January 1918 by a U-boat. The ship was carrying 279 wounded British and some German officers, plus medical staff, and was returning from Malta when it went down. Fortunately, everyone on board was saved, bar three crew members who were killed in the initial explosion.

The Germans later tried to claim that HMHS *Rewa* was carrying ammunition, and this justified its sinking. The programme makers sent the divers down and they found two 18-pounder shell cases in the wreck. Were these, they wanted to know, enough to prove the Germans right? I stood in front of an 18-pounder field gun at the museum and said the discovery of two shell cases was not enough to constitute an ammunition-carrying ship. I also explained that, if you looked at the two cases, you could see that both had been fired. To my mind, this suggested that these were two spent shell cases being taken home by a soldier for his mum as a souvenir. It was my debut in a medium I would come to love.

Chapter Twenty

One of the many positives from my time at Woolwich was the opportunity to join one of the oldest coin and medal dealers – or should I say specialist numismatic dealers – in the world.

Early in my last year at the museum I got a call from A. H. Baldwin & Sons, a London-based family firm that dates back to 1872, who were looking for someone to run their medal department. Now owned by the Stanley Gibbons Group, Baldwins is the gold standard when it comes to dealing in coins and medals, and this was an opportunity I could not afford to miss.

They wanted me to join on a full-time basis working from their new Coin Room at 399 the Strand, but I never wanted a full-time job and suggested I work there two days a week. I knew the museum was on its last legs, but I wanted to see it out and the then Regimental Colonel, Roddy Lee, was so nice about it. He also knew the museum was closing, and he knew how sad I was about it.

'I'll tell you what, Mark,' he said. 'Why don't you do one day a week at Baldwins, and we can treat that as your job resettlement course. And if you want to take a day off every now and again to accommodate your commitments with Baldwins, you can do that as well.'

Roddy was one of the best guys, and I couldn't have been more appreciative of his helpful attitude. It gave me the perfect chance to move seamlessly from one role to the next, and I've never looked back as far as Baldwins is concerned. I love my job there as the firm's medals, orders and decorations specialist, and I still do two days a week, which is ideal.

I have a shop at the office on the Strand, from where I buy and sell medals. I travel all over the country looking at people's collections, either to buy or to catalogue for sale. I have a website where I advertise medals, and once a year I write a big auction catalogue and we have an auction of medals. I also sell militaria. It couldn't be more perfect in terms of a job for someone whose passion is collecting medals and bits of military stuff.

And then there is the Victoria Cross and my talks about it, a subject that has become my speciality. Again, I owe its origin to my time at the museum. And it all started with the Victoria Cross guns at Woolwich.

When I arrived at the museum, I saw these two famous old cannons sitting out in the rain on the main parade square, and I thought that was wrong. I said to Roddy's predecessor, the aforementioned Colonel Simon Hutchinson, that we couldn't possibly leave these two historic pieces sitting outside, rotting in the weather. They were far too important for that. And eventually, after much toing and froing, I had the guns brought into the museum, and we put them in the foyer.

The Victoria Cross had already been a subject that fascinated me, but those guns sparked renewed interest in what remains the ultimate award for heroism in the face of the enemy for servicemen and women in the army, navy and air force, and for all ranks. The guns provided a focal point for early talks I would give at the museum about Queen Victoria's Medal, and I would stand between them explaining the history and how it came about.

When the medal that became the Victoria Cross was first thought of, in the mid-1850s during the Crimean War, there was a strong belief – shared by the queen and Prince Albert – that a new award was required to acknowledge the courage of soldiers and sailors serving in her armed forces. Our then allies, the French, had one with their Légion d'honneur, so why couldn't we have one too?

Prince Albert discussed the proposed medal in great detail with the queen. When he was shown an early draft of the warrant for the new 'order', as it was then conceived, he wrote on it 'The Victoria Cross' – naming it as he did so, and telling us what form it would take.

It was known that the queen did not want the medal to be made of something precious that would be worth a lot of money, because this was an award that would not be about the medal but the deed behind it – that was the important thing. Later, she made another critical intervention when she altered the motto on the medal, crossing out 'for the brave' and substituting 'for valour'. She did not want the idea to gain traction that anyone who had not been awarded the Victoria Cross was in some way not brave.

In January 1856, Queen Victoria signed the statute that created the Victoria Cross. An early version had been made of copper that did not impress her – she said her soldiers and sailors would be proud of this medal and would polish it, only to see it go pink like an old penny. Instead, someone suggested it be made in bronze, and with that an old myth was born.

The first parade for the Victoria Cross was held in Hyde Park on 26 June 1857, when the queen, on horseback, pinned the new medal to the chests of sixty-two recipients. Famously, in the case of Commander Henry Raby, the first man in line, the queen managed to stick the pin straight into his flesh under his tunic, while he stood unflinching before his sovereign. It was a couple of months before the ceremony that the *Daily Telegraph* erroneously reported that the Victoria Cross was being made from bronze taken from cannons 'captured from the Russians' at the Siege of Sevastopol in the Crimean War. A letter to *The Times* from a Crimean veteran also referred to this.

But this was not the case. The early medals were made from a stock piece of bronze acquired by Hancocks, the jewellers in London, who still make the Victoria Cross to this day. When the block they were using ran out, they tried other sources, including melting down old bronze pennies. These produced very strange Victoria Crosses from the time of the Boer War.

Then, in 1914, captured guns were suggested as a source, a solution that would bring myth and reality into line. They had to be of foreign manufacture, made of bronze and captured in battle to qualify, and two cannons kept at the Royal Arsenal at Woolwich were chosen. They had been captured at the Taku Forts in north-eastern China during the Second Opium War in 1860.

The button, or cascabel, was duly cut off the back of both guns, and between them these two cascabels have made over 800 Victoria Crosses since that time. And the great irony is that they are not Russian guns . . . but of Chinese manufacture. The notion that our highest award for valour in battle is hewn from material made in China certainly raises a few eyebrows, I can tell you.

So I would stand before these two pieces of history at Woolwich, delivering my talk about all of this, and explaining the story behind the guns and the medal. The museum had its own collection of Victoria Crosses – twenty-three in all – and I would hold one and show it to people as I talked them through the legend of the medal and the men who have been awarded it.

What I noticed from the beginning is that this small symbol – a Maltese Cross with the Royal Crown on it surmounted by a standing lion – can stop a whole room. When people see one, and they know it's not a fake, you hear an audible intake of breath. That's partly because of what the Victoria Cross stands for and partly because they remain so rare – only 1,355 people have been awarded one, three of them twice.

If you think of the Victorian period and the First and Second World Wars, something like 10 million men went out to fight, but only 643 men came back with one of these things. And those that wear that ribbon remain revered, as evidenced by the tradition that requires officers of all ranks, right up to Chiefs of Staff, to salute a Victoria Cross holder.

The more I gave those talks and the more I researched the subject, the more fascinated I became. I learned a lot about the medal from John Glanfield, whose book, *The Bravest of the Brave*, tells the history of the Victoria Cross. And I also spent a long time talking to David Callaghan who, at the time, was director of Hancocks and oversaw all aspects of the supply of Victoria Crosses by the company for thirty-five years.

I own a Victoria Cross. It was awarded to a man called George Hinckley, a then forty-three-year-old bearded able seaman on board HMS *Sphinx*. He volunteered to rescue two officers lying wounded in open ground during the bloody Taiping Rebellion in China in 1862. He carried both men to safety despite coming under heavy fire, as his citation put it, from 'musketry, gingalls and stinkpots'. That would be muskets, swivel-mounted heavy muskets and ignitable earthenware pots filled with gunpowder, nails and noxious substances. Hinckley, who lost his original Victoria Cross while attending a funeral – it was later replaced – retired from the navy as a Quartermaster and died at Plymouth in 1904.

My favourite Victoria Cross story – and there are plenty of good ones to choose from – is that of John Raynes, whose medal was part of the museum collection. He was a sergeant in the Royal Artillery who had been a policeman in Leeds before the outbreak of the Great War. Raynes was a man who simply didn't know when he was beaten and demonstrated extraordinary courage and determination in the most appalling circumstances.

On 11 October 1915, Raynes was serving in A Battery, 71st Brigade, Royal Field Artillery, north-west of the French village of Loos. They were in a hellhole next to a notorious slag heap from nearby coal mines and a line of houses dubbed

'Quality Street', just south of the Lens–Béthune road. British artillery had been hammering the German lines in the final days of the Battle of Loos, and then the Germans replied with a barrage of their own.

Aerial reconnaissance by the Germans had accurately pinpointed A Battery's position, and soon it was being targeted by high-explosive shrapnel and gas shells. There were numerous casualties, and the order was given to cease fire so that the wounded could be attended to. Raynes and his friend, Sergeant John 'Jack' Ayres, took shelter in a dugout. It was then that Ayres remembered one of the guns had been left with an unused shell still in the breech. Had it been hit, that gun would have exploded and possibly killed all its gun team.

Ayres ran out to clear it, and as he did so he was hit by shrapnel from an incoming shell. Raines's Victoria Cross citation, published in the *London Gazette* of 16 November 1915, takes up the remarkable story of what happened next:

> Sgt Raynes went out under intense shellfire to assist Sgt Ayres, who was lying wounded 40 yards away. He bandaged him and returned to his gun when it was again ordered into action. A few minutes later 'cease fire' was again ordered owing to the intensity of the enemy's fire, and Sgt Raynes, calling on two gunners to help him – both of whom were killed shortly afterwards – went out and carried Sgt Ayres to the dugout. A gas shell burst at the mouth of the dugout and Sgt Raynes once more ran across the open [ground], fetched his own smoke helmet, put it on Sgt Ayres and, himself badly gassed, staggered back to serve his gun.

It's a long citation because Raynes was awarded the Victoria Cross for his actions over two days – days that would destroy his health but see him rewarded with an appearance before the King at Buckingham Palace to receive his medal.

The day after the rescue, Raynes was in the battery cookhouse in one of the houses on Quality Street when it was hit by a German shell. The building was demolished in the explosion, burying four men in the house and four more in the cellar. The citation records: 'The first man rescued was Sgt Raynes, wounded in the head and leg, but he insisted on remaining under heavy fire to assist in the rescue of all the other men. Then after having his wounds dressed, he reported himself for duty with his battery, which was again being heavily shelled.'

What a man. Sadly, Sergeant Ayres did not survive, but Raynes did and was soon back in England, suffering the terrible effects of gas poisoning having forgone the protection of his own helmet to help his friend. Raynes was eventually discharged from the army in December 1918 and returned to work for the police in Leeds. But his health continued to deteriorate, and he died on 13 November 1929, aged forty-two. His military funeral was attended by nineteen Victoria Cross recipients, and over 100,000 people lined the route to Harehills Cemetery in Leeds, where 30,000 more attended the burial.

In a postscript that underlines how quickly and completely even our heroes can be forgotten, his grave was discovered in a state of disrepair in 2008 by Anthony Child, a West Yorkshire policeman who had been researching Raines's wartime exploits. The grave was then refurbished and a service of rededication held in November that year, officiated by the West Yorkshire Police Chaplain, the Reverend Inspector Andrew Earl.

Like so many Victoria Cross recipients, Raynes was a modest man who never believed he had done anything unusual. In an interview with a reporter from the *Sheffield Daily Telegraph* not long after he returned to England, he was asked about what he had done to earn the award. 'I have only a hazy idea of actually what did happen,' he said, 'and I naturally wish to forget the whole affair. I simply did what other men would have done in similar circumstances. It was the biggest surprise in the world when I got a telegram congratulating me.'

Over the years at the museum, I met all the living holders of the Victoria Cross bar one, and they all said something similar to Raynes did: 'Ah, I didn't do anything.'

I thought, 'There's something wrong here, something we don't understand, because we all expect them to describe something extraordinary.' So I came up with the idea that the reasons the Victoria Cross is awarded can be broken down into roughly four groups. In no particular order, they are: I want to help my friend; I want to help these people; I got annoyed; and somebody needs to do something.

At the end of my talks, I would say to people, 'Right, you are not going to ask me questions. I'm going to ask you them.' Then I would quiz them: 'Have you ever had a member of your family hurt themselves in the kitchen or fall over in the garden?' The answer is generally 'yes'.

'What did you do? Did you help them?'

'Yes.'

'Now, have you ever seen someone fall over in the street

or get knocked off a bicycle or fall down a flight of stairs? Someone you didn't know? If so, what did you do?'

'Oh, I went to help them.'

'OK. Have you ever got annoyed?'

'Oh yes...'

'And finally, have you ever looked out into the street and spotted a bit of wood hanging down and thought, "Someone should nail that up or someone's going to get hurt." And then three days later you are out there with your hammer?'

They say, 'Oh yes.'

And I say, 'Well, there you go. You've actually done the same as them. The only thing you don't ever want is to be in their situation, and that's the bit that makes this medal so special. Because what we have just talked about is in all of us. We would all do these things, but to stand up and do it at that moment, with the level of threat that they are under, that's the bit that makes them so special, even if they won't admit it.'

Queen Victoria was right. The Victoria Cross is not about being brave – it's about seeing a situation and knowing you've got to do something. These people don't say they are brave – that's the one thing they never say. They say, 'You know what? It had all gone horribly wrong, and I was in big trouble, and I thought, "Hell, I've got to get out of here"' or '"I've got to get him out of here"' or whatever it might be.

During my years at the museum, I had become a Freemason – I joined a local lodge at Loughton not far from home – and people used to come to my Victoria Cross talk at the museum and ask if I would be happy to give my talk at their lodge. And so gradually my reach expanded.

One of the first I did was during the 150th anniversary of the Victoria Cross in 2006. I was invited to talk at the United Grand Lodge of England on Great Queen Street in London. Not long before, Johnson Beharry of the 1st Battalion, Prince of Wales's Royal Regiment, who was awarded the Victoria Cross for his actions in saving members of his unit from ambushes in Iraq in 2004, came to see us at the museum. We had Victoria Cross replicas in the museum shop, and they came with a card that explained what the medal was all about. I asked Johnson, who has become a great friend, if he would sign one of the cards, and I took that along with me to the talk at Great Queen Street.

There were about 100 people there and the talk went well. At the end I told them about the card that Johnson had signed, and we sold tickets for it as part of the raffle to raise money for something called a CyberKnife for the Royal London Hospital. That's a pain-free, robotic, radiotherapy cancer treatment system. The Victoria Cross copy alone with its signed card raised about £600, and a delighted punter took it home with him.

You could tell this was something that people loved – the chance to have a signature from a Victoria Cross holder along with a replica medal. And afterwards, I had about seven secretaries from other lodges approach me and ask me to deliver the talk for their members. To start with it was always the Victoria Cross talk – 'For Valour: The Story of the Victoria Cross'. Then I developed a talk called 'The Medals on Grandad's Waistcoat'. This was the story of how medals were awarded from Waterloo up to the First World War, and I related it through what ribbons you might see on Grandad's waistcoat. Then there was a talk called 'The War to End all Wars', which starts in 1870 and ends in 1945. And then I did 'The Battle of the Somme', 'The Battle of Waterloo', plus talks on Pegasus Bridge and Rorke's Drift, and finally a talk called 'Hearts of Oak: The Victoria Cross Story Part Two', which illustrates each of the four categories of behaviour I have described that lie behind the award of the medal.

But the Victoria Cross has always been the most popular subject and the most in demand. After-dinner talks at Freemason lodges led to Rotary Clubs, u3a (University of the Third Age) meetings and Western Front associations. I spoke all over Britain and in Guernsey, Jersey and as far afield as Japan, Gettysburg in the United States and on cruise ships. The talks have morphed into one-man shows where I do an evening in a theatre with two forty-five-minute sessions, almost always on the Victoria Cross, split by an interval. And I get asked to talk about the Victoria Cross on news programmes when a new medal is awarded.

Everywhere I go, people come up to me at the end and say, 'Thank you.'

And I say, 'Oh, wow, and what for?'

And they go, 'For keeping these stories alive and telling us about these people.'

Some have even told me they wished I had been their History teacher at school because then they would have loved lessons. That's the sort of comment that is so pleasing to hear.

The Victoria Cross is an unending source for the sort of storytelling that I learned as a child at home. I must have given more than 500 talks based on it. I never make notes or even prepare what I am going to say. I rely on my accumulated knowledge of a subject I never stop learning about.

Not long ago I was asked to give a twenty-minute talk at the United Grand Lodge in London, an event that was being hosted by one of the highest-ranked Masons in the land, Jonathan Spence. There were 750 people present in the room, and as Jonathan was introducing me, I sat there thinking, 'I have no idea what on earth I am going to talk about. How can you talk about the Victoria Cross in twenty minutes?' It seemed such a random thing – how do you start it? What's the hook? What's the point?

Then it suddenly came to me – Spence wanted something about the Victoria Cross seen through the lens of camaraderie and service to the community. I had the first line in my head just as he invited the audience to welcome 'Mark Smith'. It was that close. But I never feel nervous – just a feeling of privilege at being able to share these stories of heroism and sacrifice.

I stood up and walked round the lodge, using the radio mic as I always do, and I don't know what I said exactly because I never do. But at the end, when I sat down, 750 people stood up to applaud, including Jonathan Spence. Afterwards they asked me for a copy of my script for the minutes. I told them I didn't have one. 'But you must have written that down,' I was told.

'Honestly,' I replied, 'I really don't know what I said. I just gave you a story, that's all.'

Chapter Twenty-One

Ever since the *Antiques Roadshow* was launched by the BBC in 1979, the talk in my family, led by Nan – Mum's mum – was always about how I should, or would, end up on what has been one of Auntie's most successful creations.

I'd hear it after I'd presented my latest militaria purchase to the assembled company before Sunday lunch. 'Oh yeah, Markie boy, you should be on *Antiques Roadshow*,' they'd tell me.

It used to make me laugh. Of course, who wouldn't want to be one of the experts talking to Britain every Sunday night about the stories behind the medals their dads and grandads won in wartime? But I never imagined it could ever happen to me.

But it did, and it all started when I got a phone call at the museum one day from a lady at the BBC in January 2014.

'Hello Mr Smith,' she said. 'I gather you're the curator at the Royal Artillery Museum in Woolwich.'

'Yes, good morning, that's me,' I said.

'Well, I am phoning from the BBC programme the *Antiques Roadshow* on behalf of Mr Simon Shaw who is the producer of the show.'

'Oh really?'

Actually, I was thinking, 'Oh wow! We've cracked it at last. They want to record an edition of the programme at the museum. We're going to be put on the map like never before. People are going to flock to see the place after an hour of prime-time free promotion.'

'Yes,' she said. 'Simon would like to meet you.'

I looked in my diary, which was busy at the beginning of the new year, and after a few seconds leafing through it, I suggested a date in mid-February. 'Would that be convenient?'

'Umm, not really,' she replied. 'He would like to see you tomorrow at BBC Broadcasting House at Oxford Circus at 4.00 p.m., if you could kindly make that.'

'OK,' I thought, 'they're obviously on a tight deadline...'

'I'll see him there,' I said.

The next day I went to Woolwich as normal and then got the train and the Tube and arrived at the Beeb in good time. I walked past the imposing presence of All Souls, Langham Place, outside Broadcasting House, and reminded myself that that was where my great-great-great-grandma and grandad got married.

I introduced myself at reception.

'I'm here to see Simon Shaw at the *Antiques Roadshow*,' I said.

'Oh yes, Mr Smith,' said the woman on the desk. 'Simon has actually rung in to tell us that he's running late and he's so sorry. He'll be about twenty minutes.'

I was directed to a canteen where I sat down with a cup of tea and waited, and waited... and waited. There were pictures of Daleks on the walls – it could *only* be the BBC – and there was a busy feel to the place, with people rushing in and out meeting friends and colleagues for a cuppa.

Then all of a sudden this chap walked in.

'Hello,' he said, 'are you Mark?'

'I most certainly am,' I replied.

He got himself a cup of tea and a second one for me. And then we started chatting. He talked about the museum and my life as a collector of medals and militaria – he seemed to know quite a lot about me – and it slowly began to dawn on me that this wasn't about promoting the museum or doing the show there, this was about me.

'Switch on, Smith!' I told myself, as I heard Shaw begin to talk about how he and his colleagues had been thinking I might be able to fit into the team of experts on the show as one of the militaria specialists.

'But the bit that worries us', he was saying, 'is we're not sure that you know the value of things in the way our experts need to, because museum people don't have to worry about the money side of the items in their collection.'

I thought, 'Hang on a minute . . . money and value have been second nature to me all my collecting life.'

'Oh yes,' I told him, 'I get that, but you have to remember I've been a medal collector for forty-odd years, and everything I do is based on values and going to militaria fairs and actually buying and selling this stuff.'

It seemed to do the trick because not long after that Shaw brought our chat towards a conclusion in a way that set my heart racing. 'OK, Mark,' he said, 'let's give it a go, shall we?'

'Thank you,' I said, trying hard not to shout it from the rooftops.

Inside I was thinking – broadly – 'Wow! Wow! . . . And wow! I'm going to get a chance to be on the show that my family watch every week – the one they've all said could be the perfect place for me.'

Now Shaw was talking about the practicalities. 'What we'll do is offer you something we call an "observer contract". That means that we get you to come along to a *Roadshow*, and we watch you and see how you get on. But, on the other side, you watch us because you don't know how hard this job is that you've just said you want to do. And honestly,' he added with a broad smile, 'you don't know what you've just said yes to. So we would like you to come along to two venues to start with. We're going to choose one, and we'd like you to choose the other. The one we'd like you to come to is this one here,' he said, pointing at the words 'Derby, Roundhouse' on a piece of paper that featured a long list of upcoming locations.

I stared at the collection of towns, cities and great houses and castles up and down Britain and Northern Ireland that were about to host the show, and right near the bottom, about four from the end, was 'Walthamstow Town Hall'.

'I'll do that one. That will be great,' I said.

I left the meeting walking on air. That day Helen was away on one of her antiquey things – probably a fair somewhere – so I had no one to celebrate with. But I was starving, and I was going to have a good time anyway. So I went to one of my favourite restaurants, which is sadly no longer there – the Gay Hussar on Greek Street in Soho.

I got a table for one and ordered smoked salmon, duck in plum sauce and a half-bottle of champagne. There was a painting on the wall in my little booth. It was a Dutch Old Master-type thing of a really large bloke with a bottle of champagne and oysters all over the table. He was on the wall in front of me, and I had my dinner with him and toasted him to boot.

The following Monday morning, I turned up at the museum as normal.

'You're not going to believe this,' I said to Steve Hookins and Paul Evans, 'but it looks like I'm going to be on the *Antiques Roadshow*.'

'What d'you mean?' said Paul.

'Well, they want me to have a go at doing militaria – you know, being an expert on the telly and so on.'

'Well, that *is* interesting,' replied Steve.

'What d'you mean?' I said.

Steve then told me about something I had no clue about. A week or so earlier, we had hosted the BBC daytime antiques and auctions show *Bargain Hunt* at the museum, and its then presenter, Tim Wonnacott. He had come, trademark colourful bow tie and all, to film a series of short items about bits of military kit and militaria connected to the First World War. It was part of the programme's output to mark the centenary of the outbreak of the war. Wonnacott and I sat down in front of the cameras in the Gunnery Hall to discuss an artillery piece, a Victoria Cross, some trench art – bits of shell casing turned into hats and ashtrays – and a rifle with a bullet hole through its magazine.

It seemed to go well enough, and I enjoyed it. But I thought no more of it as I left and headed home, leaving Steve to see them out. It was at that point that he heard

Wonnacott chatting about me to his director, who had been running our little shoot.

'He never said "er"', Wonnacott was saying. 'He never said "umm". He never went off the point. We filmed every single segment in one take, and we finished a couple of hours early. Are you on the *Antiques Roadshow*?'

The director replied in the affirmative.

'Well,' said Wonnacott, 'I reckon you've just found your new militaria man.'

So *that* was how Simon Shaw had found out about me...

When you are an *Antiques Roadshow* 'expert' or 'specialist', the first thing that happens is that you get sent a Call Sheet. This tells you where you need to be, what time, where the hotel is and all that stuff. The pattern for all the shows is the same: travel on day one; meet the public and do the show on day two, including all the filming; and then return home after breakfast on day three.

In this case, the filming in Derby was on a Sunday, so I left London from St Pancras on the Saturday morning. The BBC prefer you to travel by train to reduce the environmental impact of what they are doing, but it suits me because I don't like driving anyway. When I got to Derby, it was raining like it does in the Bible – hosing it down – complete with thunder and lightning.

Luckily, the station, the hotel and the Roundhouse were quite close to each other. I ran into the hotel, walked up to reception and told them I had a reservation under the name 'Mark Smith'. I was met with bafflement. There was no booking in that name. Eventually, I cottoned on.

'OK, perhaps the booking is under the BBC,' I said,

feeling a little self-conscious as I used those words for the first time.

'Oh, BBC – the *Roadshow* – of course, here we are Mr Smith,' came the almost instant response.

At that point, the one and only Geoffrey Munn, beloved longtime *Roadshow* expert on all things jewellery, appeared at the check-in desk. Then I heard the warm, reassuring voice that me and my nan knew so well from Sunday nights in front of the telly.

'Er, hello, good morning, Geoffrey Munn, BBC,' he said.

And they went, 'Oh yes, of course, sir,' and gave him his room card. He didn't know who I was from Adam, so he never said anything to me. I was just thinking, 'Wow, it's Geoffrey Munn from the *Antiques Roadshow*!'

I went to my room and then headed across to the Roundhouse. They had asked me to do a screen test before the filming day and had requested that I bring something along that I could discuss in front of the cameras. I had packed a little collection of medals, and I took them with me as I ran through the deluge to the venue.

It was pitch-black inside with thunder and lightning outside. There were lots of people running around, with cables all over the place. In one corner there was what's called the 'multi-cam' set up, with three or four cameras on tripods in a semicircle with lights to go with them. The sound people were there, the mixing-desk thing was set up, and Simon Shaw was there with all sorts of people buzzing around him.

I went over and introduced myself to them.

'Hello, I'm Mark Smith. I've come for a screen test.'

They couldn't have been more friendly. 'Oh hello, hello,

hello. Great to see you, Mark. Just wait a few minutes and we'll come and find you,' said one of the production staff.

I watched them go about their work for about ten minutes, and I could see how practised they were. This was a well-orchestrated process that I hoped to become a part of.

'OK, we're ready for you now, Mark, if you would like to come this way,' said one of the runners.

I walked over to the cameras. It seemed to me that pretty much everyone from the show was there watching. And there was a table with the 'AR' logo on it. 'This is so fantastic,' I thought as I laid my medals out for the first time. Then one of the sound guys came over and asked if he could put a mic on.

'Yeah, no problem,' I said.

'You've done this before, haven't you?'

'Well, not this exactly, but yes I'm pretty familiar with it . . .'

'Thought so,' he said.

Then the director of this little test exercise announced that they needed a 'punter' – someone to play the part of a member of the public who had brought the medals in to show me. He turned and pointed at a chap with radio sets, headphones and wires all over him. He was the floor manager, who was obviously busy and whose body language made it perfectly clear that he did not want to do this.

'OK, Dave, would you mind stepping into the breach?' said the director.

Reluctantly, Dave came forward and stood on the other side of the table.

I went, 'Hello.'

And he said – in a very sceptical almost-whisper – 'All right?'

He sounded completely uninterested . . . and bored.

I laid out my medals, and I heard the director say something about the sound level and the synchronization of the cameras, and then I heard the immortal words, delivered quietly and in a monotone: 'And . . . action!'

I turned to this bloke, and I said to him, with all the enthusiasm I could muster, 'So . . . so you've brought some medals to the *Antiques Roadshow* today. Where did you get them from?'

And he said, 'Well, I found them while I was burying the cat behind the shed . . .'

We all collapsed, and I can't remember what happened after that. Suffice it to say, the screen test was considered good enough.

That night, I walked into the bar in the hotel – word had gone round to meet up at 6.30 – and it was the whole *Roadshow* cast. They were all there – the aforementioned Geoffrey Munn, and some or all of the following: Philip Mould (pictures and prints), Clive Farahar (books and manuscripts), Hilary Kay (miscellaneous), Rupert Maas (pictures and prints), Dendy Easton (pictures and prints), Lennox Cato (furniture), Paul Atterbury (miscellaneous), John Benjamin (jewellery), Marc Allum (miscellaneous), Will Farmer (ceramics and glass), Duncan Campbell (silver), Jon Baddeley (miscellaneous), Judith Miller (miscellaneous), Susan Rumfitt (jewellery) and not forgetting the show's star presenter, Fiona Bruce.

As I walked in, I could see people in the hotel walking

round the bar, gossiping away to each other. You could almost hear them saying, 'Oh look, that's what's-his-name who does pictures, and that's so-and-so who does the furniture...'

I was standing there, and Alastair Dickenson, who used to do silver, came over and asked me who I was.

I said, 'Mark Smith. I'm filming tomorrow.'

It seemed to go rather quiet, and he went, 'Ah, so what do you do then?'

I said, 'Arms and militaria.'

He went, 'Oh, not another one. So there's only one question to ask you then, isn't there?'

I was thinking, 'Oh no, he's going to ask me something really tricky, about some ancient battle or other, or what size shoes Henry VIII wore with his armour.'

Instead, he said, 'What would you like, red or white wine?'

Chapter Twenty-Two

The routine for the first day of a *Roadshow* trip is pretty much the same everywhere we go.

Arrive at the hotel at 4.00 p.m., meet in the bar at 6.00. Me and my partner in crime on the militaria desk, Robert Tilney – yes, he's the cheeky chappie with the big moustache – will have texted each other to say we've arrived.

We all have a beer and then go to dinner together, experts and crew. Usually, the various producers and directors will stand up at some point and tell us about the day ahead, and we sort out lifts and how we are going to get to the venue. I would say most of us are in bed by 10.00 p.m. and down to breakfast at 6.30 a.m. sharp, ready for the long day ahead.

I never wear the clothes I'm going to film in for breakfast. I can't bear the thought of having tomato and egg down my shirt all day. So I come down dressed and then pop back upstairs afterwards to change. Then we get into taxis or hire cars and head off to the venue, where we park in the designated area for experts.

At that point the window comes down, we say 'experts', and the attendant often says something like, 'Oh look, it's those two off the telly.'

Then we do this wonderful walk to the venue, when we go past the people who are already queuing up. They don't say anything to start with – it's very polite and British – and then Robert and I start saying, 'Hello, hello.' And then they start 'helloing' us back. And that's when I do a few autographs and stop so that people can do selfies with us.

When we get into the venue, Robert and I will go off and find our table, and then we all gather for a pre-show briefing when the procedural stuff is gone through – fire drills, first aid, emergencies and so on. Then they say, 'Have a lovely day,' and we head back to our table where two stewards – often volunteers – will be marshalling our growing queue.

What Robert and I do is try to split it so that I get the medals and stuff, and Robert, who trained as an armourer, gets the stabby, pointy, killy things – the weapons. That's because, to be fair, he has a better chance of filming those, and I have a better chance of filming the medally bits. So we triage the queue, as it were, so the right person is dealing with the right stuff.

Then at 9.30 on the dot, the tannoy system crackles into life, and we hear a recording of Fiona Bruce. 'Good morning and welcome to the *Antiques Roadshow*,' she says in her familiar, friendly and confident delivery. And then the theme music plays and we're off.

That's when the unique buzz of a *Roadshow* starts, and the experts in ceramics, glass, silver, film and pop memorabilia, jewellery, toys, paintings, clothing and all sorts of bits and bobs start looking at the stuff that people have brought in. Soon the camera crews are busy recording the first segments which will actually appear on television. They will aim to do about seventy of them throughout a typical day, and it's all very lively and exciting as Robert and I start looking for that first thing we can each put forward for filming.

When people get to the front of the queue, they'll go, 'Hello, it's lovely to meet you.'

I tell them, 'It's lovely to meet you too, and what have you brought for me today?' It's always very relaxed and friendly.

They usually have a carrier bag. And then they get the thing out that they have brought along for me to see. And, as it comes out of the bag, I know what it is – I know what war it comes from, I know what country it comes from, I know what it's for and I always know what it's worth.

On my side of the table, it could be medals, photograph albums, uniforms, logbooks, flying helmets, the odd steel helmet, Christmas tins from the trenches, death plaques or memorial scrolls. Values can range from nothing to hundreds of thousands of pounds.

And when you ask people where they got the thing that came out of their carrier bag, and they don't say eBay or other 'bought sources', that's when I start to get more interested.

I will already have an idea of what its potential could be for telling a story, and now what I'm looking for is the hook. I want the little detail that's going to turn this from a mere object that someone owns, into something that can tell a story about their dad, their grandad or their great-uncle. My 'expert' bit is to be able to find something in that story that will work – and it's not necessarily how much it's worth. For me, it doesn't matter that it's worth fifteen quid, it's the story that counts.

If we want to get something filmed, we have to fill out

something called a Specialist Request Form. On it are the following headings – 'specialist', 'specialist's description of item', 'owner's name', 'owner's description of item, if different', 'maker/manufacturer/hallmark/signatures', 'important dates connected to the item and briefly why', and it then asks what sources you have used to check the item's authenticity.

Under 'director's notes' you write in what makes this item special, any interesting points about the owner or item, important dates, marks, markers or places, and finally any copyright issues or other points to include in a filmed interview.

The completed form goes to the director, who has to make a decision whether to film it or not. It's quite competitive when you consider that each expert in every field is also looking to get stuff filmed, and the directors are looking for a variety of material to make up each show. I usually aim to film five items during a day, and nowadays, in the post-Covid world, they tend to make three programmes out of each venue. That means I might get an item broadcast on each of the three programmes, sometimes two.

Occasionally, people come in and you find yourself with an embarrassment of riches. A lady appeared at the front of the queue once and took out a set of First World War medals, a photograph of her grandad and his medical bag, because he was a doctor. She also had a notebook and a map with a bullet hole through them, and she had the bullet.

I said, 'OK, stop, we're going to film this.'

I filled out one of the forms, and I took her and her things – she carried it all because none of us experts are insured to do that – and we went back to where the directors were. I explained to them what was so good about this. Then I left her there to begin what could be a long wait on a busy day and went back to my table thinking, 'I've got one in the bag. They're going to film that.'

I sat down and the next bloke in the queue said, 'Hello, I've got this . . .'

And he pulled out a set of First World War medals, a discharge scroll and a pocket watch that had a bullet stuck in it.

He said, 'This is the watch that saved my grandad.'

And I said, 'You're not going to believe this mate, but the lady before you had exactly the same thing. Come with me.'

I filled out another sheet and took it over to the producer. 'You know I told you the last one was the Holy Grail? Well, I've just got another one,' I told him. 'And d'you know what? I want to film them together.' And that's what we did.

People will queue for three or four hours to see us, and we might see up to 300 people in one day. I try to give everybody as much time as I can so that they have had the best day out ever. Most of them have always wanted to be part of the show and are quite happy to line up in the rain with all the other people, watching the cameramen at work, the runners dashing about, and hearing the radio sets crackling.

Then they come up to the table and meet someone like me or Robert, Will Farmer, Geoffrey Munn or my amazing friend Ronnie Archer-Morgan – faces they've seen on the telly – and they have such a good day. They know that not everyone is going to get filmed, and a lot of people don't want to be filmed in any case. They just want to come and show me their grandad.

With the ones that do come before the cameras, you

normally get one of two reactions. Some say, 'Oh wow, great!' and others go, 'Oh God, now I'm going to be scared!' With them the trick is to try to reassure them, make them feel at home and relaxed, and make it as easy as possible.

We never try to rush people through if we don't think they have something of interest. Everyone has to have a *Roadshow* experience. So our job is to smile all day long, and the first person and the last person in the queue has to have exactly the same experience of meeting their expert at the *Roadshow*. And they do. And I work very, very hard to achieve that. I chat to them, and we have a bit of a laugh, and it's all good stuff.

You can have a joke with people, but on the militaria table we often have to temper that and think carefully about who we are talking to when they are bringing up sometimes painful memories or telling shocking stories. And you have a duty of care not to be blunt and just say their story doesn't work or doesn't add up. That's because sometimes people come in with tall stories – collections of medals that would be impossible for any one individual to have won, or medals that are copies or fakes. Then you have to break it to them gently.

When it comes to handling things sensitively, one of the most heart-rending stories I dealt with was not about conventional militaria at all, but a woman who brought in three small pieces of simple jewellery made of tin. They were tiny little things, little shapes – a dog, a shield and a watering can. She told me they belonged to her mother and her grandmother, and one of them had been worn by her mother every day of her life. The daughter had removed it only after her mother had died.

The three brooches had been made for the women when they were inmates in a Nazi concentration camp at Theresienstadt, now in the Czech Republic. It was a show camp that Hitler's regime used to try to convince the world that such places were not sinister at all. In fact, thousands of Jews died at Theresienstadt, and thousands more were moved on from there to death camps like Dachau and Auschwitz.

On the back of one of the brooches were the initials 'DK' and a date in Polish: 8 July 1943. It was her mum's sixteenth birthday – one of the many days she had endured in captivity.

We talked about the camp, and I mentioned that the Nazis used to allow the newsreel cameras in.

'Exactly,' said the woman. 'My mum was in the choir – she was never a singer, but there was an amazing composer who was captured there. He managed to get an underground choir going, and they used to rehearse every night, and they managed to learn Verdi's entire *Requiem*. When the Nazis realized this was being done, they thought, "Let's showcase this – this will show them how well we treat these people", so they arranged a concert for the Red Cross and showed them off.'

'Were any other members of the family in the camp?' I asked her.

'All of them were taken there,' she said. 'My mother, her brother, my grandfather – my grandfather was taken to Auschwitz. My uncle died three days before his twenty-first birthday in Dachau.'

It was shocking to hear this woman's testimony, and she told it with impressive composure. It was great that it got airtime, too, because it drove home the tragedy of the war.

And in case you are wondering, we never put a value on things from the Holocaust. I won't do it, and it's *Roadshow* policy not to do so. We certainly didn't do it in this case.

That desperately sad story illustrates the difference between the fun that we have and the reality of what I do on the show. It's not medals, jewellery or photos that I am dealing with – it's real people. I have the honour and the privilege of talking about real people who often did extraordinary things – things that they never wanted to do or set out to do. But they did them. They stood up at that moment.

They might be a regular soldier who went out to the First World War, and people might say to me, 'Oh, these are only ordinary medals.'

But I look at them and say, 'Well, that's four years in the trenches, and that's appalling. That's an appalling thing to happen to anyone. And the only thing that represents those four years, and that bloke being terrified every second of every day, are those three medals.'

That's the bit that I am so in awe of. It's those people and being able to tell their stories. Their descendants come on and talk about their grandad, and I can bring his story to everyone who watches the show. People come up to me on the street, and they say, 'We love you, you're so respectful – you tell those stories so beautifully about all those wonderful people. Thank you for telling those stories.'

For me, that's the best thing anyone can ever say to me – and you can write that on my headstone.

Other experts say to me that I've got the hardest job on the *Roadshow* because I've got to know all the stuff about dates and battles and wars, and instantly know it too. It's true, there's usually no time to look this stuff up – you've got to know it.

But I say that I've got the easiest job in the world because all I do is talk about people's grandads. In my view, the other specialists are the ones who do the hard part. They've got to remember when whatever-he's-called made that chair – I couldn't do that, but talking about people's grandads is simple. Every time you say, 'Who was this?' and that person says 'That was my dad' or 'That was my grandad', everybody watching knows that kind of character. He was the one who sat in the corner of the room at Christmas, the one who never talked about the First World War. Suddenly I am telling his story for them, for him . . . to all of us.

We certainly have a laugh, me and Robert, and dogs at the *Roadshow* – a regular feature, as anyone who watches it can attest – can sometimes provide the punchline.

A few years ago, we were filming at the Abbey Pumping Station in Leicester, and during a typically hectic day the runners came round at about 3.00 p.m. and asked if Robert or I had had any lunch. We said we hadn't, and they ticked us off. 'You're supposed to have lunch, you know. It's all provided for you,' they told us.

They asked whether we would like some sandwiches instead. We both said yes and reminded them that neither of us likes lettuce. Well, we didn't have to worry on that score because they came back with some delicious ones made with cheese and pickle.

Now, Robert and I have been known to make each other cry with laughter, because we can be quite wicked to each other.

So I opened my sandwich and took a huge bite.

'They're top-notch,' I told him. 'No lettuce in sight,' I added as I put the sandwich back in its packet and placed it by the table leg on the floor, as the next person in line came forward.

'Hello,' he said, and then quickly added, 'please finish your sandwich first.'

I thanked him but told him there was no peace for the wicked and we should get on. So I sat there and listened to what he had to say about an RAF logbook from the Second World War, and when we had finished Robert came up behind me.

'D'you want to know something that has really made my day?' he whispered conspiratorially in my ear.

'What's that then?' I replied.

'That bloke's dog has just eaten your sandwich . . .'

Over the years, I have had the pleasure of meeting some amazing people and hearing about their often extraordinary parents and grandparents, so it feels invidious to pick out one or two. But I can't write about the *Roadshow* without mentioning Naik Gian Singh, whose story I heard during a visit by the programme to Glasgow in 2023.

A twenty-four-year-old soldier from the Punjab, Singh was awarded the Victoria Cross by King George VI in 1945 for his actions during the Burma campaign against Japanese forces.

His son, a smartly dressed and softly spoken gentleman in a black jacket and matching black turban, with a face framed by a white beard and moustache, told me the story of how his father had conducted two lone charges against Japanese positions. These happened during an assault against a Japanese-held Burmese village.

After destroying a machine-gun nest entirely on his own, his Victoria Cross citation describes what Singh did next. 'Our tanks had now moved up and come under fire but Naik Gian Singh, who had sustained several wounds, again rushed forward and annihilated a Japanese anti-tank gun crew, capturing the weapon single-handed. He then led the section in clearing all enemy positions.'

I've heard some stories of heroics in battle, but this was right up there.

'I know these things happen really just in the heat of the moment, but that still takes some bravery to do that,' I told his son, who was a lovely bloke. He replied that his father never talked about the war with his children and that he had lost a lot of his friends in that battle.

I then asked him if he had any idea what this Victoria Cross might be worth. He said he had never considered it and that his father had never wanted to be parted from it.

I had thought about this between meeting the son and the time we filmed it. As usual, I had not mentioned value during the chat at the table but waited until we filmed the segment so that what I said would have maximum impact. And I chose my words carefully to ensure that, rather than talk about thousands of pounds, I got the 'm' word in.

'It's a quarter of a million pounds,' I told him, as he threw his head back in disbelief and wiped tears from his eyes. Behind us, I could hear an audible gasp from the guests standing listening in the round.

Then he said, 'Even if it's worth 2 million or 10 million, still we won't part with it.'

'I understand that,' I told him. 'They are some of the

most iconic things we have in this country for our military all across the world, and I will tell you now that meeting your dad and his medals today has been a true honour. Thank you so much.'

It was an amazing find and one of the good ones but, in truth, they are all good as far as I'm concerned.

Collections of medals can knock your socks off. In 2015, we were filming in the gardens of Balmoral Castle, and this lovely bloke came to the table with a 1914 Christmas tin, or should I say a Princess Mary Gift Fund Box. These embossed brass tins had been sent out to soldiers on the Western Front on the initiative of Princess Mary, the then seventeen-year-old daughter of King George V, to provide them with treats for the festive period. Typically, they contained tobacco and cigarettes.

This chap opened the tin, and as soon as I looked inside, I knew we were going to film it. Later, in front of the cameras, I took the things out in turn.

'So who was this chap?' I asked.

'He was John Cargill, and he was my grandad,' replied the guest, whose name was John Henderson, a fisherman in his seventies who hailed from Wick in Caithness.

'What did he do?' I asked.

'He was a merchant seaman and a fisherman,' he said. 'I remember him very well. He had a small fishing boat, and I would go to sea with him before school. He would say to me, "You need to get to school," and I would say, "Don't bother, I'm happy where I am."'

The first things I pulled out were a trio of medals, the 1914–15 Star, the British War Medal and the Victory Medal.

As I laid them on the table, I explained that they were for someone who fought in the First World War who was in the Black Watch regiment. Then there was a Military Medal, a bravery award which Mr Henderson did not know anything about, having found it only after his grandad had died in 1980.

Then there was a Divisional Gallantry Card – another bravery award. But that wasn't the end of it – this was an old Christmas tin that kept on giving. Then I got out a 1939–45 Star, an Atlantic Star and a War Medal. And then I pulled out a Distinguished Service Medal (DSM), the Royal Navy equivalent of a Military Medal, which is two away from a Victoria Cross.

So now John Cargill had a George V Military Medal and a George VI DSM. I asked what he had done for the DSM, and Henderson told me his grandad had been on an anti-mine trawler. A mine had got caught up under the bow, and he had gone forward to cut it free so that the boat didn't blow up.

'That's incredible,' I said. 'But it doesn't stop there, does it?'

And that's because, before all the other medals were bestowed on him during the two world wars, Cargill had served as a Quartermaster aboard the RMS *Carpathia*. This was a transatlantic passenger steamship owned by the Cunard Line. It became famous in the immediate aftermath of the sinking of the *Titanic* in April 1912 when it altered course to find survivors in the icy waters of the North Atlantic.

After arriving at the scene four hours after the sinking, her sailors in rowing boats – nineteen-year-old John Cargill among them – managed to rescue 705 *Titanic* survivors, including babies. For that he was awarded a bronze Carpathia Medal. These were issued to crew, while officers were given silver ones.

Henderson explained how his grandfather, who lived at Gourdon on the Aberdeenshire coast, had ended up on the *Carpathia*. 'He was a fisherman, and when things were tough he would take himself off to earn some money,' he said. Later in Cargill's life, at an event reuniting *Titanic* survivors with their rescuers, a woman who was saved as a child by *Carpathia* crewmen recognized Cargill and approached him to thank him.

I was shaking when I held that Carpathia Medal – I'd never touched one before. The collection was astounding – it was hard to imagine anyone being awarded a Military Medal, a DSM and a Carpathia Medal all in one lifetime. It was virtually impossible, and this was undoubtedly one of the rarest groups of medals anywhere in the world.

'You have made my year,' I told Henderson. 'You have one of the most amazing groups of medals I have ever seen.' On that day I valued the collection at about £10,000, but that was a figure I was advised to use because the *Roadshow* had dealt with complaints in the past about valuing items from the *Titanic*. If I saw them today, I would probably say £75,000.

It can be highly emotional hearing the stories behind medals, and I know people cry when they watch some of them on the *Roadshow*. And that goes for one or two people in high places. I know this because, after I got run over, I started doing talks to raise money for the London Air

Ambulance. They had ferried me to hospital that day when I was knocked down in Leytonstone.

When the service took delivery of two new helicopters, Helen and I were invited to help celebrate their arrival at an event at RAF Northolt where guests also included David Beckham, who was charming. The star guest, though, was Prince William, and we were duly presented to him in a line at the base.

When his equerry introduced me, he told the prince I had been one of the Air Ambulance's patients, and that I appeared on the *Antiques Roadshow*. William said, 'I know. I don't watch the *Antiques Roadshow* myself, but my wife does. And when I told her I was going to meet you, she said, "Ah, he's the one that makes me cry every week."'

Finally, a word about Fiona Bruce, who has been the presenter of the *Antiques Roadshow* since 2008 when she took over from Michael Aspel. When I first arrived, I was in awe of her because she was the star of the show. But Fiona is down to earth and a warm, friendly and fun person to work with. She is certainly not aloof. She is part of the team, and she joins in and is very, very good at what she does – a complete professional. I would say that, in real life, she is pretty much exactly like the person you see on telly.

Chapter Twenty-Three

In March 2017, I fell down the stairs.

I still think about it every time I linger on the landing, preparing to go out, and wonder how I did it.

It happened on a Friday morning, and I know that because I was getting ready for the first of two lunches that year held by the Benevolent Autocrats' Leisure and Luncheon Society. They were always on a Friday at the RAF Club on Piccadilly, and at the time I was the president.

The society was created in 1991 after the First Gulf War among a group of us working at the MoD by Stuart Cloke – incidentally, my best man. It has since grown to about 140 members made up of people from all walks of military and service life – soldiers, sailors, airmen, policemen, firemen and ambulance men. We get together, have a great lunch with wine taken, and then raise money through raffles and auctions for good causes. They have included stroke and diabetes charities, and the armed forces charity Blesma that helps limbless veterans. During my ten years at the helm, which ended in 2022, we raised over £30,000.

That morning, I was planning to meet up with fellow society member Chris Balm, an old friend who shares my passion for medal collecting. We were going to rendezvous at Charing Cross and then make our way to the club. I had been in the library at home – aka my study – and I came out onto the landing at the top of the stairs and called the dogs. They needed to go out first.

'You two ready for a quick walk?' I said, watching Tilly and Molly respond with their usual dizzying pirouettes. Having come bounding out to meet me, they stampeded down the thirteen stairs to the hallway leading to the front door. Down there, tails wagging, they were looking up at me.

'Come on then – we're ready, let's go,' they were saying as I pulled my jacket on.

I don't know how my right foot slipped on the carpeted top step, but it did. It came up in the air and, as I tried to stop myself falling, arms flailing, the other foot slipped off the edge of the step too. Our stairs are quite steep, with wooden bannisters on the right-hand side as you look down, and I had generated enough forward momentum to clear the first three steps and land on my back on the edge of the fourth one. Then I hit the next step just below my neck, before tumbling down the rest of them and landing in a heap at the bottom.

I heard an enormous thump when I hit the steps for the first time, and afterwards I lay there with the wind knocked out of me and the dogs fussing around me. Instinctively, I started to shout, and that's when the pain hit home. It was agony. After several minutes I had got my breathing under control, and I gingerly made my way back upstairs, where I thought I would lie down on the bed.

But I couldn't lie down. It was too painful. So I thought

I would sit down. But I couldn't do that either. So I sort of leaned against the bed thinking, 'God, this hurts.'

It was not long after that that I realized I was going to need an ambulance. But first things first, and me being me, I would have to shave and wash before they came to get me.

Somehow, I worked through the – it has to be said – extreme discomfort, and got myself ready, shaving and brushing my teeth, and then I phoned for help. It must have been about forty minutes after I'd fallen.

'Who is the casualty?' I heard the lady at the other end ask.

'It's me,' I mumbled.

She must have misheard, because her next question was, 'Is the patient breathing?'

'Yes, I would say so – he is,' I answered, inducing a spasm of pain in my chest as I suppressed a giggle. At that stage, I thought I must have broken several ribs. I knew a bit about that from previous accidents, after all.

'What have you done?' she was asking.

'I've fallen down the stairs and hurt my back,' I said.

She wanted to know if I was on my own, which I was – Helen being already out at work – and whether I could open the front door, which I could. She told me the ambulance was on its way.

I carefully manoeuvred myself back down the stairs, and sat on the bottom step where I called the dog-walker and explained what had happened, and then waited.

After about twenty minutes, two blokes appeared at the door in all their kit. I let them in.

'OK, what have you done?' one of them asked.

'Ah, I fell down the stairs,' I told him.

'And where does it hurt?'

'My back, it's my back,' I replied.

'Oh, OK, you've probably just knocked the wind out of yourself. You'll be all right. D'you think you can walk to the ambulance?'

I went out and crossed the road, climbed into the back and sat in a chair on the left-hand side.

'You feeling all right?' the other one asked me.

'I'm going to be honest, no I'm not. This really hurts,' I said.

He went, 'OK. We'll pop you up to Whipps Cross where they can take a look at you, OK?'

When we got to the hospital, they put me in a wheelchair and rolled me into reception where the guy leaned over the desk and looked down at me from what seemed like a great height.

'What you done, then?' he asked in a matter-of-fact way.

'Ah, fell down the stairs,' I said.

'How many?'

'All of them,' I said.

'How many of them were there?'

'Thirteen,' I said.

And at that point everything changed. People started rushing around me, and I got taken out of the wheelchair and put on something I remembered from being run over on Leytonstone High Road – that old friend the spine board.

It was about as horrible as I recalled from the first time round, as I lay in a cubicle stuck on its hard surface with my neck in a brace, staring at the ceiling and listening to a family saying goodbye for the last time to an old boy next door.

Eventually they took me down for a CT scan – another familiar experience from the aftermath of the accident in Leytonstone – and then left me back in the cubicle, staring at the ceiling for about another hour.

After what seemed a lifetime, someone leaned over my face and said, 'Mr Smith?'

'Yes?'

'Well, we've had a look and you've broken your back in two places.'

'Really? Oh great.'

'Yes. Two vertebrae are cracked, but the injuries look stable and we are going to fit you with a brace, which should do the trick.'

I was delighted to be released from the board, but the brace was hardly much better. It was a black waistcoat-type thing with metal rods inside it, and it looked like a cross between a stab vest and a flak jacket. It was secured with a series of Velcro tabs. It was to be my ever-present instrument of torture, twenty-four hours a day, for the next six weeks.

They helped me get dressed, gave me a squirt of morphine in my mouth and sent me on my way. Once again, my near neighbour and dear friend Siobhan Tyrrell – who is also on the *Roadshow*, specializing in jewellery and medals for women – came to the rescue, turning up in a cab to take me home. She also got hold of Helen for me and explained what had happened. 'Markie's had a bit of a tumble,' was how she started that conversation.

That brace thing was monstrously uncomfortable. It was

like the plaster cast from hell that you could take off only when you wanted to wash. It was all I could do to get through the prescribed six weeks with my upper body encased in it, helped by regular doses of painkillers.

To start with, I overestimated my ability to deal with the pain and discomfort. We had been given a voucher the previous Christmas for tea for two at Fortnum & Mason, and the following weekend we had booked to go. Helen had offered to cancel but I insisted. 'Sure, I can handle this,' I thought.

I put my clothes on and the flak jacket under my sports jacket, and we got the train to Liverpool Street and then the Tube to Green Park. That's a lot of walking and stairs, incidentally. It was by the time we were making our way down Piccadilly that the thought finally occurred that this was too much. 'You can't do this – this is hideous,' I muttered to myself.

We got to Fortnums, where one of the other customers recognized me off the *Roadshow* – it was one of the first times that had happened to me – and we had tea. But I knew there was no way I could get home the way we had come. At that point I gave in to the inevitable, and we called a cab to take us all the way back to Walthamstow.

I've recovered, but ever since that accident I've been dealing with a long-term back problem, with the pain registering about two out of ten on an average day. When I spend a lot of time typing up medal catalogues, or standing talking on a battlefield for hours, it can go up to eight or nine on the scale. It never stops . . . right between the shoulder blades all the time. But I've got used to it, and life carries on.

Chapter Twenty-Four

I don't think I'll ever forget hearing Stevan Bennett mention that he had been trying to track down a lady called 'Hilda Shirt'.

What he said, standing in the hall of a golf club near Poole in Dorset one evening a couple of years ago, stopped me cold. In fact, Stevan himself would later describe me as looking as if I'd been shocked by a cattle prod.

That's because, in the militaria world, you could liken the impact of hearing what he said to me winning the lottery. It was that unlikely he would say those two words and that I would be there to hear them.

Hilda Shirt was, of course, Harry's mum – Dad's best friend's mum – and how Stevan came to be looking for her is a lovely story. How I found out about it was an amazing coincidence, and it would lead to one of the best things that's ever happened to me, something that would bring me closer than I ever thought possible to Dad and his Catalina flying boat in the war.

It was Paul Evans, my former No. 2 at Woolwich, who initiated the series of events that would see me meeting Stevan. And not only meet him but end up the proud possessor of the flying boots worn by my dad's pilot, Flight Lieutenant John Ayshford, a priceless memento of their time together in the RAF.

After the Royal Artillery Museum closed, Paul got a job working as Communications Officer at Hamworthy Barracks in Poole where the Special Boat Squadron is based. As Remembrance Sunday approached in 2022, he asked if I would come down and give my Victoria Cross talk at a local golf club.

I was very happy to do so and got on the train, arriving in plenty of time to entertain a room full of about 150 people sitting at round tables. They were tucking into a roast dinner, and then it would be my turn to get up and deliver my talk. There was a stage in the room, but I couldn't stand on it because it was full of all sorts of bits of militaria – a Bren gun, a parachute, uniforms on dummies, sandbags and so on.

When I arrived and mentioned to my host that it was great to see that stuff on show, he explained where it had come from.

'Oh yes,' he said, 'there's a bloke in the village who offered it to us when he heard that you were coming. It's his private collection, and he'd love to say hello if you have a moment at some point.'

'Oh, that's great,' I said. 'Is it all right if we do it at the end? It would be good to get the talk done first.'

'No, no, that's no problem,' he said.

With the talk duly delivered, we were chatting again and the host ushered this chap over.

'Mark, this is Stevan,' he said.

I assumed he had said 'Stephen' and got that wrong at the

first go. Stevan brushed that to one side and said how lovely it was to meet me as we shook hands.

'It's lovely to meet you too,' I said. 'You've got some nice stuff up here,' I added, gesturing at the stage behind us.

'Yeah, I've got some good things,' he said.

'I particularly like the Bren gun,' I said, and we carried on chatting about it for a few moments until we moved on to flying kit – one of my favourite topics. It was at that point that I noticed a pair of brown boots sitting among all the other kit.

'Oh wow, incredible. I like your flying boots. Where did you find those?'

'Ah, well,' said Stevan, 'there's a good story with them.'

'Oh yeah?'

'Yeah, I bought them at a militaria fair a few years ago. And when I got home I found a letter inside one of the boots, and it was from the mother of a lad who had been killed on this chap's aircraft.'

'Hmm, that's pretty cool,' I said, not thinking for a moment that those boots and that letter might have anything to do with my dad or Harry.

I was actually thinking, 'That's such a cool thing to have found.' And thinking too how much I would love to find an old flying boot with a letter inside. I knew something like that could be the starting point for a whole world of fascinating research that could lead to identifying someone and what they did. I'd heard about letters like that and seen letters from the First World War from mothers to senior officers about their sons, and from the Second World War too.

Stevan then moved on to the punchline. 'Yeah, it really

got to me because it's such a nice letter, and I thought, "D'you know what? I'm going to try and give this back to the family." And I have spent the last eight years or so trying to track down this lady called . . ."

And that's when he said, 'Hilda Shirt.'

And I stood there, staring in disbelief at him.

What I said next was, 'The lad who was killed was Flight Sergeant Thomas Henry Shirt, 240 Squadron, B Flight, and the boots belong to a man called Flight Lieutenant Johnny Ayshford.'

Now it was Stevan's turn to stare in disbelief. 'How on earth d'you know that?' he asked.

I told him that Harry was Dad's best friend, and that he had been killed standing next to him on board their Catalina flying boat by Japanese machine-gun fire during a night operation over northern Sumatra.

'What?'

'Yes, and I knew Johnny Ayshford and had lunch with him and my dad not long before Johnny died.'

You could sense the collective amazement, shock even, among the people standing round listening to this exchange, as Stevan and I filled in all the gaps on both sides of this incredible story.

Stevan then showed me the letter Harry's grief-stricken mum had written to Ayshford from her home in a little village in the Peak District of Derbyshire, three weeks after Harry's funeral in Madras. I read it for the first time, moved by the depth of sadness she was feeling at the loss of her 'dear boy' whose death had preoccupied my dad's life until the day he died. Seeing her handwriting, in neat blue fountain pen, it all felt so real and immediate, even though nearly eighty years had elapsed since she wrote it.

Flt Lt J. M. Ayshford
240 Squadron
RAF
South East Asia Air Force

Station Road
Dove Holes

23/5/45

Dear Flt Lt Ayshford

I thank you for your letter concerning the death of my son, Harry. I am so sorry not to have replied before, but the shock of Harry's death has made me very unwell, and I did wait to reply to you myself. I do wish to thank you most sincerely and to all the members of your crew for all you did for my dear boy.

It breaks my heart to think of your desperate journey back with him. What an ordeal it must have been for you all. Harry was, I know, very happy with you all and, in almost his last letter, said how very fortunate he was to be with such a grand lot of fellows. His letters were always so cheery [that I felt I was there with you] so much.

Sorrows such as these seem almost more than we can bear, and if it were not for the comfort of our friends around us, we should never survive them. I have this morning received the photographs of Harry's funeral.

It has been most kind of the squadron commander to send them, and I am writing to thank him. It does give us some little idea of where he is laid.

I should like to send out some money to buy flowers, and I wonder, if I can manage to send some, if you would kindly see to this for me. When I feel a little better, I will make enquiries.

May I thank you again for the sympathy and kindness conveyed in your letter, and also for the nice things you say about my dear one. I should be very pleased to see you when you return. May God keep you all and bring you all safely home to your dear ones.

I am yours sincerely

Hilda Shirt

This brought back so many memories and so many stories my dad had told me about his crew and about their life in India, and it reminded me that I had promised him I would go out to visit Harry's grave. On that score, a few days after I met Stevan, he emailed me a copy of a photograph from a local history book about Dove Holes. The picture was of Harry's funeral in Madras in St Mary's Cemetery on 4 May 1945, and there, clearly visible, was my dad. I had never seen it before.

At some point after our meeting, Stevan wrote to the *Antiques Roadshow* and told them about this story. They then got in touch with me, and I explained that this was really quite an amazing thing by anyone's standards. And so they invited Stevan to come to one of our shows at Swanage Pier in Dorset in 2023.

Stevan brought along the boots and the letter. On camera, on a fine summer's day, we told the story together of that dramatic first meeting in Hamworthy. We explained how we had worked out how the boots linked Hilda, Harry, Johnny Ayshford, my dad, me and Stevan.

And drawing on our earlier conversations about the night Harry was killed, Stevan explained that I would not have been there in front of him that day in Swanage had not Harry and my father exchanged places in the aircraft a few minutes before it was hit by a fusillade of gunfire that left Harry mortally wounded.

'Had they not swapped places, you wouldn't be standing here talking to me today,' said Stevan. I tried to read out Hilda's letter, but the powerful emotions under the surface quickly got the better of me. 'I can't do it. I can't do it. You go,' I told Stevan, who then read it out himself.

Afterwards, I explained how Dad was in a state of shock on the way back from the mission and wouldn't accept that Harry – who was lying in the starboard bunk on the plane – had died. 'He held Harry's hand for pretty much all the way back, and the doctor, when they landed, told him that Harry was gone. And you showed me a photograph of Harry's funeral, which I'd never seen before' – it duly appeared on screen – 'and here is my dad, standing at the back.'

Then I produced something Stevan had not seen before. It was a photo my dad had taken three weeks before Harry's death. 'And there's Harry,' I said pointing at him in the picture. 'There's my dad. And there's Johnny Ayshford, the owner of your boots.'

'It makes me quite emotional,' said Stevan, looking at it. I had to agree.

'Yes, I think that one got me as well,' I said.

Then came something I was not expecting. 'Well, there is one last final surprise,' Stevan told me. 'Johnny was your dad's pilot, so I believe these boots belong to you. And they're going back with you no matter what.'

He handed them to me, and I hugged him. 'Thanks mate. Dad says thank you . . . blimey!' I said with tears in my eyes.

Later, I told the programme what having those boots meant to me. 'They are incredible. To have something from my dad's crew again – just incredible. I will treasure them forever,' I said.

And indeed, they are treasured. They sit under my chair at my desk at home, and I often think that if the house burnt down they would be one of the only things I would rush to chuck out of the window. The connections with them are so strong. When I met Johnny Ayshford he was an old man, but in the wartime photos he looks like a big kid with a huge moustache. It's funny because they all thought he and Don Hendrie, the Navigator/Bomb Aimer, who was thirty when he joined the crew, were so old. But you look at Johnny and he was only a youngster, really.

I often think about this and wonder what brought Stevan and me together. What are the chances of finding a bit of an aeroplane, or something that was in an aeroplane, that your dad flew in? Virtually nil. What are the chances of finding the medals of someone from your dad's crew? That's almost impossible, too. So to have someone turn up out of the blue, not only with a pair of boots that were there at the time, but with the letter of the mother of the man I had heard about almost every single day of my life, was incredible. I can hold that letter from Hilda Shirt in my hands. Hers was a name I had known so well for all those years. I always knew that Harry lived in Dove Holes in Derbyshire – I've always known this stuff – and now I have the proof.

The year 2025 was the eightieth anniversary of Harry's death, and meeting Stevan and being given Johnny's boots seemed to underline that it was now the right time to undertake my long-planned trip to visit him in Madras. In doing so, I would be honouring that promise I made to my dad shortly before he died.

Postscript

Years ago, probably in the early 1990s, the Commonwealth War Graves Commission announced that you could write to them about the grave of any soldier, sailor or airman buried anywhere in the world and they would send you a photo of that grave.

I told Dad about this, and he duly wrote off. A few weeks later, he got back a photo of Harry Shirt's headstone in Madras. It came in a little folder thing.

The day it arrived, Dad was sitting in his usual armchair opposite the telly in the front room at Mum and Dad's, and I was sitting opposite him. After he'd shown me the picture, I said, 'I'm going to go and see him one day.'

'Oh yeah?' he said.

'Yes, Dad. I'm going to go out to Madras and find that grave. Why don't we go together?'

But he said he didn't want to go, and with a finality that made it clear to me he had made up his mind. I think it had all come too late for him.

'OK,' I said. 'Well, I'll go and see Harry on your behalf.'

As the years ticked by and we lost Dad, and then came the remarkable story of Johnny Ayshford's flying boots, the feeling that I had to go steadily intensified. Then, almost before I knew it, it was the eightieth anniversary of Harry's death in April 2025, and I could sense this tunnel leading me towards India. It was a country I'd been to on holiday several times but without going anywhere near Madras, or Chennai as it is now called.

The final impetus came from the process of writing this book. After telling the story not only of my life, but of my father's wartime exploits and of the impact that the death of Harry had had on him, it seemed the natural conclusion that the story demanded. I simply had to go to India.

Because of what turned out to be a minor health issue (I pulled a muscle in my chest swinging a new golf club, and everyone – including me – thought I had had a heart attack), I missed the actual anniversary of Harry's death, 26 April. Instead, I found myself at Heathrow alongside Helen and our old friend Annalise Bush in early July 2025. Annalise had always wanted to visit India and jumped at the chance to join us when I asked her if she would like to come.

It was to be a five-day trip. Its sole objective was to find Harry's grave and pay homage to the young man from Dove Holes in Derbyshire, as I had promised my dad and myself that I would do years earlier. With that in mind, Helen created a little WhatsApp group for us. It was called 'The Hunt for Harry'.

I've been on planes so many times for work, for holidays, but never a flight of this duration for something like this – to visit a cemetery and a single grave on the other side of the world. And in the dead of night, as we cruised eastwards towards the sunrise over Chennai, I sat fretting about whether we would succeed in our mission.

On the Commonwealth War Graves Commission website, it told you where Harry's grave was. It was in a plot on the south side of St Mary's Cemetery, an overgrown Victorian, Raj-era British graveyard not far from the centre of Chennai. But it said the plot was inaccessible due to 'health and safety' issues. A wall was falling down, and the place was no longer safe to enter. This was tormenting me. I thought to myself, 'I'm flying all the way to India, and when I get there I'm not going to be able to visit Harry's grave.'

Chennai airport was noisy, hot, stuffy and full of exotic smells, even at three o'clock in the morning. That day the temperature hit 44 degrees, and the humidity was off the scale. It was a Thursday, and we had arranged a guide and a driver to take us from our hotel in the centre of the city to the cemetery on the Saturday. We filled in the time with a trip to a local food market on the Thursday afternoon, and to a church full of memorials to old British soldiers from the 1700s and 1800s on the Friday.

Then the day I had been waiting for arrived. The guide and driver were ready for us at lunchtime as we stepped out of the hotel, me with a Royal British Legion wreath in hand that I had brought out from England. I had written on the card 'Harry. Always Remembered' – a message from all of us, but also from Harry's great-niece, Katie Tanfield, who was aware that we had gone to India to find him.

'You really want to go to *this* cemetery?' said the guide, pointing at a spot on the city map with barely concealed incredulity after we explained what we wanted to do.

'Yup,' I said firmly, though I was still not completely

certain we would be heading to the right cemetery in the right part of town.

We set off down a busy trunk road heading out of the city. The road was chaotic, but luckily we were only on it for about ten minutes before the guide asked the driver to turn abruptly to the left through what looked like a hole in a wall, barely big enough to fit a car.

Then we drove down a little track for about fifty yards and stopped.

'This is it – we're here,' said the guide as we got out in front of some wrought-iron gates with a big padlock on them. Alongside them was a doorway, and we went through to find a little hut where the man who looked after the graveyard lived. There were toys lying around outside, washing hanging from the trees, and plastic shoes lined up outside the door. There was a brief discussion and much shaking of heads between the cemetery man and the guide.

'I'm afraid we have a problem,' said the guide.

I knew what was coming. It was health and safety, and they were going to say we couldn't get in.

'I've flown 5,000 miles for this, and we do *not* have a problem,' I announced politely but firmly once again.

It seemed to do the trick because we then set off through this old graveyard, which was a bit like Highgate Cemetery in North London, except a hundred times more overgrown and with probably a million snakes and 45 gazillion spiders. We kept to the gravel path as it wound its way through the gravestones of British men, women and children who had lived in Madras during the Raj.

Then the path changed. Instead of crushed stones and

brick, it had become grass, clipped and neat, and it led to a small metal gate with a familiar sign fixed to it: 'At this location there are Commonwealth War Graves'. There was also a sign saying the cemetery was temporarily closed. It said 'Inconvenience caused is deeply regretted'.

Beyond the gate, the scene took my breath away. There in the sunlight lay an immaculately tended graveyard with rows of headstones set out on a billiard-table lawn, just as you might find in France or Belgium, and with a large white stone cross standing sentinel over them. There were roses and shrubs growing in front of many of the graves, and the plot was surrounded by beautifully clipped hedging. It all sat shimmering in the heat, and we could hardly believe our eyes. You could tell that this place was loved and looked after.

The crumbling wall was quickly circumvented as the cemetery manager showed me a place where he, myself and the guide could climb over it and gain access. Helen and Annalise remained outside but were never more than a few yards from me as I began walking through the 125 graves of British officers and men from familiar service backgrounds.

There were men buried there from the Hampshire Regiment, the Wiltshire Regiment, the Royal Berkshires, the Devonshires, the Royal Engineers, the Royal Artillery, the Royal Corps of Signals, the Royal Navy and, of course, the Royal Air Force.

'So who are we looking for?' asked the guide.

'His name is Shirt,' I said as we continued walking up and down the neat rows. 'Harry Shirt.'

I had gone up the first line and Harry wasn't there. Then I walked back down the second line and Harry wasn't there either. Then I walked back up again and got to the very end of the next row and there he was, over by the wall. As I turned the corner, I saw the letters T. H. Shirt carved into the headstone of grave No. 108, and I heard myself say out loud, 'Hello Harry. You don't know me, but I've come on behalf of Les.'

I called out to Helen and Annalise to come round to be close to where I was, and we all stood quietly trying to take it all in. I said to Helen, 'Look, it's Harry,' and she burst into tears. Then Annalise burst into tears, the guide started crying, and so did the chap from the cemetery. I just stood there and said, 'Harry, mate, we've come to see you.'

Then I stepped forward, placed the wreath against the headstone, stepped back and stood to attention. I could almost hear Harry saying, 'Who are you and what on earth are you all doing here today?' In my head I tried to explain who I was and why I had come all that way.

I went behind the headstone as I do for every soldier, sailor or airman that I take people to see on battlefield tours, and, with both hands placed firmly on the top of the stone, I recited the immortal words from Laurence Binyon's 'For the Fallen'.

> 'They shall grow not old, as we that are left grow old:
> Age shall not weary them, nor the years condemn.
> At the going down of the sun and in the morning
> We will remember them.'

With tears in all of our eyes once again, we stood for another minute or so in silence before I enunciated the Kohima Epitaph.

'When you go home, tell them of us, and say
For your tomorrow, we gave our today.'

And then I stood there for a while because I couldn't do anything else. There was nothing else to do.

Eventually, I pulled out the photograph Stevan had given me of Harry's funeral and, even though some of the features of the wall surrounding the plot had changed, I was able to match the scene. It brought home to me that this was exactly where Dad and his crew led by Johnny Ayshford had stood just over eighty years previously, burying their fallen comrade with full military honours.

This was more than a special moment. It was a moment in my life I will never forget.

Out of all of the thousands of headstones that I've seen on battlefield tours over the last forty years, this is the one headstone that means more to me than all of the others. Because with all the others, I've seen the photographs of the men concerned, or their medals, but this is the only one I've ever been to for a person I actually thought I knew. He wasn't just a photo, and he wasn't just a headstone, and I don't mean that disrespectfully to all the others, but bless them, I didn't know them. But to turn that corner and see 'T. H. Shirt, Royal Air Force Volunteer Reserve, Died 26 April 1945' genuinely stopped me in my tracks.

We were probably the only people to have visited that grave from Britain in the last eighty years, and I'm very conscious of that fact. I often say to people, 'If you've got someone in France or not too far away, please go and see them because, even if you just go once, they do just deserve it. Just once.' And there's a bit of me that says, 'One day, sometime, I'll go and see Harry again. I will.'

On the way out, we all thanked the cemetery manager profusely for the excellent work he does looking after a graveyard that so few people from Britain visit. He smiled warmly at us as we left.

That night, Helen, Annalise and I toasted Harry at dinner. Between us there was a wonderful feeling of mission accomplished. We did it.

Acknowledgements

This book is not only an account of my life, but an acknowledgement of almost all the people to whom I owe my thanks and who have been part of my world. So rather than pick anyone out, I would like to say thank you to every one of them.

Mark Smith
November, 2025

Picture Credits

Insets

All pictures care of the author except:

p.1 bottom two, source unknown
p.2 top left, Crown Copyright
p.3 top right, Crown Copyright
p.4 top left, Crown Copyright
p.5 top, Crown Copyright
p.10 top, Wikimedia Commons
p.15 middle, Wikimedia Commons

Index

accidents
  aircraft 81, 121–2, 127, 130
  car 107–10, 212–15, 221
  stairs 277, 278–82
  trains 79–81, 117
Accrington Pals 169–72
After the Battle (magazine) 29, 86–7, 88, 90
air accidents 82, 121–2, 127, 130
Air Gunners
  brevet badge 19–20
  training 79, 117–22
air-sea rescue missons 196–8
aircraft *see also* Catalina flying boat
  B.E.2 biplane 158–9
  Blenheim bomber 17–18
  Botha bombers 82, 117
  de Havilland Dominie 79
  Harrier jump-jets 107
  Harvards 118–19
  Lysanders 118–19
  Oxfords 119–22
  Percival Proctor 79
Aircrew Association 36

Airfix kits 17–18
airshows 18
Akrotiri, Cyprus 182
Albert, Prince 239
Alexandra Palace 211
AMOT (Army Museums Ogilby Trust) 218, 219–20
Ansell (office manager), fire-watch duties 40–1
ant attacks 193–4
Antiques Roadshow
  Balmoral Castle 2014 episode 272
  Derby Roundhouse episode 254, 256–7, 259–60
  dogs 270
  Étaples Military Cemetery episode 174
  Glasgow 2023 episode 270–2
  Harry Shirt's story 289
  Mark joins 251–4
  people's stories 31, 266–9, 270–4
  roadshow routine 256, 261–6
  screen test 257–9

Antiques Roadshow – cont'd.
  Walthamstow Town Hall
    episode 60–1, 254
Apex Badge 100
archaeology 104–5, 134–5, 219
Army Foundation College,
  Harrogate 235
army pensions 14–15
Arras, Battle of 160–1
Atlantic convoys 127–9
Australian 8th Brigade 154–5
Austria, War Museum of
  Military History, Vienna
  189–90
Ayres, John 'Jack' 243, 244
Ayshford, John M.
  appearance 290
  background 124
  Catalina captain/co-captain
    36, 195, 198
  death 286
  flying boots 284, 286, 289,
    290–1
  jaundice 132
  letter from Hilda Shirt
    287–8, 289, 291

badges
  Air Gunners 19–20
  car accidents 110
  Combined Cadet Force
    (CCF) 100
  Sweden travel souvenir 209
Baldwin & Sons, A. H. 237–8

Balm, Chris 277–8
Barbed Wire Tours Ltd 163
Bargain Hunt (TV series) 255–6
Barker, Chris 107–10
Battle of Britain 88–9, 92
*The Battle of Britain: Then and
  Now* (Ramsey) 88–9
battlefield guiding 163–70,
  172–6, 235
Bay of Bengal 194–5, 198
BBC Broadcasting House 252–4
B.E.2 biplane 158–9
Beckham, David 275
beer rent 103–4
Beharry, Johnson 247
Benevolent Autocrats' Leisure
  and Luncheon Society 277
Benghazi, Libya 131
Bennett, Stevan 283, 284–6,
  288–9
Binyon, Laurence 298
Bird, Mr (Dunkirk survivor)
  148–9
Bizet, Georges, *The Pearl
  Fishers* 54–5
Björling, Jussi 54
blackmail 182–3
Blackpool 75, 123
Blenheim bomber 17–18
Blesma 277
Bliss, Georg 93–4
Blitz 9–10, 23, 38–41, 44–7
BOAC (British Overseas
  Airways Corporation) 207

Boer War 8, 240
Bolden, Theresa 113–14
Botha bombers 82, 117
Braight, F/Sgt 120, 121–2
The Bravest of the Brave
  (Glanfield) 242
British Museum 104
The British People, 1902– 1975
  (Smith & Mauger) 209
broadsword, basket-hilted 32–3
Brouillet, Madame 136, 140
Bruce, Fiona 262, 275
Bryant, Sergeant 102–4
Buchan, William 143
Burma 194–6, 201, 270–1
Bush, Annalise 211, 213, 214,
  294, 297, 298
butchery 12, 49–50

cabinet of curiosities 99
Cairo, Egypt 131
Callaghan, David 242
car accidents 107–10, 212–15,
  221
Carew Cheriton,
  Pembrokeshire 119–22
Cargill, John 272–4
Carpathia, RMS 273–4
Carr, Jason (JJ) 87, 107–10
Cason, Harry 41
Catalina flying boat
  Atlantic anti-submarine
    patrols 127–30
  Burma service 194–5

flight time 3, 124
journey out to Madras 130–2
landing on water 126–7
lands in Kyaukpyu 201–2
Les's flying hours 1
Mark's flight over London 1–5
'Nickel II' sortie, leaflet
  dropping, Japanese attack
  198–202
photography 127, 195
rudder control system 4
size and design 123–4
Special Duties Operations,
  Japanese territory 195–202,
  207
Ceylon 132
Chamberlain, Neville 224
Chapman, Annie 50
charities 188, 235, 247, 274–5,
  277
Chennai (Madras), India 130,
  193, 203, 294–6
Child, Anthony 244
Christmas Day storytelling
  9–10, 14
Churchill, Winston 78
cinema 113, 115
Civil Service exams 147, 177
claymores 32–3
Cloke, Stuart 277
Coates, Tom 125, 132, 202
coins 237
collecting
  completing sets 27

collecting – *cont'd.*
  Mark's First World War collection 33–4, 143–4, 151–61
combat, unarmed 97–8
Combined Cadet Force (CCF) 95–8, 100–4
Commonwealth War Graves Commission (CWGC) 152, 172, 235, 293, 295
concentration camps 266–8
conservation 219
coral poisoning 132
Cormack, Peter 217–18, 219
Coppersmut, Mrs 235
Crawford, Vic 125, 199, 200–1
Culloden, Battle of 33
curtain purchase 185
Cyprus 182

D-Day 169
Darby, Jane 179
Das Boot 113
Davies, Charlie 98
Deadman, Frank 39
Deep Wreck Mysteries (TV series) 236
DHSS (Department of Health and Social Security) 133–4
Dickenson, Alastair 260
Dickerson, Henry (ggg grandad) 8, 96
Distinguished Service Medal (DSM) 272

dogs 111–12, 269, 278
Downing, Jimmy 155
Downing Street, IRA bomb 181
Duerden, Orrell Taylor 170–2
Dunkirk 37–8, 148–9
Dunstan, Edward (brother-in-law) 191, 213
Dunstan, Helen (wife)
  antiques fairs 211
  background 191–2
  career 191
  curtain purchase 185
  learns of Mark's accident 213–14
  marriage 78, 191
  meets Mark 191
  visit to Harry Shirt's grave 294, 297, 298
Dunstan, Lizzy (sister-in-law) 9, 214
Dunstan, William (nephew) 3

Earl, Andrew 245
East Lancashire Regiment 156–7, 169–72
Egypt 131
Egyptology 104
Elizabeth Line 234
Epping Forest 56–7, 65
Étaples Military Cemetery, Boulogne 174
Evans, Paul 234, 255, 283, 284
Evanton, Scotland 79, 81, 117–18

Fairburn, Arthur 145
Fairburn, William 145
Field, John 41–2, 43
Firepower 230, 233
First Gulf War 179–80, 277
First World War *see also*
    medals; Somme
  Arras 160–1
  chronology 144
  Fromelles 154–6, 164
  letters home 159–60
  Loos 242–4
  Mark's first interest in
    collecting 28
  Pals battalions 169–72
  Princess Mary Gift Fund
    boxes 272
  scale of death 163, 165
  Ypres 144–5
fishing, Mark Smith's
  childhood 51–2
floods, military aid 188
football 11–12, 65–6, 85
'For the Fallen' (Binyon) 298
Forest School, Snaresbrook 29,
  83–6, 99–100, 111
The Forgotten Soldier (Sajer)
  87–8
Fortnum & Mason 282
Foster, David 84–5
Foster, Don 2, 36–7, 124
Foster, Steve 2
Foulkes, Charles Clarence 173
Foulkes, John 173–4

Foulkes, Peter 173
Franz Ferdinand, Archduke
  190
Freemasons 110, 246–7, 249
Fromelles, Battle of 154–6, 164

Gardner, Andrew 84
Gay Hussar restaurant 254–5
George Gascoigne Secondary
    Modern School,
    Walthamstow 208
George VI 47–8
Glanfield, John 242
Goldsmiths College, University
  of London 209
Great War *see* First World War
Griffiths, Edmund 156–7
Gulf of Martaban 195
guns in museums 231–2

H. M. Stores, army surplus 56
Hackney Wick stadium 65
Hale, Corporal (Accrington
  Pal) 171
Hamburg, German army staff
  college 211
Hamworthy Barracks, Poole
  284
Hancocks, makers of
  Victoria Cross 240,
  242
hand grenades 99–101
Harbottle, David 107–10
Harding, Vic 67

Harrier jump-jets 107
Harvards 118–19
hats, fishy 72
Heeresgeschichtliches Museum,
    Vienna 190
helicopter payments 179
*The Hell They Called High
    Wood* (Norman) 138
helmets
    fire watcher's 28
    German 29, 32, 89–90, 95
Henderson, John 272,
    274
Hendrie, Don 124,
    199–200, 201, 290
Hinckley George 242
Holditch, Ray 153
Holmes, Richard 98–9
Holocaust 266–8
Home Guard 14
Hooglede, Flanders 175–6
Hookins, Steve 234, 235, 255
Hooton Park, Wirral 119
Hutchinson, Simon 217, 220,
    229, 230, 238
Hyland House Primary School,
    Walthamstow 10

Imperial War Museum 105, 133,
    142
India Club restaurant 226–7
India Service Medal 29–30
IRA bombs 180–2
Iron Cross medals 90–2, 93–4

Jack the Ripper 50
The Jam 112–13

Kay, Hilary, great uncles
    174–5, 176
Killadeas, Northern Ireland 123
Kohima Epitaph 298–9
Königsberger, Walter 175–6
Kosovo 184–7
Kyaukpyu, Burma 201, 202

Lancashire Fusiliers, 1st
    Battalion 142–3
Larkhill, Wiltshire 234
Leadenhall meat market 50
Lee, Roddy 237–8
Leigh, Yeovil, Somerset 107
letters to and from home
    159–60, 205, 287–8
Lewis, Martin 84, 85, 98, 101
Leyton Orient football club 14
Lidell, Alva 130
Liverpool Street station
    44–5, 46–8
living-history 232
logbooks 22–6
London Air Ambulance 235,
    274–5
London Fire Brigade Retired
    Members Association 166,
    167–8
London Medal Club 93
London Olympics 59
Longmoor army camp 100, 103

Loos, Battle of 242–4
Lough Erne, Northern Ireland 123, 125–7
Luftwaffe oxygen masks 70–1
Lynn, Vera 223, 233
Lysanders 118–19

McKeniry, Roisin 215
Mackness, Herbert 153–6, 164
Madras, India 130, 193, 203, 293–5
Maguncor Lodge 110
Malins, Geoffrey 142–3
Manchester United 65–6
maps 100–1
Markhouse Road Secondary Modern School, Walthamstow 208, 227
Martaban, Gulf of 195
Masonic lodges 110, 247–8, 249
Mauger, Peter 209
medals
 Baldwin & Sons, A. H. 237–8
 British War Medals, sold for cash 156
 Carpathia Medal 275
 Distinguished Service Medal (DSM) 272
 fakes 92, 93
 India Service Medal 29–30
 Iron Cross 90–2, 93–4
 Les Smith's 27–8
 Mark's current collection 31–2
 Mark's early collection 29–31, 33, 90–1
 Mark's First World War collection 33–4, 143–4, 151–61
 Military Medal 273
 Mr Bird senior 149
 Orders and Medals Research Society (OMRS) 149–51, 233
 researching names 151–2
 time machines 32
 Victoria Cross 238–49, 270–2
Merrill, Robert 54
Merriman, Alan 37
metal detectors 138–9
militaria fakes 92–3
militaria shops 89–90, 92–3, 136
Military Aid to the Civil Community 188
Military Aid to the Civil Powers 188
Military Medal 273
Ministry of Defence (MoD)
 D Mov Ops RAF 179–82
 Defence Intelligence 13 183–7
 Director Finance Policy 187–91, 211, 215–16
 IRA bombs 180–1
 library 152
 S9 (Air) 178–9
 security vetting 182–3

Mods 112, 113–15
Morse code 75–7
Mortledge, Wendy 234
Munn, Geoffrey 257
Murphy, Paul 93
Museum Studies Master's
  degree 230–1
museums
  AMOT (Army Museums
    Ogilby Trust) 218
  British Museum 104
  Imperial War Museum 105,
    133, 142
  Royal Artillery Museum,
    Woolwich 32–3, 216–20,
    223–4, 229–36, 237–9, 241,
    252, 255
  Royal Navy Fleet Air Arm
    Museum, Yeovilton
    107
  War Museum of Military
    History, Vienna 189–90
music 54–5, 111, 112–13

Napoleon Bonaparte 166
National Archives 37
NATO in Kosovo 184–7
Nato Training Group Financial
  Sub- Group 189–90
New Year's Day 59
Nobo, Phil
  background 10–11
  career 12
  Epping Forest cycling 56–7
  fishing and taxidermy
    attempts 52
  Les Smith's service
    number 19
  Mark's MoD security vetting
    182–3
Norman, Terry 138
nostalgia 59–60
numismatics 237

Oban, Scotland 129, 130
Ogilby, Robert 218
Old Soldiers Never Die
  (Richards) 137
Olympics, 2012 London 59
Omaha Beach 169–70
opera, *The Pearl Fishers* (Bizet)
  54–5
Operation Panda 78
Orders and Medals Research
  Society (OMRS) 149–51,
  233
orienteering 100–1
Over the Top with Smudger's
  Battlefield Tours 163
Oxfords 119–22
oxygen masks, Luftwaffe 70–1

Pals battalions 169–72
Parry, Colin 195, 198
'Partner for Peace' countries
  189–90
Paxton, Roger 190
photography 127, 195

Plaistow Press 90
Poole, Hamworthy Barracks 284
Poole Pirates (speedway) 65

Queen Mary, RMS 129–30

R&R Militaria 89–90
Raby, Henry 240
radar training 119
RAF *see also* Catalina flying boat
  Les Smith signs up 42–4, 48
  No. 1 Signals Depot, West Drayton 78
  Operation Panda 78
  Special Duties Operations, Japanese territory 195–202, 207
  training 17, 73–8, 79, 117–22
RAF Club, Piccadilly 277
Raidan, Abe 214
Ramsey, Gordon
  appearance and character 88
  battlefield visits with father 88, 135
  battlefield visits with Mark 141, 143, 144–5, 156
  early collection 89
  Luftwaffe oxygen mask 70–1
  meets Mark 29, 85, 86–7
  Orrell's story 172
  Plaistow Press employment 90
Ramsey, Winston 88–9, 90
Rawlinson, Henry 170

Raynes, John 242–5
Red Baron 158–9
Red Hills Lake, Madras, India 130, 193, 198, 203, 205
Regimentals (shop) 90
Rewa, British Hospital Ship 236
Richards, Frank 137
Richardson, Gladys (wife's grandmother) 78–9
Richthofen, Manfred von, Baron 158–9
Riley, Brenda (aunt) 69
Riley, Joan *see* Smith, Joan
Riley, Ted (grandfather) 14, 15–16
riots, military aid 188
Robinson, Gavin 195, 201
Rockers 114
Rose, Hermann 176
Roudeix, Alain 86
Royal Artillery Museum, Woolwich 32–3, 216–20, 223–4, 229–36, 237–9, 241, 252, 255
Royal Flying Corps 158
Royal Green Jackets headquarters, Winchester 96, 97–8
Royal London Hospital 247
Royal Navy Fleet Air Arm Museum, Yeovilton 107
Royal School of Artillery 234
Royal Warwickshire Regiment 159–61

Sajer, Guy 87–8
Salisbury Plain 76–7
SAS transport, First Gulf War 179–80
Schmidt, George (g grandfather) 12, 49–50
Schmidt, George (gg grandfather) 12
Schmidt, Jacob (ggg grandfather) 12
Schmidt, Walter (Dick) (grandfather)
  Army pension bet 14–15
  education 50
  fire-watch duties 28, 39
  First World War 13–14
  name change 12–13
  opinion of RAF 26
  service number 19
Scott, Joe 98–100
search-and-rescue helicopter missions 179
Second World War
  Atlantic convoys 127–9
  Battle of Britain 88–9, 92
  Blitz 9–10, 23, 38–41, 44–7
  Burma 194–6, 201, 270–1
  Chamberlain's announcement 224
  concentration camps 266–8
  D-Day 169
  Dunkirk 37–8, 148–9
  Les Smith's memories 18–19, 22–4
  Mark's first interest in collecting 28
  medic's dressing stations 149
  Operation Panda 78
  Special Duties Operations, Japanese territory 195–202, 207
  Victory in Europe Day 206
  Victory over Japan Day 207
Sharp, Dave 85, 103, 107–11
Shaw, Simon 251, 256
Sheriff, Marc 234
Shirt, Harry
  background 125
  death 1, 4, 202, 203, 225, 286
  Egyptian fortune telling 131
  funeral 203, 204–5, 287, 289, 299
  grave 293–4, 296–300
  leaflet droppping, injured by bullet 199–202
Shirt, Hilda 283, 286–7, 289, 291
Singh, Naik Gian 270–2
Smith, Ernie (great uncle) 65
Smith, Helen *see* Dunstan, Helen
Smith, Joan (mother)
  appearance and character 51, 69
  death 25, 227
  engagement 119
  first flight 25
  love letters 10, 21
  marriage 123

meets Les 69
name 69–70
sees Les off to RAF training 73
shopping trips 51
wartime stories 70–1
Smith, John Basil 159–61
Smith, Kathleen (Auntie Bob)
　birth 7
　height 64
　shopping trips 53
Smith, Les, Collections
　Manager 234
Smith, Les (father) *see also*
　Catalina flying boat
　Aircrew Association lecture
　　36–7
　ambition to join RAF 39,
　　40, 41
　appearance and character
　　64–5
　birth 69
　BOAC employment 207
　childhood illness 71
　clerk work 38, 44–5, 46–8
　comments on Chamberlain's
　　speech 224
　coral poisoning 132
　death 227
　education 71
　Egyptian fortune telling
　　131
　engagement 119
　final illness 223–5
　first job 71–2

flying hours 1, 206
funeral 21, 227
hospital stays and ant attack
　193–4
joins RAF 42–4, 48
logbook 22–6
malaria 104
marriage 123
medal collecting 29–31, 90
medals 27–8
meets Joan 69
memoirs 35–6, 37
photographs 17
RAF training 17, 73–8, 79,
　117–22
refuses to go on battlefield
　tours 141–2
retirement 209
service number 18–19
smoking 226
talking 63, 227
teaching career 208, 227
train accident 79–81
trauma 207–8, 209, 225–6,
　289
uniform 19–20, 21–2
university career 25, 209
war souvenirs 20–1
watch and wedding ring 20
Smith, Mark *see also* medals
　battlefield guiding 163–70,
　　172–6, 235
　birth 7, 60
　cadet force 29

Smith – *cont'd.*
car accidents 107–10, 212–15, 221
career aspirations 21–2, 104–5
Catalina flight 1–5
childhood 9, 10–12, 17–20, 21–4, 27–9
Combined Cadet Force (CCF) 95–8, 100–4
current collection 31–2
education 29, 83–5, 99, 104, 230–1
eyesight 22
first flight 25
first interest in collecting 27–9, 85, 87
first TV appearance 236
fishing 51–2
Freemasonry 110, 246–8, 249
jobs, *Antiques Roadshow see* Antiques Roadshow
jobs, Baldwins 237–8
jobs, first at DHSS 133–4
jobs, Ministry of Defence *see* Ministry of Defence
jobs, museum curation 32–3, 216–21, 223, 229–36, 237–9, 241, 252, 255
jobs, Social Security Medical Appeals Tribunal 147–8
meets and marries Helen 191
Nan 7, 27–8, 65, 101–2, 251
note to self 221
relatives and oral history 7–8, 9–10, 14, 15, 23
Somme visits 135–41, 143
speaking career 235, 247–9
stairs fall 277, 278–82
taxidermy attempts 52
visit to Harry Shirt's grave 293–300
Smith, Rodney (Gypsy Smith) 57
Smith, Vic (uncle)
birth 7
fire-watch duties 39
speedway 65
wartime stories 10, 23
Smithfield meat market 12, 119
Social Security Medical Appeals Tribunal 147–8
Socrates bet 15
Somme
Accrington Pals 169–72
aircraft 158–9
Dick Schmidt's experience 13–14, 138
hand grenades 173–4
Mark's visits 135–41, 143
Sunken Lane, Beaumont-Hamel 142–3
Switch Line 13, 138
Ted Riley's experience 15
Thiepval Memorial 140, 143, 172, 173
South East Asia Command 130, 206

Special Boat Service
    Association 235
speedway 65, 66–7
Spence, Jonathan 249
Sphinx, HMS 242
Sri Lanka 132
stairs fall 277, 278–82
Stanley Gibbons Group 237
Steward, Derek 227
storytelling
    childhood experience 7–8,
        9–10, 14, 15
    speaking career 248–9
submarines 127–30, 195
Sullivan, Jim 125, 200–1, 202
Sumatra 198–200
Sun test 188
The Sweeney 95
swords 32–3

Taiping Rebellion 242
Tanfield, Katie 295
taxidermy attempts 52
Theresienstadt concentration
    camp 266–8
Thiepval Memorial 140, 143,
    172, 173
Thistlethwaite, Paddy 125, 202
Thomas, Barry 66
Tilney, Robert 261, 262, 269,
    270
Timbers, Ken 217, 232, 235
Titanic, RMS 273–4
Tollervey, Amos George 158

Tottenham Hotspurs 65–6
toyshops 53
train accident 79–81, 117
Transylvania, HMS 154
trauma 207–8, 209, 225–6,
    289
Trotman, Peter 203–4
Tyrrell, Siobhan 214, 281

U-boats 128, 236
unarmed combat 97–8
uniforms
    Combined Cadet Force
        (CCF) 97
    H. M. Stores, army surplus 56
    Les Smith's 19–20, 21–2, 73–4
    Mark Smith's childhood
        purchases 56
United Grand Lodge of
    England 247, 249
University College London
    230–1

Vandenburg, Darren and Isobel
    213, 214
Victoria Cross 238–49, 270–2
Victoria, Queen 239–40, 246
Volksbund Deutsche
    Kriegsgräberfürsorge 175

Wakeham, Derek 97, 99–100
Walthamstow
    1970s-80s 57
    Antiques Roadshow 60–1, 254

Walthamstow – *cont'd.*
  early history 49
  fire-watch duties 39
  market 55
  Orford Road 57–8
  schools 10, 208, 227
  shops 29, 51, 53–4, 55–6, 59, 68, 90
  Smith family home 9, 49, 50–1
  town hall 60
Wapshott, Peter 163, 235
War Museum of Military History, Vienna 189–90
War Walks (TV series) 99
Warcop Training Area 102
Waterfall, Stan and Bunty 107
Waterloo 166–8

Weatherley, Steve 67
Welch, Eric Arthur 157–9
Wheeler, Stephen 150–1
White Hart Lane 65–6
Whitechapel 50
Wigg (office boy) 41
William, Prince 275
Willmott (RAF Morse Code cadet) 77, 78
Winchester, Royal Green Jackets headquarters 96, 97–8
wine 67–9
Wonnacott, Tim 255–6

Yatesbury, Salisbury Plain 76–7, 78–9
Ypres 144–5